TURBULENT
IRAN

Recollections, Revelations
and a Proposal for Peace

SIR ELDON GRIFFITHS

July 2010

SEVEN LOCKS PRESS

Santa Ana, California

Seven Locks Press
P.O. Box 25689
Santa Ana, CA 92799
(800) 354-5348

Individual Sales. This book is available through most bookstores or can be ordered directly from Seven Locks Press at the address above.

Quantity Sales. Special discounts are available on quantity purchases by corporations, associations, and others. For details, contact the "Special Sales Department" at the publisher's address above.

Printed in the United States of America

Library of Congress Cataloging-in-Publication Data
is available from the publisher
ISBN 1-931643-92-X

Cover and Interior Design by Heather Buchman

To Betty

TABLE OF CONTENTS

FOREWORD

by Ambassador Bruce Laingen,
held captive in Iran for 444 days

For most Americans, Iran and its leadership are largely beyond comprehension. Iran first comes to mind as a place where American diplomats were held hostage, where bearded clerics arbitrarily rule, back movements such as Hezbollah, and who now seem determined to acquire nuclear weapons. But here is a book by an Englishman, now living in America, in which the author reminds us in a series of personal vignettes that Iran is much more than that; a country and a people rich in culture and purpose, deeply proud of their history and now of considerable strategic consequence for the entire region and for American interests therein. Americans, he tells us, need to look beyond the box in which they place Iran.

He can speak with authority. Sir Eldon Griffiths knew Iran before its revolution, watched it change over the years as a Member of the British Parliament and government minister and has traveled there since—wearing both British and American hats. Now living in Southern California in the midst of its large Diaspora of Iranian-Americans, still fascinated by Iran's culture as there transplanted, he is active as a leader in the World Affairs Councils of America in efforts to build a better American understanding of the Middle East and today's Iran.

Having been one of those hostages and having served in Iran in the American Foreign Service in the hostage period and for two years in an earlier period, I share Sir Eldon's fascination with that country and with its people. I went there first in the immediate aftermath of the Mosaddegh affair in 1953, including a temporary assignment as the American Consul in the Holy Shrine city of Meshed. In the years that followed I watched from a distance as our embassy grew, in both size and involvement, as the Shah resumed his throne and the U.S.–Iranian relationship began its expansion into what became America's principal security anchor in that part of the Middle East. The Islamic Revolution of l979 ended all that, and I returned in June l979 as the *chargé d'affaires* of the embassy to a much-reduced presence, eventually becoming a hostage with my fifty-two colleagues for those 444 days. As the expression has it, the rest is history.

That history has seen our two countries without formal diplomatic relations for all that time. For more than quarter century, the United States has had no dialogue with Iran. That has made no sense, for either country. It has complicated our relations with every other country in the region. It *must change*. It ignores the many shared interests we have with Iran, including the transit of oil through the Persian Gulf, efforts to staunch the flow of narcotics across Iran to the West from Afghanistan, stability in Central Asia and, not least, a shared human interest in the Iranian Diaspora community in the United States—so large as to make America the second largest Persian speaking country in the world. Above all, the U.S. and Iran have a shared interest in political stability in Iraq—our future relationship with Iran will depend heavily on what evolves politically in Baghdad.

Despite all that, Iran and the United States still have not been able to overcome the painful legacy of their past. The crisis over Hezbollah's attacks on Israel and the Israelis massive counter-offensive strikes against Lebanon underline this. Mutual distrust sees the U.S. persisting until now as an outrider among the powers seeking an understanding on the nuclear issue, even though all concerned know full well that a resolution is not possible without direct American concurrence. The U.S. has now, however, announced its readiness to join with its E.U. partners at a negotiating table with Iran, provided it "verifiably suspends" all its uranium enrichment procedure. Iran's immediate negative response was predictable, but so is the likelihood of a continuing bargaining period ahead.

What is needed, as Sir Eldon so eloquently argues in his sensitive historical analysis, is a deeper mutual understanding on the part of all concerned that a further spread of nuclear weapons into the volatile security situation of the Persian Gulf region is so compelling a danger as to call for statecraft of the highest order.

Regrettably this is proving hard to come by.

—Bruce Laingen

PREFACE

After Iraq—Iran? That is the question that haunted policymakers and many ordinary Americans and Brits as President George W. Bush and Prime Minister Tony Blair grappled with the interlocking conflicts that in fall 2006 threatened to engulf the Middle East in the most dangerous conflagration since the second world war.

Israel invaded Lebanon in an effort that failed to destroy Hezbollah's guerrillas. Civil war menaced Iraq, destroying U.S. and British hopes of an orderly withdrawal. Tribal warlords as well as Taliban insurgents once again were on the rampage in Afghanistan.

From Egypt and Jordan to Syria, Saudi Arabia and the United Arab Emirates, there were well-grounded fears of a new wave of intifadas, suicide bombers and revolutionary coups aimed at replacing pro-Western rulers. Convulsive anti-Americanism and hatred of Israel ruled the Arab street and media.

The overriding impression was of a comprehensive failure of American and British foreign policy in a strategically vital region that supplies two-fifths of the world's oil, and in recent years, has given birth to its most savage terrorist cells and bitterest religious rivalries.

And over it all loomed a dark new cloud—the prospect of Iran's Islamic regime getting its hands on nuclear weapons.

For years the theocratic government in Teheran has been regarded by the United States as a "threat to world peace." The State Department accuses it of arming and financing Hezbollah. The CIA identifies the Islamic regime as "the No. 1 supporter of terrorism." Iran in response calls the United States the "Great Arrogance" and describes America as the "crusader enemy of Islam." Its President Mahmoud Ahmadi-nejad says Israel should be removed from the map of the Middle East. Thousands of his youthful acolytes have pledged to sacrifice their lives to wreak vengeance on the Great Satan.

The most dangerous issue separating the two sides is Iran's nuclear power program. The Bush administration says this is a cloak behind which the ayatollahs are reaching out for atomic weapons that would enable Iran to dominate the Persian Gulf, threaten U.S. forces in the Middle East region, and possibly attack Israel. Iran replies that its reactors are intended to produce nothing but electricity and that as a sovereign nation it has an "inalienable right" to do this.

International inspectors report that they have no evidence to confirm that the Iranians have the will or the ability to produce the enriched uranium needed to make nuclear warheads, but no responsible government in Washington or London can fail to address this danger. Atomic weapons in the hands of the Islamic regime in Iran would inject a new and destabilizing element into an already chaotic region.

Yet Iran is critically important to any lasting resolution of every one of the Middle East conflicts in which the U.S. , Britain and their allies are involved.

Only if Iran concurs will Hezbollah call off its war against Israel, collaborate with the U.N.-sponsored peacemakers and subordinate its military forces to the Lebanese government in Beirut.

Likewise in Afghanistan. Without Iran's compliance the warlords of the Farsi-speaking western provinces will not yield to the authority of the elected Afghan government in Kabul.

Iran, too, is critical to the future of Iraq because of the Iranians long-standing involvement with the Kurds in the north, and their near control in the south of Iraq's waterway to the Persian Gulf. Iran is the home of the Shiite version of Islam and the principal supplier of weapons, training and funds for Iraq's Shia' militias.

Iran's mullahs exert an increasing influence over the Shiite majority in central and southern Iraq and on its national assembly and government. The fiercer the conflict between Iraqi Sunnis and Shias becomes the closer the Shias draw to Iran, where many of their leaders took refuge from Saddam Hussein's persecution.

U.S. and British commanders have other anxieties about Iran's influence in Iraq. Short term, they worry that Iranian intervention might force their troops into a fighting withdrawal, more like Dunkirk or the U.S. exodus from Saigon, than the peaceful handover to a united and democratic Iraq that Bush and Blair once visualized.

Longer term, the Americans and Brits worry that once their troops depart, the influence of Iran inexorably will extend to the southern shores of the Persian Gulf, overawing Saudi Arabia, Kuwait and the United Arab Republic. Most of Bahrain's population is of Iranian descent. Many of the oil workers in Saudi Arabia and the UEA are Shiites. Oman owes a debt to Iran for its help in securing its independence against invaders from Yemen in the 1970s.

These anxieties about Iran succeeding America as the postwar overlord of the Persian Gulf crystallized in Washington when defectors brought intelligence about Iran's enriching uranium to levels that could be used to produce a nuclear bomb. President Bush's response was that the U.S. "would not allow Iran to obtain nuclear weapons or the means to make them."

Some Americans and more Israelis urged military action to ensure this.

By spring 2006, there was a danger that threat and counter threat could escalate into a Catch 22 situation in which American hawks screamed "attack Iran before it gets nuclear weapons," and Iranian peacocks cried, "get nuclear weapons quickly, to prevent an American attack."

This war talk alarmed America's allies, including the Brits. So did the deteriorating situation in Iraq, where the last thing U.S. commanders—or most U.S. Congressmen—wanted was to open up a second fighting front with Iran.

Facing such pressures, the administration in July 2006 changed tack. After refusing for twenty-seven years to engage in talks with the Islamic regime, the White House ordered American diplomats to join European, Russian and Chinese representatives in negotiations with Iran. This was a wise, if overdue, decision, for Iran is in no position to produce an atomic weapon for at least four and more likely five or six years, even if that is what its rulers are hell bent on doing. There is no need for America to stumble into a further unwinnable war in the Middle East.

Prudence, experience and the overstretch of U.S. and British forces in Iraq, Afghanistan and in support of a U.N. peace-force in Lebanon, all point to the wisdom of examining the origins and scope of Iran's nuclear program and of understanding why the Iranian people, as well as the mullahs support it, before the U.S. decides on any drastic action.

Hence this short book which seeks to shed light on Iran for Americans and Brits. It is not a scholarly work, only a narrative of one man's encounters with some of the Iranian movers and shakers, who over the past half-century have shaped an ancient and turbulent land with which I fell in love with as a child.

Understanding Iran is difficult, perhaps impossible for any outsider. The more one studies its people, the more they become as Einstein said of the universe, "not more intelligible but more mysterious."

But Iran is more than a mystery. It is the largest, strongest, proudest and most populous nation in the oil rich gulf that bears its ancient name—Persian.

Territorially, Iran is the land bridge that links—and separates—the Arabs to the south and west from the Turks and Russians to the north and the Afghans, Pakistanis and Chinese to the east. Culturally, it is the heir to one of the world's most brilliant civilizations. Though largely mountainous and desert, it is endowed with immense reserves of oil, gas and other minerals.

For the first half of my adult life, Iran was the partner and ally of the country of my birth and the country of my adoption. It is a land I like and admire. Among its handsome, talented and often infuriating people, are many I am proud to count as close friends.

Part One therefore offers some glimpses of the people, places, events, anecdotes, mishaps and humor that make up the multicolored carpet of Iran. I hope you will enjoy them.

Part Two is more analytical. It tells the story of how Iran got into the nuclear power business, where its nuclear facilities are located and whether Iran is in violation of the international treaties that forbid the spread of nuclear arms. This is pretty technical stuff: skip it if you feel uncomfortable with the details of how the United States, France and Germany, having designed and helped to build Iran's reactors, ever since have sought to prevent the Iranians using them to enrich their fuel to the levels that are required for nuclear weapons.

Part Three is very short. It offers an old man's suggestions about how in the broader context of the Middle East crisis, both sides can draw back from the armed confrontation into which in mid-2006 the U.S. and Iran appeared to be sliding. No one save the author is responsible for these proposals for new initiatives to end the Cold War between the United States and Iran. They are radical as well as contentious—first, a Persian Gulf non-aggression pact, then a nuclear détente whereby Israel as well as Iran renounces atomic weapons in the context of a future NATO guarantee.

The United States needs to think outside the box into which it has sought for a generation to confine its approach to Iran. A different Middle East is dawning, as religious passions, oil, the internet, terrorism, the revival of Russia and the rise of China bring new forces to bear on a region that links Europe, Africa and Asia and contains three-fifths of the world's known energy reserves. The key to it is Iran, and the time to move forward is now.

ACKNOWLEDGEMENTS

This book could not have been written without the help of hundreds of others, many of them Iranians in America and Europe as well as in Iran.

In Geneva I benefited from the collection of papers and photographs assembled by Ardeshir Zahedi, former Foreign Minister of Iran; in New York from the shrewd advice of Akbar Lari and Ahmad Teherani, a former Iranian ambassador to South Africa; in Los Angeles from the wisdom of Ali and Anousheh Razi; in Orange County from the suggestions of Bijan Kian and Fred Ameri, my successor as Chairman of the World Affairs Council of Orange County. Invaluable too was Vojin Joksimovich, a nuclear safety engineer, whose experience in the atomic power industries of Britain and the United States enabled me to understand and narrate the tangled story of the Iranian nuclear power program.

I benefited greatly from many fine books about Iran, notably *The Shah's Last Ride* by William Shawcross, *The Last Great Revolution*, by Robin Wright, *The Last Shah of Iran* by Houchang Nahavandi, *Shia Revival* by Vali Nasr and *Persian Sphinx* by Abbas Milani who is now engaged, monumentally, in writing the biographies on one hundred fifty of the last century's most eminent Persians. *Crisis* by Hamilton Jordan refreshed my memories of Jimmy Carter's tergiversations over admitting the Shah to America; *From Cold War to Hot Peace,* by Sir Anthony Parsons, recalled Margaret Thatcher's change of front in regard to the Pahlavis. *Shopping for Bombs* by Gordon Corera provided a masterly analysis of the Pakistani scientist, A.Q. Khan's black market contributions to nuclear proliferation.

My thanks are also due to Peggy Beale and Ayumi Hakaoka in America and Wendy Woodward in England who fought their way through the thickets of handwritten scraps of paper which, along with any errors, were the author's contribution to the manuscript of this book, and most of all to my darling Betty. For her patience, and the thousands of hours she spent transliterating my scribble, I thank her and dedicate to her a book the first word of whose title aptly describes the experiences we both had to endure to get the final manuscript to my editor, Heather Buchman and publisher, Jim Riordan of Seven Locks Press.

PART ONE

DISCOVERING PERSIA AS A SCHOOLBOY

All should be free to worship their God without harm.
— Cyrus, King of Persia

The first time I spoke up for Persia was as a child. This arose from my grammar school's practice of organizing its pupils into four houses, Romans, Trojans, Spartans and Vikings. The first three were classical, befitting a school that grounded its students in Latin and Greek, but the Vikings were an anomaly since these Scandinavian raiders did not appear on the coasts of England until Rome, Troy and Sparta long since had ceased to exist. I therefore asked my house master why we did not have a house named for the Persians, since they were civilized contemporaries of the Romans, Trojans and Spartans, while the uncivilized Vikings were not. His one word answer was "Herodotus," naming the Roman scribe whose chronicles of the Greeks and Persians did most to fix their stories in the minds of generations of English schoolboys and politicians.

Explaining, the housemaster averred that there's no such thing as history: only historiography. The narratives of those who write about past events inevitably are colored by the sources available to them and by the cultures and attitudes of their times. So the Greeks, as chacterized by Herodotus and most of the European historians who later relied on him, nearly always emerged as "the good guys," as per Socrates and Alexander the Great, while the Persians were the "bad guys," black bearded Asians who no self respecting English grammar school would want to be identified with. "That's wrong," said my housemaster, reaching up for a thick volume on his bookshelf. "Read this if you want to know more about Persia."

Persia and the Persian Question is a 600-page classic by Lord Curzon, an early twentieth century foreign secretary, viceroy of India and with the exception of Winston Churchill, perhaps the last of the great British imperialists. Devouring his book (which still adorns my bookshelf), I copied into my notebook the paragraph with which he ended it.

"For all its present debility, Persia is a country that should excite the liveliest sympathies of all Englishmen; with whose government our own government should be in terms of intimate alliance; and in the shaping of (whose) future the British nation have it in their power to take an honorable lead."

From Curzon I moved on to the collection of books about Persia that were to be found in my school library. From these, as a fourteen-year-old, I acquired a superficial yet abiding interest in the 4,000-year-old story of Iran as it now is called.

For here were fascinating tales of the Persians' ancestors, then known as Elamites, winning their independence from Babylon in 1749BC; of the Assyrians under a king with the intriguing name of Ashurbanipal, wiping out their great city of Susa in 639BC; most of all, of the Achaemenian dynasty and Cyrus the first great king emperor, invading Mesopotamia, capturing Babylon and carrying Persian power as far as Egypt to the south and Afghanistan to the east. I cut out from a schoolboy magazine that long since has ceased publication a picture of the stone relief at Persepolis of Darius the Great, King of the Persians from 521 to 486BC and another of his son, the warrior Xerxes I silhouetted against a gate flanked by winged bulls with human heads. A turning point came on my fifteenth birthday when I was given a set of the Encyclopedia Britannica, the equivalent in the 1930s of Google as a search engine. From its densely packed pages, I copied out poems by Ferdowsi, the equal of Homer, Dante or Shakespeare about Iran's perpetual struggle between the crown and the turban, and descriptions of Cyrus's bodyguard, the 10,000 strong

Perspepolis bas relief: officer (left) respectfully addressing Darius I

Ceremonial procession of tributary kings bearing gifts, as depicted on the walls of the Persepolis

immortals so named because when one fell, another instantly took his place. I also drew a map of the all weather highways built by the Persians to link an empire that centuries before Rome, was ruled by laws based on a text that Cyrus required all his governors to abide by:

All should be free to worship their God without harm.

No one's home shall be destroyed and no one's property looted . . .

World War II put an end to my teenage love affair with classical Persia. In 1939 Nazi Germany invaded Poland and partitioned it with Communist Russia, occupied Denmark and Norway, and unleashed the blitzkrieg that smashed through Holland and Belgium and forced France to surrender. Britain in 1940 stood alone in the face of threatened German invasion. Only after the RAF defeated the Luftwaffe in the air battles over England did Hitler denounce the Nazi-Soviet pact that had enabled his war machine to concentrate on Western Europe, and turn the full weight of the *wehrmacht* against the Soviet Union. This made Britain and Russia allies leading Winston Churchill a lifelong anti-Communist, to explain this by saying, "If Hitler had invaded hell, I would have come to this House [of Commons] and said a few kind words about the devil."

As the Germans thrust deeper into Russia, my father pinned a map onto our kitchen wall, showing the land mass between the Baltic Sea and the Persian Gulf. Across this, he drew red arrows, one showing the German Afrika Korps thrusting its way across Egypt and thence into Palestine and Iraq, the other arching down from the Ukraine and the Caucasus across Iran to the Persian Gulf. The British Eighth army, Dad assured me, would beat back the attack on Egypt (as it did). But there was only one way to stop Hitler from getting his hands on Middle East oil. "The Russians will decide this," he said "If they lose, we lose. We have to keep the Red Army in the war."

There were only two ways to get the guns, tanks and ammunition the Russians desperately needed into the Red Army's hands. One was by ship via the Barents Sea and the ice free port of Murmansk, a route along which hundreds of British merchant ships were sunk by German submarines; the other via the roads and railways of Iran to Russia's southern front in the Caucasus. I duly marked the Iranian route on my father's map, sticking yellow pins onto cities with romantic names like Khoramshar, Shiraz, Isfahan and Tabriz. Officially, Iran was neutral, but its ruler, Reza Shah, an army officer who the Brits had supported when he put an end to the Qajar dynasty and crowned himself king in 1926, was more pro-German than pro-British. Hitler had promoted the notion that the Aryan master race, destined to inherit the earth, had its origins in Iran, the name to which Reza Shah had changed the ancient name of Persia. Germany in the 1930s had become Iran's most important trading partner. German engineers helped build its cement plants, highways and Reza's most ambitious project, a railroad linking the Persian Gulf to the Caucasus. This was the vital supply route that in 1941 was needed to transport tanks, guns and ammunition to keep the Russian army in the war.

That summer the BBC announced that German expatriates employed on the Iranian railways were sabotaging the land route to

Russia. Dad and I rejoiced to hear that on August 25, 1941, British and Russian troops moved into Iran to keep the supply lines open. The Brits also removed Reza Shah whose contacts with Hitler had enraged Churchill and exiled him first to Mauritius, then to South Africa (from which later I was to help return his four poster bed to Teheran). His twenty-two year old son, Mohammad Reza Pahlavi, was placed on the throne in his place.

At the time this made good sense. There was a war to be won. It did not occur to us that in Iranian eyes, the Anglo-Russian intervention would be regarded as an "occupation" or that the young Shah would never forgive the Brits for removing and humiliating his father. Nor did I know that some Iranians at the time asked President Roosevelt to intervene and "reverse" the British action. There was never any prospect of this. Only after Pearl Harbor did America become a world player.

BRITS AND PERSIANS

Underneath a Mullah's beard, you'll find a label,
"Made in England."
— Persian saying

I paid little further attention to Iran until World War II ended and I went up to Cambridge University where scores of Iranian students were attending the medical school and the economics and geology departments. In my college was a former British army engineer who had worked on Iran's roads and seaports and an older man named Percy (whose last name I have forgotten) much of whose life had been spent in the Khuzestan desert with the Anglo Iranian oil company. Percy's only son had died at childbirth in the searing heat of the Persian Gulf, when he and his young wife lived in a tent during the early stages of construction of the world's largest refinery at Abadan on the Shatt al Arab waterway.

At Cambridge I learned a lot about the Brits involvement in Iran. About the adventurers and explorers who had penetrated its trackless deserts and reopened trade routes that had not been used for a thousand years; about the East India Company's dispatching troops and warships in 1802 to prevent the French under Napoleon moving into

British empire troops built roads over which they marched across Iran, from the Persian Gulf to Teheran to the Caspian.

Naser-el-din, the pride of Persia

Iran from Egypt; about a regiment of the British army in India marching 2,000 miles from the Persian Gulf port of Bushehr where Iran now operates its nuclear power station to help Naser-el-din Shah, most famous of the Qajar shahs, repulse Russian incursions into his Azerbaijan province in the north.[1]

Amongst these Victorian pioneers were some extraordinary characters. John Malcolm, known as "Boy" because he was commissioned as an officer at the age of thirteen, was one of seventeen children born to a Scottish crofter who seized Kharg Island in 1839 and led a hundred cavalry men and 1,200 muleteers to Teheran where he established the first British legation. Henry Layard, stirred by his childhood memories of reading the *Arabian Nights* in the 1840s, floated 300 miles down the Tigris River on a raft supported by inflated goatskins and joined a caravan of nomads headed into Iran's wild Baktiari country where, dying his hair and beard, he became a confidante of one of its khans whose son's life he saved with large doses of quinine. Layard sailed a steamer named *Assyria* up the Karun river to the rapids above Ahwaz, dismantled it to avoid a seven mile stretch of white water, then reassembled the vessel so as to steam on to a river port from which cargo could be carried over the mountains to Iran's second city, Isfahan. And then there was Henry Rawlinson who having visited the ruins of the great desert city of Persepolis, founded by Cyrus and burned to the ground by the Greek army of Alexander the Great, made up his mind to unlock the secrets of the wedge-shaped scripts chiseled into an 800-foot high wall that towers above the desert flats at Bisitam, near Kermanshah. Rawlinson without rope or ladders, risked his life again and again to edge along the vertical rock face and copy the 2,000-year-old letters from the long lost language of Darius II. Translated, these revealed the sophistication and wisdom of a civilization that in its day matched and in some ways surpassed those of Luxor and Athens.

Reading about these pioneers led me to the works of the founder of the Persian studies school at Cambridge, another Victorian Brit who fell in love with Iran. E.G. Browne, as he was known, translated into English the *Ruba-iyat of Omar Khayyam*, a treasure house of wit and wisdom composed in the eleventh century AD, at a time when Mongol invaders were sacking the cities of northern Persia and Islam's priests were fastening on the rest of the country the same kind of religious strictures as the ayatollahs impose today. The Ruba-iyat celebrates the joys of wine, women and song, just as most modern Iranians do, whenever they are free to do so.

This was a point underlined to me by Peter Avery, a former oil company executive who thanks to his command of the language and culture of Persia became the professor of Persian poetry at Cambridge University. Dr. Avery occupied a set of rooms facing the entrance to Kings College chapel. His updated translation of Omar Khayyam's great poem is illustrated with some of Iran's most beautiful and sensuous pictures. This taught me that neither the flagellants who whip themselves into a bloody frenzy to commemorate the killing of Imam Hussein, the founder of the Shiite version of Islam, nor the unsmiling mullahs who presently rule the roost in Teheran are typical of the Persians.

Martyrdom, it is true, it is a quality that the more religious Persians are brought up to admire. In the process they have developed some unique characteristics. One of these is a yearning for the apocalypse. Somehow, somewhere, Iranians expect a messiah, a Mahdi to reappear and resolve their problems. Young and old alike are also devoted to conspiracy theory: they feel compelled to blame someone, anyone other than themselves (until recently the Brits, now more often the Americans) for their own and Iran's pain. A case in point is the unshakable belief of an old Persian lady now living in Washington that the Islamists, who seized her assets and forced her to flee, were installed by the British in revenge for the former Shah's raising the price of oil. "Underneath a mullah's beard," she says, "you'll find a label, 'Made in England.'" Even more far-fetched are some of the Iranian theories applied to the Americans. President Bush was charged by some Iranians with invading Iraq at the request of the Iranian mullahs in return for their investment of trillions of dollars in Texas.

Such fantasies, combined with the polemical language of Iran's mullahs and politicians, makes it easy to demonize the Iranians. Herodotus, the Greek, did this twenty centuries ago; pundits on America's TV shows do the same today. My experience is that no generalization, except this one, comes near to fitting the Iranians. Nine out of ten of them are Shiites, though there are also vigorous communities of Jews, Zoroastrians and Bahais, but within the boundaries of Iran there is as rich a variety of people as there are colors in a Persian carpet—Arabs along the Persian Gulf coast, Baluchis (literally "wanderers") in the mountains that border Pakistan, Lors and Baktiaris in the south and west, Turkmen traders and farmers where Iran merges into the republics of central Asia. Kurds preponderate on both sides of the frontiers between Iran, Iraq and Turkey. Azaris, the largest minority are to be found in the northwest, along the shores of the Caspian.

Among this melange of tribes and races, there is no mistaking the majority Persians who mingle with Afghans, Indians and Mongols in the teeming cities of Iran.

They may be moon-faced, hatchet-faced, tall, squat and angular, dark and fair complexioned—but they do not fit the caricatures of Persian rug dealers or morose-looking mullahs. The Iranians I have come to know and (mostly) to enjoy being with, love to haggle, gossip and argue, dance, eat, gamble, sing, drink and make merry. As a species, despite the mullahs, they are as warmhearted, hospitable, impulsive, generous, quarrelsome and sexy as any people on earth.

Historically, and linguistically, they have also held onto their identity. Unlike the other classic empires, Babylon, Assyria, Egypt, Greece and Rome whose cultural imprint remains but whose political identity has disappeared into the mists of time, Persia remains unmistakably Persian. That is why its people are so proud.

MOSADDEGH LIFTS HIS NIGHTGOWN

*At the appropriate moment, he could transform himself from a frail
decrepit shell of a man into a wily, vigorous adversary.*
— Report to U.S. State Department

Ipaid my first visit to Iran in 1951. By then I was a foreign affairs
writer at *Time* magazine and the big story of the day was the
seizure of Abadan by a fiery Iranian nationalist named
Mohammed Mosaddegh. The Brits first struck oil in Iran in 1908 and
used it to provide cheap fuel for the Royal Navy. Post World War II,
Abadan became for a new generation of Iranians a symbol of foreign
exploitation of their country.

I first heard of Mosaddegh's attempt to take control of the Anglo-
Iranian oil company (AIOC) over lunch at the Yale Club of New York.
A ticker tape in the cloakroom said
"World's biggest oil refinery faces clo-
sure as mob in Iran invades Abadan."
With three friends, one a Brit, two
Americans, I sent an impertinent
telegram to Prime Minister, Clement
Attlee at No. 10 Downing Street. This
said, *"Possession nine tenths of law.
Send in parachute brigade. Hold
Abadan and negotiate but do not give
it up stop."*

It was no surprise that Mr. Attlee
did not reply!

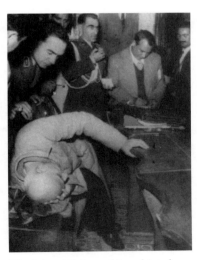

*The Prime Minister of Iran fainted
when it suited him.*

Mosaddegh is still revered by most though not all Iranians. He was an unlikely liberator. Appointed as prime minister in his late seventies, following the assassination of his predecessor Ali Razmara, he was a French-educated landowner, prone to throw fainting fits when his passions got the better of him. He delighted in telling tales about his craftiness in getting the better of his opponents by pretending to be at death's door. It was Mosaddegh's eloquence that persuaded the Iranian Majlis in 1950 to unanimously demand the nationalization of the Anglo-Iranian Oil Company and confiscation of Abadan. The Brits had no objections in principle to nationalization. Attlee's government had nationalized Britain's own coalmines and railroads. But as AIOC pointed out, with some justice, it was the oil company, not the Iranian government that took all the risks of prospecting for and discovering the oil and gas in what previously was a sandbox where no Iranian trod. Attlee therefore refused to accept Mosaddegh's seizure of Abadan without compensation or any guarantee that its oil would continue to flow to Europe.

Mosaddegh then threatened to arrest all the U.K. citizens in Iran and expel the four hundred in Abadan. British troop reinforcements rushed to their bases in the Persian Gulf. The drums of war were beating as a Royal Navy carrier took station offshore. Preparations were made for a British invasion force.

It was at this point that the United States, which in those days played only a minor role in the Persian Gulf, reluctantly offered the good offices of one of its most experienced diplomats, Averill Harriman.

I had several times met Ave Harriman who later was to

Abadan: The world's largest refinery from the 1930s–1960s

become one of my bosses at

Newsweek. He was liked and trusted by the Brits as a former U.S. ambassador and director of the Marshall Plan. Arriving in Teheran on July 15, 1951, the six-foot five-inch American was greeted by tens of thousand of Iranians shouting "Death to Harriman." He drove to his quarters in the government guest house through a city that resounded to the sound of gunfire and rioting between Mosaddegh's supporters and opponents whose placards said "Mosaddegh is mad."[1]

Next day, Harriman met Mosaddegh in an encounter he described as "different from any in my long diplomatic experience." Accompanied by an interpreter, Vernon Walters, who later was named the deputy director of the CIA, he was ushered into the prime minister's bedroom where the Iranian leader reclined, half-dressed, on his bed. Walters, a hefty U.S. colonel was directed to climb onto the bed and sit there crosslegged while translating a conversation that included Mosaddegh's assertion that, "Iran's problems have always been caused by foreigners. The whole problem began with that Greek, Alexander, who burned Persepolis."

The Americans pleaded for a compromise over the oilfields. But Mosaddegh wasn't listening.

Harriman reported to the State Department:

> *Mosaddegh projected helplessness (but) relented on nothing. Under pressure he seemed to have only a tenuous hold on life itself as he lay in his pink pajamas, hands folded on his chest, eyes fluttering and breath shallow. At the appropriate moment though, he could transform himself from a frail decrepit shell of a man into a wily vigorous adversary.*

It was Harriman's efforts to find a diplomatic way out of the impasse over Abadan that led to *Time* magazine's first cover story on Iran. I wrote this in March 1951 when Mosaddegh visited New York to plead Iran's case at the U.N.

On arrival, he checked into the Waldorf Astoria but insisted on sleeping on a camp bed so that photographs of his stay in American

Mossadegh as prime minister 1950–53 nationalized the Anglo-Iranian Oil Company precipitating the first Middle East oil crisis

would not portray him in such luxurious surroundings. He then went to a New York hospital for tests to determine if he was well enough to address the Security Council. Pronounced fit, he still asked the council to indulge him on account of his "long journey and failing health." An aide read his two hour long speech following which Mossy, as *Time* labeled him, dramatically limped to the U.N. podium.

"My countrymen lack the bare necessities of existence," he said. "Their standard of living is probably one of the lowest in the world. Our greatest natural asset is oil (yet) living around the largest oil refinery in the world, they are suffering in conditions of absolute misery."

The Afro-Asian loved this. Many of the delegates applauded when Mosaddegh accused the Brits of "making a great parade of their love of peace when concentrating warships along our coasts." He ended with a flourish. "They are trying to persuade world opinion that the lamb has devoured the wolf."

The dialectic outcome of the U.N. debate was a draw between Mosaddegh and the British ambassador, Gladwyn Jebb with whom most Monday mornings I shared an early train ride from Connecticut to New York. But politically, no one won. Then, as now, the Security Council's decision was to postpone taking a decision, establishing what James Reston of the *New York Times* described as the "principle of total loss. Everybody loses; the large powers, the small powers and the United Nations itself."

Mosaddegh before going home traveled to Washington to meet President Truman.

Staying at the Shoreham hotel, he claimed to have been kept awake all night by the sound of gunfire (there was none) and had his embassy put out a press release that described him as the George

Harry Truman greets Mossadegh who described himself as the George Washtington of Iran

Washington of Iran. At the White House he told Harry Truman, "Mr. President, I speak for a very poor country, just sand, a few camels, a few sheep . . ."

"Yes, and with your oil just like Texas," interjected Secretary of State Dean Acheson.[2]

Truman's chief concern was that if the oil crisis spun out of control, Iran might fall into the hands of the Soviets who were "sitting like a vulture on the fence, waiting to pounce." If the Soviets take Iran, he warned, "they would be in a position to wage a world war."

During talks at Mosaddegh's bedside, U.S. officials repeated the President's warnings and urged him to come to terms with the Brits— allowing Iran to have sovereign ownership and control of its oil resources but providing a "neutral" company to operate and manage Abadan and leaving B.P. to market the oil. Vernon Walters who paid a final personal visit to make sure that he had not had a last minute change of heart, said:

> *Dr. Mosaddegh, high hopes have been raised that your visit would bring about a fruitful result, and now you are returning home empty-handed.*

Mossy's response was telling:

> *Don't you realize that in returning empty-handed, I go*
> *home in a much stronger position than if I returned with*
> *an agreement which I would have to sell to my fanatics.*[3]

My *Time* cover story on Mosaddegh which was re-published in *Readers Digest*, was based on advice from U.S. and British oil experts and reflected Averill Harriman's memoranda which were leaked to *Time's* Washington bureau (as well as to *Newsweek* whose foreign editor I later would become). One of my colleagues, James Bell also had a brief interview with Mosaddegh that included a unique incident. Perhaps he was sending a message, more likely he was responding to the same kidney problems as made him weep but at one point in their discussion, the prime minister climbed out of his bed, turned his back and lifted his robe. He then relieved himself in a blue chamber pot!

Time magazine made Mosaddegh its 1951 Man of the Year, hardly its best editorial judgment. The British gave up Abadan and Iran's oil production dropped sharply, despite higher oil prices. The politics of both the U.S. and Britain meanwhile underwent major changes. In London, Winston Churchill and his resurgent Tories ousted the Labour party. In Washington, Dwight D. Eisenhower ended nineteen years of Democratic control of the White House to become America's first Republican president since the Depression in 1933. These changes which before long were to catapult me back from America to England, transformed the situation in Iran.

THE AMERICANS MOVE INTO IRAN

More like a dime-store novel than serious foreign policy.
— Dwight D. Eisenhower,
President of the United States

It was Churchill who first decided that Mohammed Mosaddegh must be removed by force. The military invasion that the Brits initially had planned to safeguard Abadan's technicians effectively, was vetoed by U.S. opposition, and the reluctance of the then Labour party to support Churchill in military action. But something had to be done. Output at the giant Masjid-Suleiman field slowed to a trickle. Thousands of Iranians were thrown out of work. Shortages of fuel and of imported food and medicine led to violent demonstrations in Teheran, whose bewildered and hungry people had expected oil nationalization to lead quickly to better times. The Tudeh (Communist) party urged Iranians to turn to the Russians for help.

No less disturbing for the U.S. and U.K. was the wider diplomatic context of 1952. President Eisenhower had been elected on a strongly anti-Communist platform, yet week after week the headlines told of Soviet advances and American setbacks. The U.S. army had been hurled back from North Korea by the Chinese. The Soviet Union tested its first H-bomb. Berlin was again under pressure. Mosaddegh, capitalizing on the success he had scored with the Afro-Asians at the U.N., signed a friendship treaty with the Egyptian dictator, Nasser, who before long would follow his lead and nationalize the Suez Canal.

Once in office President Eisenhower appointed two anti-Communist brothers to his Cabinet. One was John Foster Dulles, the new Republican Secretary of State, the other Allen Dulles who was named as deputy director, then head of the CIA. The two men were very different. When Foster, a stern Presbyterian, came to lunch at *Time* magazine, I got a note from its owner, Henry Luce describing him as "a great Christian secretary of state," and adding, "be sure to help him carry his burdens." Allen who I met at the Washington apartment of their sister, Eleanor who also, though unofficially, worked for the CIA by contrast was a *bon viveur*. A wine-loving, tennis-playing partner of the New York law firm Sullivan & Cromwell, Allen Dulles saw the U.S.S.R. as a threat to what he grandly called "the accumulated civilization" of the American century. Both brothers were determined to reverse the worldwide advance of communism. Foster talked of rolling back the Soviets out of east Europe.

It came as no surprise when I learned that British intelligence agents were actively discussing with their opposite members in Washington how best to "take out" Mohammed Mosaddegh. The leading Brit was one of my future colleagues in the House of Commons, C.M. "Monty" Woodhouse who as chief of British intelligence in Iran ran a network of undercover agents and associates. Woodhouse, later Lord Terrington, teamed up with Kermit Roosevelt, a rising star in the CIA's still embryonic operations in the Middle East. Both men had served as intelligence officers during World War II and accompanied President Roosevelt and Winston Churchill when they met Stalin in Teheran in 1943.

Woodhouse in his talks with leading figures in Washington concentrated on the risks of a chaotic Iran becoming a satellite of the Soviet Union. He and Roosevelt were both convinced that the Communists in

U.S. Secretary of State Foster Dulles and brother Allen Dulles, head of the CIA. Both were determined to roll back the tide of communism.

Iran would support Mosaddegh as an activist front man to overthrow the Shah, and would then discard him in favor of an Iranian Peoples Republic with fraternal links to Russia. The Tudeh party already had printed postage stamps of an Iranian Peoples Republic.[1]

To prevent this, the Brits proposed to mobilize a coalition of Iranian tribal leaders, army officers, mullahs and elder statesmen to oppose and remove Mosaddegh who would be replaced by a new pro western leader ready to negotiate a settlement of the oil crisis with U.S. and British firms. The British code name for these complex activities was "Operation Boot." It depended heavily on the network of agents Woodhouse had left in post in Iran and in particular on three remarkable brothers, Sayfollah, Asadollah and Qodratollah Rashidian to whom the British secret intelligence service (SIS) paid a retainer of $10,000 per month.

The Rashidians' nominee to replace Mosaddegh was General Fazlollah Zahedi, a former chief of the Teheran police district, former senator and former minister to the interior, with a distinguished record as an infantry commander who had fought against the Russians in Azerbaijan. General Zahedi who already had made it known that he was interested in becoming prime minister, ironically had been arrested and jailed by the British for his pro—German activities in World War II. Zahedi's overriding objective were to save Iran from the Communists. His U.S.-educated son and closest aide, Ardeshir Zahedi, was to become a prime mover in the subsequent history of Iran,

General Zahedi and his son and aide, Ardeshir (left). Prime movers in ousting Mossadegh and returning the Shah to the throne

ambassador to London and Washington, and one of my closest Iranian friends.

The CIA accepted Monty Woodlouse's plan, subject to fleshing out its details.

The U.S. embassy in Teheran, now headed by an ambassador, Loy Henderson with closer links to the Brits than his Democrat predecessor, surreptitiously began making contact with some of Woodhouse's agents. I knew nothing of these activities until I learned that the SIS had moved its Middle East headquarters to Cyprus and that its chief, Sir John Sinclair, head of British intelligence, then known only as "C," had met Allen Dulles in Washington. Secretary of State Dulles then told the U.S. National Security Council at its meeting with the president that "If Iran succumbed to the Communists, there was little doubt that the other areas of the Middle East with 60 percent of the world's oil reserves would fall into Communist control."[2]

The die was cast on June 14 when President Eisenhower finally agreed with Churchill that Mosaddegh must go. Operation Boot was renamed Ajax. Kermit Roosevelt took over command. "This is how we get rid of that madman," said Foster Dulles. The White House was more skeptical. Mr. Eisenhower later wrote in his memoirs that Roosevelt's account of Operation Ajax sounded "more like a dime store novel than serious foreign policy."

Looking back, I think Ike was right. Given what they knew at the time of Stalin's Russia which only recently had forcibly incorporated Poland, Czechoslovakia and Hungary into the "evil empire" that had encouraged the North Koreans to invade South Korea, the U.S. and Britain were entitled in their own interests to seek to prevent the Communists from bringing about the same result in Iran. But in the event it was the Iranians or more accurately the Teheranis who provided the people power that overturned Mohammed Mosaddegh.

To be sure, most Iranians cheered Mosaddegh when he seized Abadan. "How proud we were to translate B.P. (British Petroleum) as Benzene Pars, Iranian Oil," wrote Farah Diba, the wife of the Shah in her memoirs.[3] But Mosaddegh didn't know when to stop. He went too far, too fast, and too irrationally for his own and his countrymen's good. He threw away the opportunity for Iran to reap the benefits of his seizure of Abadan And large numbers of Iranians recognized this at the time. A note I received from one of the shrewdest contemporary observers said this:

> He lead the country into an impasse. As oil revenues fell, the economy deteriorated. Unemployment soared. Inflation was out of control. Many of Mosaddegh's key supporters abandoned him. The most prominent members of the religious establishment turned against him because they feared his policies would lead to a seizure of power by the Communists.[4]

Mosaddegh's response to criticism was to trade on his medical infirmities. In the full flood of his oratory he would suffer or feign fainting spells. Once when the Shah, seeking to prevent the prime minister's storming out of his office after threatening to resign, stood in the doorway to block the exit, Mosaddegh fell to the floor apparently in a dead faint. These antics were an embarrassment for most of the Teheranis I met at the time. Far from idolizing Mosaddegh, they blamed him for the loss of their country's oil revenues, and could not wait to see the back of him.

The last straw was Mosaddegh's dissolution of the Majlis in early July. The elected parliament, he said it was "not worthy of the Iranian people." That left Mosaddegh a virtual dictator, ruling Iran from his bedroom by decree.

The events that followed were dramatic (and are still argued about in Iran) My recollections are as follows:

Early August, 1953: Kermit Roosevelt returned to Teheran. I met him in the Hilton Hotel where we talked about Yale and his private school, Groton. I had no idea what he was doing in Iran. The big news was Mosaddegh's demand for control of Iran's armed forces. The Shah as commander in chief refused.

August 14: The Shah signed two *firman* (decrees), one dismissing Mosaddegh, the other appointing General Zahedi in his place. Mosaddegh refused to accept his dismissal. The army colonel who handed the Shah's *farman* to him was arrested.

August 15: Headlines in the Teheran press said that Mosaddegh's next step would be to abolish the monarchy. The Shah and Queen Soraya fled to their summer home at Kelardasht, a village on the coast of the Caspian Sea, and later flew to Baghdad (then British controlled).

August 16: Mobs supporting the Shah clashed with mobs supporting Mosaddegh. Mosaddegh's security agents arrested large numbers of royalist supporters. General Zahedi went into hiding. The Shah was reported to have flown from Baghdad to Rome.

August 17: Teheran was in chaos. Iran's army officers were reported to be deeply divided. Should they back Mosaddegh as prime minister? Or the nominee of the Shah to whom they had sworn allegiance. Most opted for General Zahedi.

August 18: Pro Mosaddegh supporters surrounded the equestrian statue of the Shah's father, Reza Shah. When they tore this down, most Army officers were appalled.

August 19: The speaker of the Majlis came out against Mosaddegh. In the streets, the tide turned in favor of the Shah. Groups of weightlifters from Zurkhaneh clubs where Iranian athletes built up huge Schwarzenegger-like muscles marched through the bazaars, shouting "Death to Mosaddegh."

August 20: General Zahedi drove in an Army tank to the radio station. He declared himself to be "the lawful prime minister, by the Shah's order." Zahedi sent a telegram to Rome telling the Shah that

Iranians were "counting the minutes" until his return. Mosaddegh surrendered, and was held prisoner in the Army officers club. Teheran radio announced that the Shah was on his way home.

So ended one of the last century's most extraordinary bouleversements. Six days in August 1953 saw the Shah of Iran fleeing and Mosaddegh on top, then Mosaddegh torn down and the Shah back on his throne.

To what extent was this an Anglo-American coup, as Iranian nationalists ever since have insisted? Kermit Roosevelt certainly disbursed large quantities of U.S. dollars to gang leaders and members of the clergy whose followers filled the streets of Teheran with anti Mosaddegh demonstrators. Among them were the Zurkhaneh weight lifters. Roosevelt also made contact with some of the agents and sympathizers that the SIS had recruited. On this basis, the CIA and Roosevelt himself, in his book, *Counter Coup: The Struggle for Control of Iran* (pub. McGraw Hill 1979), gave most of the credit for Mosaddegh's removal and the Shah's return to U.S. and British boldness.

General Zahedi (top at left with stick); Mossadegh supporters and Communists tear down the statue of Iranian national hero, Reza Shah; General Zahedi greets supporters as he drives to office as prime minister; crowds of Teheranis welcome the return of the Shah

Scores of TV shows and spy movies have since embedded Operation Ajax into the literature of American successes in the Cold War.

My sources in Iran have always described these claims as more fiction than fact. *Counter Coup,* for instance, is replete with errors. Thus, Roosevelt says that he spoke in German with General Zahedi. In fact, Fazlollah Zahedi did not speak a word of German, only Farsi, Turkish and Russian. Roosevelt also says that Zahedi was hidden in a house occupied by a member of the U.S. embassy. Zahedi said that he never met any American in August 1953 nor did he ever meet Kermit Roosevelt, despite the book's claims that he did. Most fanciful is *Counter Coup*'s claim that Roosevelt told the Shah that the BBC would interrupt its Persian language service at twelve noon on a specified date with a pause that would signal that his mission had the personal approval of President Eisenhower. The BBC's broadcasts to Iran were never aired at twelve noon, and the BBC both denied this and successfully sued Roosevelt's publishers for damages.

The truth, I believe, is that Monty Woodhouse's intelligence assets and Kermit Roosevelt's leaflets and largesse, contributed to Mosaddegh's fall—but only because enough Iranians followed General Zahedi's lead and went out into the streets to resist Mosaddegh's reach for absolute power.

Ardeshir Zahedi, who was at his father's side throughout the August crisis, says:

> *Mosaddegh was overthrown by a popular uprising that started in the poorest districts of Teheran. It was not the result of any CIA plot. None of the U.S. embassy officials or CIA operatives spoke Persian or had any real experience of the country. A handful of men with no knowledge of the language and customs could change a regime only in a TV serial like* Mission Impossible.

Vernon Walters who was to become deputy chief of the CIA agreed with Zahedi. "The CIA takes more of the credit for this than they deserved," he wrote in his memoirs.

The Shah gave most of the credit for his safe return to the throne to Teheran's people. "Workers and craftsmen, students and members of the liberal professions, soldiers, policemen, even women and children took an extraordinarily courageous stand against the frenzied dictator," he wrote in his diary. The Shah too was exaggerating. It was not for love of him or the monarchy that the Iranians, as he put it, "reversed the situation." Yet the Shah's description of those tempestuous days seems to me to be nearer the mark than either the Hollywoodized version that appeals to Americans' preference for drama over facts, or the Iranians penchant for believing that everything they disapprove of is the product of a conspiracy cooked up by the Brits or a plot engineered by the Americans.

The irony remains. By trumpeting American and British ownership of the operation to get rid of Mosaddegh, *Counter Coup* and the spy literature it spawned, assisted in the creation of a legend. A charismatic but irascible old orator who threw away the opportunities of oil nationalization was transformed in the eyes of subsequent generations of Iranians into the "old lion," the "liberator," even "the George Washington" of Iran. So it is that the first demand Iranians make of anyone seeking to bridge the gap between Iran and the west is that the U.S. and Britain must apologize for bringing down Mohammed Mosaddegh!

THE SHAH'S DREAMS AND ILLUSIONS

Only if prices rise to levels where you cannot afford to burn oil inefficiently will America look for alternative sources like nuclear power.
— Shah of Iran

My first face to face meeting with the Shah who returned to the throne when Mosaddegh was removed, took place in the Niavaran palace, overlooking Teheran. We met in his office, a cool corner room with tall windows, gold plated telephones and inkwells, to which I was escorted through a labyrinth of mirrored corridors. I already had written extensively about Mohammed Reza II, describing him in *Newsweek* magazine as an Iranian version of his autocratic French contemporary, Charles de Gaulle. Since then the Shah had launched his White Revolution, white because he proclaimed that its program of drastic reforms could be carried through without spilling a drop of blood. He had also, in American and British eyes, amply justified his restoration to the Peacock throne by whole heartedly committing Iran to the Western side of the Cold War and cushioning the shock of higher oil prices by using its petro-dollars to purchase U.S. and U.K. armaments.

Shah and Shahbanon (Empress) in Imperial regalia, with children (center), Shah's twin sister (right), older daughter Shahnaz and Queen mother (far left)

The context for our meeting was the Shah's intention to pay a state visit to the United States at the

— 28 —

invitation of President Nixon. Of special interest to Americans was his pretty French-educated wife, Farah Diba who six months earlier had become the toast of Paris when the royal couple visited France as guests of President De Gaulle. Asked by the media, "Of all the wives of heads of state you have met, which one do you like best?" De Gaulle replied, "Farah."

"What about Jackie Kennedy?"[1]

"She is very pretty too," said the general, "but Farah has an impish quality which gives her something *extra*!"

I noticed three photographs of Farah Diba on the Shah's desk. The largest showed her cradling their son and heir to the throne, Reza Pahlavi, born in 1960. Peering down from the wall was a portrait of the Shah's father, Reza Khan in Cossack uniform.

Dismissing his aide, the Shah stubbed out a cigarette and motioned me to a dark red sofa. "I understand that you are British and American," he said in quiet accented English. "Both your countries are friends of Iran so you are most welcome here."

Time and my advancing age long since have erased the details of the conversation that followed. But three points that the Shah ticked off on his well-manicured fingers still are etched in my memory—land reform, women and oil.

On the first, he flattered me by saying that he understood I knew something about farming. He had been well-briefed by the embassy in London—at the time I owned a pig farm. Launching into a passage about the need to give every peasant a stake in owning his own land, the Shah said that he was setting an example by breaking up the royal estates into small owner-occupied farms. The landed aristocracy and the mosques, who between them owned two-thirds of Iran's farmland, would be required by law to to do the same. The Shah was especially interested in the U.S. government's Point 1V self-help program designed to improve yields by offering farmers fertilizers, equipment and know how. He commended the work of William Warne, an

American, sent to Iran at the suggestion of Ardeshir Zahedi who had studied agriculture at Utah State University.

Turning to women, the Shah recalled a visit he had paid to Salt Lake City. "In Iran," he said with a smile, "we treat women better than the Mormons do. Iranian women can vote, become members of parliament and no-one makes them wear veils." The Shah claimed credit for emancipating Iranian women from the servitude and harems that had traditionally been their role. "A nation is like an airplane, to fly it needs two wings, one male, the other female."

How different it is in Islamic Iran today.

I raised the question of oil and Iran's decision to double the price, leading Saudi Arabia and all other members of OPEC to do the same. The Shah said that he needed the money to finance education, roads and power stations. When I commented that this had stoked up inflation in Europe and Japan and caused havoc on the New York stock exchange, he got up from his chair and walked about the room. "Oil," he said, "is too finite a resource to be blown out of the rear of all your millions of big motorcars. But that is what Americans will keep on doing if oil remains so cheap that you waste it."

There followed an exchange that previewed the collision over nuclear power between the U.S. and Iran today.

Shah: "Only if petrol prices rise to levels where you cannot afford to burn oil inefficiently will America look for alternative sources like nuclear power."

E.G.: "Nuclear power stations are already being built in the U.S., U.K. and France."

Shah: "Iran will build them too. Westinghouse Corporation is designing the first of our nuclear plants, which will be built at Bushehr."

The Shah and Queen Farah Diba meet Iranian ladies at court. Veils no longer were needed.

That was the first indication I received that Iran was getting into the nuclear power business. And when I checked with U.S. and British officials, they confirmed that the Shah was right. Forty years ago, Abbas Hoveyda, then the Iranian Prime Minister asked President Lyndon Johnson for help in developing a nuclear power program and LBJ agreed. He told the Shah that the U.S. would "cooperate with Iran in building nuclear power stations."

A detailed account of American and European collaboration in the development of Iran's nuclear power program appears in Part Two of this book. This disposes of the notion, much favored by neo-cons in Washington, that it was the bearded ayatollahs of the Islamist regime who launched Iran into the nuclear power business. They didn't. The Shah did, with U.S. support.

Did the Shah intend that Iran one day would have nuclear weapons? Akbar Etemad was the managing director of the Iranian Atomic Energy Organization in the 1960s. Dr. Etemad wrote in his memoirs that neither he nor Prime Minister Hoveyda "inquired too deeply into the question of whether the fuel would be enriched to make plutonium for nuclear weapons. But early on we easily understood what (the Shah) had in mind. I pretended not to know, but I could see the pieces of a large mosaic were coming together."[2]

I later met Asadollah Alam, for twelve years the Shah's closest confidante who became his Minister of Court. Alam, who kept a diary recording their conversations, described the Shah's "great vision for the future of Iran," and added. "This, though he denies it, probably includes our manufacturing a nuclear deterrent.[3]

The only other formal audience I had with the Shah of Iran occurred in the mid-1960s after my election to the British parliament. That was when he visited London and stayed at Buckingham Palace as a guest of the Queen. He addressed nine hundred businessmen and

The Shah was handsome and beautifully tailored with a politician's knack of remembering names and faces

bankers in the Guildhall of the City of London and met the Conservative party's foreign affairs committee of which I was honorary secretary.

At close quarters the Shah, in his prime was as persuasive an advocate as any of the world leaders I have met, except for such giants as Winston Churchill (with whom I briefly coincided during my first year in Parliament) and Richard Nixon (after he ceased to be president). Speaking without notes for fifty minutes, the Shah gave us a tour d'horizon whose lucidity and mastery of detail were matched only by the crispness of his replies to questions. Handsome and beautifully tailored in the days before wealth made him arrogant and flattery clouded his judgment, he had a politician's knack of remembering names and faces. He recalled, for example, the interview I had with him as the chief European correspondent for *Newsweek*. "Is it up or down you have gone between press and parliament" he enquired?

We spoke about Bahrain, where I had got to know Sheik bin Issa al-Khalifa, one of whose flashy gift watches the Shah noted I was wearing. Issa, a Sunni Arab, was scared stiff of Iran, as his successor still is today. More than half the population of Bahrain are first and second generation Iranian immigrants of the Shiite faith and the Shah, like his father, regarded all the islands in the Persian Gulf as historically and culturally theirs. British troops had been based in Bahrain for generations but to save money and fend off a revolt by left wingers in the parliamentary Labour Party over the cost of health service prescriptions, Harold Wilson's government had decided to phase the troops out. That left Bahrain vulnerable and the Shah contemplating the island's falling into his lap like an over ripe peach. It did not work out that way. Sheikh Issa was relieved—and the Shah displeased—when the U.S. navy started to move in as the British battalions moved out.

The Shah was also concerned, as I was about the Sultanate of Oman. This was "off limits" to foreign visitors in the 1960s, denied gas, running water or electricity until the Brits replaced its tyrannical old ruler, Sultan Said bin Taimur, better known as Shakbut, with his bright young son Qaboos, the present Sultan. Qaboos is a graduate of the British Army's officer training academy at Sandhurst. He spent six months in my parliamentary constituency of West Suffolk learning the ropes of local government finance and ever since has favored the "Suffolks" when appointing Brits to serve in his armed forces and police. When a private hospital in my district made an appeal for funds, the largest donation came anonymously from Sultan Qaboos.

The Shah's concern over Oman arose from the attacks being launched across its southern border by Soviet armed invaders from the Peoples Democratic Republic of Yemen (PDRY). Sultan Qaboos sought military assistance from Britain and Iran, and both responded, the Brits with units of the Special Air Service (SAS) backed up by missile batteries, Iran with a sizeable force of infantry, artillery and armored vehicles that was flown into Sallala by the Iranian air force. I visited Muscat as the guest of Sultan Qaboos and flew down to the Dhofar region of southern Oman to see the SAS in action. While there I met several of the senior officers in charge of the very much larger Iranian contingent deployed in the mountains alongside a battalion of Jordanians provided by King Hussein to help his fellow Sandhurst graduate, Qaboos.

Dhofar is one of the many forgotten Western success stories of the Cold War. The invaders were repulsed and Iran played its part on the same side as Britain and America. Should the Soviet-backed PDRY have gained control of Southern Oman, the oil tankers that then carried three-fifths of the West's oil supply from the Persian Gulf to the U.S. and Europe would have been at risk to Communist interdiction.

AMBASSADOR EXTRAORDINAIRE

A man who made—and unmade—
more friends for Imperial Iran than any other.
— Chairman, British-Iranian Group,
House of Commons, London

One result of the Shah's visit to London was that I got to know the most energetic and olympian Iranian of any of the hundreds I have met. Ardeshir Zahedi was married to the Shah's oldest daughter, princess Shahnaz. It was he who had taken the lead in finding a new wife for the Shah when having divorced Soraya, his second childless wife, the Shah was on the look-out for a new lady to share his throne. In Paris, Ardeshir found and introduced to the Shah a tall, good-looking Persian art student named Farah Diba. Aged eighteen, Farah accepted the Shah's hand and went on to bear two royal daughters and the crown prince, Reza Pahlavi.

Ardeshir Zahedi by any measure was—and still is—one of the most extraordinary figures to have occupied the center stage of Iranian politics and diplomacy over the past fifty years. The son of Prime Minister Zahedi who toppled Mohammed Mosaddegh, he was twice ambassador to the United States, ambassador to Britain, and before the revolution, the most powerful of Iran's foreign ministers. Yet what gave and still gives him a special place in the loves and hates of Iranians is his warm heart, his brutal honesty, above all his compulsive generosity, a quality that for me is the most attractive of Persian characteristics. Ardeshir is an Iranian patrician. He was brought up to ride and shoot on his family's estate at Hamadan before he was seven years of age. As a schoolboy, he wore German-style uniforms and organized anti-British protests; as a student at Utah State University, he gypsied around America washing dishes to pay for his lodgings. As a critic of Mohammed Mosaddegh he was slapped in the face by a government minister, jailed and beaten by a guard, a blow from whose rifle left the young Zahedi with an injured spine that ever since has forced him to walk with a slight, distinguished-looking limp. Along the way, Zahedi acquired a well-earned reputation as a playboy, big spender and Casanova, but beneath the smooth exterior is a man who all his life worked hard, played hard and arguably made—and unmade—more friends for imperial Iran than any other of its leaders.

One of Ardeshir's first public appointments was as an adjutant to the Shah. In 1959, he was named as Iranian Ambassador to the United States where the buzz at *Time* and *Newsweek* was that Zahedi had the ear of Vice President Nixon but had upset the Kennedy brothers and would not last long in Washington if the Democrats were to win the 1960 presidential election. Sure enough, when JFK was elected, Ardeshir Zahedi returned to Iran. His wife, Princess Shahnaz, wanted their next posting to be Rome where she enjoyed the sunshine and dressmakers; but Ardeshir insisted on London and they went their separate ways. Ardeshir's aim in Britain was to bridge the gap that had opened up between the Brits and his father, General Zahedi, who had stepped down as prime minister within two years of succeeding Mosaddegh. Neither side had forgotten that the Brits had jailed the general for his support of the Germans in World War II.

In London, Ardeshir Zahedi transformed the Iranian embassy refurbishing it with some of his own carpets and priceless ornaments, hiring

Ardeshir Zahedi (left) as aide to the Shah and bridegroom at his wedding to the Shah's daughter, Shahnaz.

cooks and an English butler who made his dinner parties the talk of the town. To the chancellery at Princess Gate and the ambassador's residence next door came a never ending stream of visitors, Persians and Americans as well as the political, cultural and social elite of London. No one I knew in the House of Commons or the City of London refused an invitation from the polished and amusing ambassador of Iran. Among his friends were Edward Heath, prime minister 1970–74, Lord Mountbatten, uncle of Queen Elizabeth and Sir Alec Douglas Home, prime minister 1963–64 and foreign secretary 1970–1974.

Ardeshir Zahedi and I became good friends. He knew of my interest in Persian history and painting. I knew of the role he had played in the revolt of the people of Teheran against Mohammed Mosaddegh. We shared an interest in America where as a journalist I had reported on Richard Nixon's campaigns in California and had got to know Iran's strongest champion in America, Secretary of State Henry Kissinger when, still a Harvard professor he worked as a Soviet expert for *Time* magazine.

In the spring of 1966, the ambassador arranged for me to visit Iran as the guest of his government. Flying into Tehran, I was met by a government car that ran into a traffic jam at the point where the airport road connected with Eisenhower Blvd. as the city's main highway to the west had been renamed.[1] Siren-blasting, blue-light-flashing my police escort tried and failed to

Iranian Ambassador to London with British friends Edward Heath (top left), Lord Mountbatten (right), and Sir Alec Douglas Home (right)

force a way through the mass of vehicles encircling the Middle East's biggest 1960s building site, the Shah-Yad monument. Yad is the Persian word for memory and the Shah-Yad was the nearest thing to an Egyptian pharaoh's pyramid, except that this vast Iranian pile was being constructed out of steel and concrete as a symbol of Teheran's advance towards the twenty-first century, AD.

I got out of my car to look at it. Despite the dust and noise the immense size of what my guide described as Iran's "reach for the stars" immediately became apparent. The centerpiece is a giant tower of soaring marble pillars that reach one hundred fifty feet up to a massive twelve-sided turret. Beneath, around a huge square, separate yards depict all thirty of the Persian dynasties and culminated when I was there in a still unfinished monument to the Pahlavi Shahs.

The Shah-Yad is not in the same league of national self advertisement as the Statue of Liberty in New York or the Arc de Triomphe in Paris. There is none of the loveliness in stone of the Lincoln monument in Washington. The architect was Hussein Amanat who as a twenty-two-year old student had seen a notice in one of Teheran's newspapers advertising a competition to design a structure that would memorialize 2,500 years of monarchical rule in Persia. Amanat, a Jewish Iranian who became a convert to the Bahai faith, sketched his ideas on the back of an envelope and translated them into blueprints in less than a week. Amanat's concept was to build Shah-Yad with 2,500 huge white stones at a cost of less than one million dollars. This beat out

Shah-Yad by day and night. A symbol of Tehran's advance towardst the twenty-first century.

the design of Queen Farah Diba's candidate but his success infuriated the architectural establishment of Teheran, leading to extraordinary claims that Shah-Yad represented the Shah's desire for phallic immortality. There were allegations that the final costs ran into millions, but as I discovered on later visits, Amanat delivered the Shah-Yad to budget and on time. He used new methods of laying concrete that had been devised by another young Persian who won the contract to lay the foundations for Australia's bicentennial Sydney Opera House.

Hussein Amanat went on to design some notable Bahai temples and less usefully to build several of the Shah's Miami Beach style vacation homes. He was forced to flee for his life when the revolutionary regime took over, but Shah-Yad survived the Islamists wrecking ball and was renamed Azadi Square, meaning freedom. It is now the site where the Ayatollahs' followers congregate each year to celebrate the down fall of the man who ordered it to be put up—the last of the shahs.

My chief host in Teheran on this trip was Hussein Ala, an impeccably dressed old aristocrat who had served as ambassador to London and briefly as Prime Minister. Hussein Ala was now Minister of Court. He showed me how to drink tea in the Iranian manner, by placing a sugar lump on one's tongue and sucking the hot liquid through it so that the sugar dissolved. Dr. Ala also took me to a nightclub and summoned a buxom belly dancer to sit on my lap. She had a huge ruby in her navel and spoke English with an Oxford accent. Asked about the ruby, she said that she had attended a famous girl's school in England, where her classmates had "stretched" her navel so as to accommodate a much larger stone than her parents otherwise would have given her on her sixteenth birthday!

Hussein Ala arranged for me to see the Shah's collection of jewels housed in a vault underneath the Central Bank of Iran. On the way, I paid a courtesy call on the governor of the bank, a distinguished looking man named Mehdi Samii whose initially reserved manner broke down when we got into conversation about his love of soccer and ability to quote Shakespeare's plays. The governor was in the throes of organizing the Shah's belated coronation ceremonies and choosing a crown for the Queen which Farah Diba wore for the first time in 1966. He was one of the first Iranians to become a chartered accountant having been trained in England by Harold Lasky, a professor at the London School of Economics for whom, as a conservative I found it easy to contain my admiration. Lasky, a Socialist theoretician, inspired the post-World War II British government to nationalize large sections of the British economy, but Mehdi Samii assured me that he had shed these Socialist ideas when he returned to Teheran. Samii helped to draft Iran's first Law on the Encouragement and Protection of Foreign Investment. More than anything else, this attracted overseas companies to set up manufacturing plants in Tehran and Isfahan in the 1960s. Mehdi Samii's only concession to the egalitarian ideas he had acquired in London was the Central Bank's staff café where clerks, drivers and secretaries for the first time ate and drank with its board members and senior executives. On the walls were magnificent oil paintings by the Persian masters.

Deep in the vaults below the Central Bank were—and still are—the crown jewels. At the entrance was the most spectacular, the Peacock throne, described as a divan but to me more like a golden double bed with four legs and two raised sides, every square inch of which is encrusted with emeralds, rubies, pearls and diamonds. Gleaming under a spotlight, the throne gets its name from the peacock shaped patterns, surrounded by flowers, leaves and fruit, into which these stones are carved. Deeper in the vault, I saw—and counted—forty glass showcases filled with a collection of jewelry that rivals, perhaps surpasses the one in the Tower of London. There were gem encrusted egg cups, diamond tiaras, silver bangles and an all gold chastity belt weighting seventeen pounds, "worth more than the contents" said the curator. Hussein Ala told him to open one of the showcases containing a globe of the world ordered by

Nasser el Dinh to whose rescue in 1804 a British force from India had marched from the Persian Gulf shore to the Azerbaijan frontier to help repel a Russian invasion. The globe weighted seventy-five pounds and was encrusted with 51,000 precious stones, the continents marked with rubies and sapphires, the oceans with emeralds. Two of the emeralds denoting the north and south Pacific each weighted more than 200 carats. A huge ruby covering Texas weighted seventy-five carats.

Hussein Ala and the curator, a descendant of Nasser el Dinh, sketched in some of the history of this fabulous collection which still forms the basis of the Bank of Iran's reserves. Afghans and Seljuk Turks had plundered Persia during successive invasions in the sixteenth and seventeenth centuries and made off with much of its wealth: but a non-commissioned officer in the imperial army not only seized power, as the Shah's father did two centuries later, but drove out the invaders and followed them to India where he retrieved a good deal of the loot. For good measure, he sacked and burned scores of Indian temples and returned home with wagonloads of pillaged treasures including the Peacock throne and the 182-carat Sea of Light diamond. Still rated as the world's largest uncut diamond, until recently was on display beneath the Central Bank of the Islamic republic.

The Peacock Throne and other treasures of the Persian Empire, now part of Iran's reserves

Author on one of Darius II's 2,500 year old monuments,
Persepolis, 1968

During this visit to Iran I flew south to Shiraz and was driven to Persepolis, the great ruined desert city I had wanted to visit since childhood. Only the Great Wall of China has ever made so stunning an impact on me. Halfway between Isfahan and Shiraz, Darius I, son in law of Cyrus began the construction of the first terrace of Persepolis in 518BC. Xerxes his son and successor (486–465BC), completed the harem and vast *apadamal* (reception room) and began work on a hall of one hundred columns that Darius' grandson Artazerxes declared open thirty years later.

Walking alone under a full moon with stars glittering like diamonds in the purple sky, I entered the ruined central hall of Persepolis through a portico guarded by sixteen foot tall winged bulls, two with human heads. The staircases are ornamented with processions of horsemen and archers bearing gifts from twenty-three vassal countries to the Persian king of kings. So smooth is the stone in Darius's waiting room that this huge room is rightly described the Hall of Mirrors.

Persepolis persuaded me that Alexander the Great committed one of history's greatest acts of vandalism when, in a drunken fit, he ordered the destruction by fire of a city that in 330BC surpassed anything in contemporary Greece and matched if it did not exceed Abu Simnel in Egypt and Petra in Jordan. Herodotus, I decided had been wrong and my classics master right about the Greeks being overrated and the Persians under rated in the text books of my old school!

FALLING IN LOVE WITH IRAN

Haunted by those plains of amber, those peaks of amethyst,
the dignity of that crumbled magnificence,
that silence of two thousand years.
— Lord Curzon

I paid a further visit to Iran soon after Ardeshir Zahedi became its foreign minister. He was pressing Iran's claims to a number of small islands in the Persian Gulf that the Brits believed were the territory of the Arab emirates of Sharjah and Ras al Khaimah. This led to heated clashes with the British ambassador, Sir Denis Wright with whom I stayed at the embassy in Teheran. British aircraft patrolling off Bahrain were alleged to have buzzed an Iranian vessel. Ardeshir threatened to send Iranian planes to intercept and shoot them down. Ardeshir banged the table angrily and only the intervention of the Court Minister, Asadollah Alam got both sides to cool down.

Yet Ardeshir as foreign minister never wavered in his courtesy and friendship to me. He wanted me to see the progress that Iran was making in the economic and social fields and to this end, he introduced me to Plan Organization, the state agency charged with channeling oil revenues into infrastructural projects.

The Director of Plan Organization was a man whose name I at first found hard to get my tongue around, Khodadad Farmanfarmaian. Among Iran's self-styled "Thousand families" who owned most of its land, the Farmanfarmaians were pre-eminent in wealth and virility. Khodadad was one of thirty two children of his patriarch father who never doubted that his clan was better bred as well as richer than the "jumped-up" Pahlavis.

Farmanfarmaian—meaning he who issues a *farman* (order)—was the title given to Khodadad's forebears by the Qajar kings of Iran. Educated at an English boarding school and at Stamford University, he taught economics at Princeton and served as a governor of the Central Bank of Iran before moving to the Plan Organization. Khodadad's style and language struck me as more American than Iranian. He opened our conversation by saying, "Call me Kodi," and offered me a coke. He was more convinced than I was of the merits of central planning. Iran's five-year plans were about much more than economic advance, he said. He and the Shah believed that they would recreate the twentieth century's equivalent of the Achaemenian monarchs' Great Civilization. Later, when he fled from Iran to London, Kodi and his brothers became supporters of Margaret Thatcher's free enterprise approach to government. One of his sisters, by contrast, was a Communist who set up Iran's social services department and survived the Islamic revolution.

The Plan Organization provided me with a car and driver and a magnificently proportioned guide named Monir who took me to see a village where the planners had built packing plants for the farmers, maternity clinics for the women, schools for the children and recreational centers for the men (no women appeared to use them). There was something vaguely socialist, even Soviet, about this. I preferred the old Persia we visited during a week of driving across the deserts and mountains to ancient cities like Isfahan, Yazd and Kerman, each of them boasting more palaces, mosques, bazaars and civic virtue than any other in Iran.

One of the first stops was at Qom, the sacred university city of Iranian Schiism, nestled between red rock mountains that reminded me of Zion Park in Utah. The center of Qom was a labyrinth of winding streets and a bazaar where turbaned clerics and Afghan laborers jostled one another among piles of fruit and marrows. On arrival in Qom, my guide Monir for the first time covered her auburn tresses with a black head dress. At a shop where rows of bearded men were playing chess and smoking hashish, I ate two bars of sticky saffron-scented pistachio nuts, washed down with glasses of scented tea made in a tall blue porcelain samovar. This I was told would strengthen my virility.

Dominating Qom is the shimmering blue dome of its ancient monastery and nearby the shrine of Massomeh, the wife of Shiism's founder, the prophet Hussein. Schiism, I was told, had ensured that Iran retained its identity. Together with their long history and culture, that is what made the Iranians different—distinct from the Arabs and Sunni Moslems. I wish I had been able to stay longer in Qom which has since replaced Najaf in Iraq as the fountainhead of Shiism's influence throughout the Middle East. Inside its monastery wall were two powerful ayatollahs, one Seyyed Kazem Shariat-madari whose wise counsel might well have saved the monarchy if the Shah had listened to him. The other, at the time his junior, was Ruhollah Khomeini, the fiery preacher whose hostility to the Shah's reforms, in particular women's rights, was to inspire the Islamic revolution that set Iran on its collision course with the West.

Heading south from Qom, we drove across deserts and mountains to Iran's second city, Isfahan, a place of metal bashers and textile manufacturers with a civic motto that claims "Isfahan is half the world." At its center is a vast central plaza where its founder, Shah Abbas I, the greatest of the sixteenth century Safavid kings, played polo. Isfahan plaza is larger than Tiananmen Square in Beijing. At one end is an

Mosques in Qom

Isfahan: "Half the World," it claims

enormous bazaar where I bought a samovar and two glass vases, at the other an ugly seven story building misnamed the "Sublime Gate" where the city's government was housed. Isfahan was Monir's home town. Proud of its history, she rattled off the dates and some of the horrors of successive invasions by Turks, Mongols and Afghans, then showed me how the Iranians had "bounced back," to build some of Central Asia's most magnificent palaces, gardens and mosques. Removing my shoes, I entered the Imam mosque and lay on my back to gaze up at the inside of its cavernous dome. This is so perfectly engineered that when I clapped my hands, the echo could be heard six or seven times before it died away.

Close by the mosque is the Palace of Forty Columns, although in fact, there are only twenty. The rest are reflections in a long narrow pool that reminded me of the one at the Taj Mahal in India. According to one of the gardeners, the reflecting pool at Isfahan added a new meaning to the word for forty in the local Isfahani dialect. Because its twenty real pillars are made to look many times that number when the water ripples, *chehel*, the Farsi word for forty, had come to signify, I was told, anything between scores and a hundred. I tried this on a street corner merchant but he said that I'd got it wrong. My guide said he was ignorant. More likely I failed to pronounce the word *chehel* correctly, and made it sound like *chel*, which means crazy. The merchant still offered me a special deal on a rug. How much in U.S. dollars? Waving his hands he said, "*Chehel*."

The Iman Mosque

Palace of Forty Columns

Before leaving Isfahan, I met a group of its officials and business-men assembled by the Plan Organization's local office. One of them brusquely rejected my anodyne comment that Isfahan seemed pros-perous and peaceful. Like Monir, he recited the number of times the city had endured sieges, famines and massacres at the hands of for-eigners, and added another, the Russian occupation in the World War II. This he said had been "arranged by the British and the Americans."

"Didn't we also get the Russians to leave in 1946?" I asked.

"No," said the official. "They were driven out by the Persians."

I asked each of these Isfahan worthies to identify the city's great-est achievements, expecting them to mention its prowess as a great manufacturing center, its importance as the entry point for trade between the Middle East and central Asia, perhaps even its renowned soccer team. Instead, as one by one I went around the table, the city fathers' answers were the same. Isfahan's greatest pride was to have served six hundred years ago as the cradle of Shiism.

Why was that more important than the city of Isfahan's other claims to fame?

"Surely you can understand this," said one of the businessmen who had attended a school in London. "King Henry VIII gave England its own identity by embracing the Protestant faith that separated it from Rome. We Persians have had our identity for 4,000 years but it was in danger of being submerged by the Sunnis until Isfahan embraced Shiism."

I recalled that conversation when Isfahan ten years later became the center of some of the earliest Shiite riots against the Shah. During the Iran-Iraq war that followed the Islamic Revolution, many of the most fanatical youngsters who sacrificed themselves in the name of Islam to halt Saddam Hussein's invasion were also Isfahanis. Religion and Persian nationalism may well have fused earlier and their identification may well be stronger in Isfahan than anywhere else in Iran. Perhaps that is why Isfahan claims to be the most Persian of Persian cities.

During the rest of my drive across the center of Iran, I was often desperately hot and far from comfortable. Our car bounced over potholes in the winding mountain roads and paper-thin strips of asphalt that crossed the desert saltpans. It was an experience that made me aware of Iran's vast size (put one end on Seattle and the other reaches beyond Atlanta), and of the variety of its people (Baktiari, Kashgais and Baluchis to name just a few of its tribes).

Along the way, I came close to falling in love, partly with the red-brown vastness of the mountain chains that turned into liquid gold as the sun set, and mainly with Monir who shared with me her favorite quote from the Persian poet Rumi, "Whoever travels without a guide needs two hundred years for a two-day journey." Monir later came to see me in New York and I took her on the Staten Island ferry to visit the Statue of Liberty. But unlike most of the Teheran ladies who later emigrated to the U.S., the girl from Isfahan fond it difficult to settle in America. In Iran she only once covered her head during our thousand-mile drive, but in Manhattan, where she worked for six months at the U.N., she took to wearing a veil. At the time I put this down to feminine contrariness; but Monir insisted that the veil provided two assets that many women find it hard to come by in America—privacy and mystery!

Before long, she returned to Isfahan and I never heard from her again. But I shall always be grateful for the opportunity she—and the Plan Organization—gave me to see the high turrets of the Zagros Mountains, the dry air and cool nights of the vast central plateau, the oasis towns and villages of sun-dried brick and flat roofs. One of my parliamentary colleagues had previously written some words that described how Lord Curzon felt about Persia.

"He was forever haunted by those plains of amber, those peaks of amethyst, the dignity of that crumbled magnificence, that silence of two thousand years."

Fifty years after Curzon, I felt the same way about Iran.

BEE-PEE AND A TOPLESS BEACH

Her Royal Highness believes that charity starts at home.
Her own of which she has many.
— Sikh guide on Kish Island

My connections with Iran widened and deepened in the late 1960s. Memories of the Abadan crisis faded as British oil companies shifted the bulk of their drilling operations from the Middle East to the North Sea and Alaska. Britain's relations with Iran improved. I was elected to the executive committee of the Conservative party's most influential body in the House of Commons and served as honorary secretary and later chairman of the British-Iranian Parliamentary group.

This brought me into contact with the large Iranian community in London and with dozens of old Persian hands, among them Geoffrey Keating, who had served as an aide to Field Marshal Bernard Montgomery, Britain's World War II army commander. Keating had spent several years in Iran as a PR man for the Anglo-Iranian Oil Company and was a trustee of its pension fund which looked after many hundreds of Iranians as well as Brits.

Keating, through his many friends in Iran, arranged for me to visit the head office of the now nationalized Iranian Oil company (NIOC) in Teheran and to tour its tanker terminals on Kharg Island in the Persian Gulf. Together we flew to Ahwaz and hired a car to drive to the oil fields. A sand storm blew up, giving Keating, an Anglo-Irishman an excuse to tell a tall story about the former Anglo-Iranian Oil Company (AIOC) changing its name to BP.

According to Keating, a bee flew into the Rolls Royce car of AIOC's chairman when, like us, he was being driven through the desert to Abadan. The chairman tried to swat it with his copy of the *London Times* but his driver, an Iranian, stopped the car, coaxed the bee onto his hand, and it flew away, unharmed. Later, when they ran into a sandstorm, the Rolls Royce's wipers could not cope with the grit on the windshield. There was not enough water in its reservoir. A cloud of bees led by the one the chauffeur had released, then appeared and covered the windshield with moisture, enabling the chauffeur to see the road and avoid an accident.

"Bee pee," explained the Iranian. AIOC was duly re-named!

To get us to Kharg Island, NIOC's manager sent a helicopter to Abadan. Arriving at the tanker terminal at night as the loading berth's lights came on, I felt like a gnat intruding into an electrified cobweb of pipework, pylons, steel towers and writhing cables. Years later, during the Iran-Iraq War of the 1980s, wave after wave of Saddam Hussein's French-built fighter bombers would bombard Kharg with Exocet missiles, setting fire to most of its oil tanks and destroying the tanker terminals. NIOC replaced them with jerry-built oil loading facilities on islands further to the east where its engineers ingeniously converted what then was the world's largest supertanker, the Liberian-registered *Seaview Giant*, into an oil terminal. This handled a sizable portion of Iran's western oil exports until the French equipped Iraqi bombers with long range fuel tanks, enabling them to sink the *Seaview Giant* and put a large portion of the NIOC's substitute facilities out of action. To keep supplies of Arab oil moving, U.S. and British warships then took over the job of escorting Saudi and Kuwaiti tankers through the war zone. Kuwait's tankers were re-flagged with the Stars and Stripes entitling the U.S. navy to use lethal force to protect them. The U.S. destroyer, *Stark* was severely damaged in one of the Iraqi air attacks which killed twenty-two American sailors, but Washington by then had tilted so far in favor of Iraq that the U.S. accepted an apology from

Saddam Hussein and retaliated against Iran instead of Iraq. Two NIOC oil rigs and six Iranian coastal vessels were sunk by the U.S. navy.

All that was for the future when Geoffrey Keating and I arrived on Kharg Island and spent two days clambering up and down steel ladders, chatting to Texan and Scottish oilmen, lunching on board a tanker with a German captain and his Filipino mate, gossiping about cricket with a gang of Pakistani laborers. As the sun went down, we drank whiskey in a club manned by an Irish bartender and Indian waiters. Keating won a small fortune playing mah jong.

Kharg was now owned and operated exclusively by NIOC. Close to a million tons of oil, 4 percent of the world's supply, funneled through the maze of pipes that linked it to Abadan. Yet during my visit to Kharg, I saw very few Iranians. Most of the managers and technicians were still Brits, Americans, Ethiopians and Sudanese. The only Iranian I remember was an official who glanced at my passport when we arrived and again when we departed. On both occasions, this gentleman got up from an armchair, said welcome or goodbye, then subsided into his chair where he sucked smoke from a tall brass jar. Above his head a sign in English and Farsi said: No smoking, No drugs, No alcohol.

From Kharg I flew east in one of the oil company airplanes heading for Kish Island at the entrance to the Straits of Hormuz. This was a six-

hour journey in a cloudless blue sky, hugging the shore of southern Iran. Piloted by a Pakistani, I saw only one large city, Bushehr where the British East India company for more than a century had based its Persian Gulf naval squadron. A few miles outside Bushehr was a cloud of dust and fumes rising from

Iran's first nuclear power plant, circa 1980, Americans and Germans designed, Iraqis destroyed and Russians helped rebuild it, at Bushehr on Persian Gulf

— 50 —

the construction site of what was to be Iran's first nuclear power station. We did not land at Bushehr and my camera was not good enough to take any aerial photographs, but at the time there were no objections to Iran's building a nuclear reactor. Germans and Americans had designed this, Indian and Lebanese companies were handling much of the civil and electrical engineering, Sudanese and Somalis, according to my pilot, were swinging the picks and shovels for the benefit of the next generation. Thousands of proud Iranians who visited Bushehr in the 1970s took home with them picture postcards of what the finished power station would look like.

From Bushehr to Kish Island is less than two hundred air miles. The island is a sandy spit with a fringe of palm trees on the Persian side of the Straits of Hormuz. To the south as my plane approached, I saw three large tankers steaming towards the twenty-three mile wide channel through which half the world's oil supply then traveled from the terminals of Abu Dhabi, Bahrain, Saudi Arabia, Kuwait, Iraq and Iran. Escorting the tankers was a minesweeper of the imperial Iranian navy. Years later, I sailed through those waters on board an Omani gunboat. My son-in-law, stationed in Bahrain, served in a Royal Navy guided missile destroyer that guarded the U.S. battleship USS *Wisconsin* during the first Gulf war. Times change, history moves on. On my first visit to Kish Island, the long craggy coast of Iran was friendly territory. Today, the U.S. and British warships that ply the Persian Gulf treat it as hostile land.

My oil company airplane landed on a half-finished runway that, according to the pilot, was being lengthened to accommodate supersonic Concordes. The

The Shah's vacation/dream island: white sand, warm sea, no fresh water and temperatures of 110°F

Shah had ordered three Concordes (though he long since had crashed before the planes were to be delivered). The thermometer in the Kish terminal showed a temperature of 112 yet the official who met me wore a military overcoat and a pair of old army boots. An Indian Sikh immigrant, he said that Kish was traditionally the lair of pirates who looted the dhows carrying silks and jewels from India to the Persian Gulf sultanates. Sinbad the Sailor, he claimed, made his home on Kish Island. The Brits since then had several times bombarded Kish to drive out pirates but never occupied the island because it has no water of it own. The Shah had nevertheless ordered Kish to be developed for his family and his people, though I saw very little evidence of the latter. Kish's waiters, gardeners and ditch diggers were nearly all guest workers from India, Somalia and Sudan.

We drove along the future Kish Riviera. Millions of dollars were being spent on luxury villas, beach clubs and private cinemas. One of the restaurants was said to be a favorite of the Prime Minister Amir Abbas Hoveyda and his wife, Laila.

Mohammed Reza Shah in his heyday: on the beach with his family; in foreground, Crown Prince Reza

The Shah's beach house was on a long curling spit where he and Farah Diba on their rare visits to the island, exercised his Great Dane dogs and frolicked in the warm sea. They were protected by life guards swimming thirty yards off shore to scare off sightseers and sharks. Occasionally, I was told, the royal family would ride through the surf on retired race horses that had to be brought in each day by airplane because Kish had no water or grass. Even the golf courses that were still being built would rely on water being pumped many scores of miles from the mainland. The queen was said to swim and paddle topless. The offshore lifeguards enjoyed this but no cameras were allowed within half a mile of the royal residence.

During the afternoon I spent on Kish Island, nothing whatsoever happened. The whole place went to sleep and so did I, under a mosquito net and fan kept in motion by a string that led to the big toe of an Arab lad known by the Indian name *panka wallah*. As he moved his foot up and down, the fan turned and stirred the air but when the boy fell asleep it stopped and the heat became unbearable.

That evening I dined on inedible squid and fried rice and was taken to see the harbor, which the Shah had declared a free port. To make room for a shopping mall with glass fronted stores offering duty free cameras and toasters, an ancient bazaar had been bulldozed, infuriating the older merchants. Haute couture salons offered mink coats to keep women tourists warm in the fierce air conditioning (which the government guest house lacked). The casino had only recently been opened and was owned by a charity, the Pahlavi Foundation. The head of this, I was told, was the Shah's twin sister Princess Ashraf who was also reputed to own shares in several others in Teheran, Shiraz, Paris, London, Geneva and New York.

"Are they all for charity?" I asked.

"Yes sir," replied my Sikh guide. "Her Royal Highness believes that charity starts at home. Her own, of which she has many."

Cutting the cards at the black jack tables in Kish casino were some of the most gorgeous croupiers I have ever seen. The English manager kept referring to them as "crumpets." None were Iranians, most were Chinese and Russian girls. The most expensive and inventive, he said, were the French and English ladies specially flown in from Madam Claude's, the 1960's most celebrated Parisian bordello.

I did not especially like Kish. There was nothing Persian about it. It struck me as a candidate to match the worst of 1950's Miami Beach,

Kish resort 2006: At the seven-star Flower of the East hotel Sharia law is relaxed to allow guests to wear bikinis and play poker

garish, hopelessly expensive, and unbelievably hot. The resort was officially opened by the Shah but closed in less than a year. Came the Revolution and Iran's mullahs held up the casino as an example of how Persian civilization was being degraded by Western vulgarity and ostentation. The royal beach house temporarily became a vacation home for hard-pressed ayatollahs.

Yet the Shah's dreams for Kish Island have not died. In its free trade zone, Iran in 2005 opened an international energy market, offering oil and gas in euros instead of dollars. French and German hotel chains have opened two new vacation resorts on Kish, one named Dariush Grand whose Las Vegas-style buildings ape Persepolis at its height. Another, Flower of the East has a seven-star and two five-star hotels, scheduled to be completed by 2009. With jet skiers and scuba divers pouring into the island Kish's promoters say that Iran's Sharia law and Islamic dress codes are far more relaxed than they are on the mainland. The casinos have been reopened, but no queens, as far as I know, any longer run topless along its shimmering white beach.

A RED-HAIRED LADY AND
A BLUE MARCHIONESS

Her fortune commanded the attention of at least
three merchant bankers.
— Sir Peter Tapsell, MP, London
stockbroker

O ne of the odd jobs I did in Parliament was to serve as
Minister for sport and recreation. This brought me into contact with the International Olympic Committee during one
of whose meetings I was introduced to the founders of Special
Olympics, a charity set up as a memorial to President John F. Kennedy.
This enables mentally disadvantaged people to compete in athletics,
swimming, field sports and gymnastics under the rubric, "Let me
win—but if I cannot win, let me be brave in the attempt." Eunice
Kennedy and her husband, Sargeant Shriver invited me to join the
international board of Special Olympics and to set up a British chapter, SOUK. As chairman I was tasked with promotion which I enjoyed
and fundraising which I hated.

For help I looked among others to my Anglo-Iranian pal Geoffrey
Keating, now a trustee of BP's pension fund. Characteristically he
replied that he invested in only one charity, himself, but that one of his
mah jong partners, an Iranian lady who had recently arrived in
London, had the means as well as the kind heart needed to help. After
a late night vote in Parliament, Keating drove me to a fashionable
home on Chester Square where we were welcomed by a red-haired
lady who turned out to be the former wife of Joe Mazandi, my correspondent in Teheran when I was foreign editor of *Newsweek*.

Homayoun Mazandi had moved to England when she and Joe parted but the couple remained good friends and Joe made ample provision for Homayoun and their two children. Her fortune, in the words of one of London's top stockbrokers, Sir Peter Tapsell, MP, "commanded the attention of at least three merchant bankers." When Keating introduced us, Homayoun had just returned from a posh dinner with a group of socialite friends at one of the west end of London's most fashionable night clubs. With her was one of the best looking women in London, the

Lady Renwick, London's answer to Perle Mesta, Washington's hostess with the mostest.

Marchioness of Milford Haven, wife of a second cousin of the Queen.

I told Homayoun about Special Olympics and said we were on the lookout for funds to help launch its next national tournament. Her response was to fish in her hand bag and bring out a fat roll of bank notes.

"I won this tonight," she said. "I have not counted it but if it will help please take it." I did. There was close to nine hundred pounds, a useful sum in those days.

Within months of her arrival in England, Homayoun Mazandi's picture appeared on the cover of one its leading fashion magazines. Gossip columnists described her as Britain's answer to Perle Mesta, Washington's hostess with the mostest. At her elegant dinner table, heaped high with the fruit and flowers that characterize Persian hospitality, I met painters, writers, bankers and businessmen, many of whom pressed me to visit their families in Iran. Once, when the table was cleared, I was hauled up onto its polished top and coerced into trying to dance as Homayoun pirouetted around me to the sounds of a zither and tambourines.

But Homayoun Mazandi was—and is—more than a pretty face. One day she flew to Paris and was one of the few women ever to be granted an interview with the Ayatollah Khomeini. Posing as a journalist, she arrived at his office

Ayatolah Khomeini meets Homayoun Mazandi, "This woman is a danger to every Iranian man," he said.

without a head scarf and was told by his staff to cover herself. Homayoun refused until the Ayatollah himself persuaded her with the unassailable argument, "You are most welcome in my house. As in yours, we ask our guests to observe the customs of the host."

On her departure, forty minutes later, Khomeini observed, "This woman is a danger to every Iranian man between the ages of eighteen and eighty." That was an asset, not a problem in London. Before long, Homayoun remarried, this time to Harry Renwick, an English peer. Her name is now Lady Renwick and she still throws grand parties in Chelsea.

Another Iranian woman who made her mark in London in the 1970s was Hamoush, the well-born wife of an Anglo-Irish engineer named Ian Bowler. The Bowlers commuted between Chelsea and Teheran when they had me to stay at their elegant villa in the hills overlooking the city. Ian Bowler had designed and supervised the construction of two of Iran's longest pipelines, IGAT I and IGAT II carrying oil and later gas from Khuzestan to the border of Russia. His home in Teheran, where Ian doffed his business suit in favor of a Persian gown was surrounded by a high wall inside which he and Hamoush planted a garden of hanging shrubs and tinkling waterfalls. Most evenings they served *chelo kebab*, literally pilaf and roast meat accompanied by piles of aromatic rice and stews of walnuts, onions, pomegranates, dried limes and saffron.

It was chez Bowler that I first participated in an Iranian celebration of Nirooz, the annual spring holiday. One of the rites is *chahar shanbeh souri,* literally jumping over a row of bonfires symbolizing the Zoroastrian fire gods, while making a wish that any yellow color in one's face, denoting jaundice will be replaced with the red cheeks of good health. The Bowlers taught me to enjoy Persian food and music, both of which Hamoush imported to England when she and Ian purchased the Chelsea studio of the portrait painter, Augustus John, as their London home.

In the summer of 1969, Ardeshir Zahedi arranged for me to attend meetings in Teheran with his defense and foreign policy colleagues and afterwards to spend a long weekend on the coast of the Caspian Sea. My companions on this trip were the owner of the *Observer* newspaper, David Astor, and Homayoun Mazandi's friend, Janet, the Marchioness of Milford Haven. Janet's wardrobe in Iran consisted of short skirts and sleeveless dresses. These kept her cool in the 100 degree heat of the Persian Gulf, but the Caspian was a different matter. We were taken to a sturgeon cannery where the temperature in the packing shed was well below freezing point and the manager felt duty bound to leave no detail of fin or tail unexplained. As he escorted us along the cutting line where the giant fish were being sliced open to reveal the caviar, Janet Milford Haven began to shiver but kept a stiff upper lip. Gradually her colour changed. It was the first time that I had seen a marchioness turn blue. Leaving the sturgeon cannery, she was the same color as the Caspian Sea!

There was, for me, another sequel to this first of my visits to the Caspian. A telegram from London said that a motion I had put down for consideration at the Conservative party's 1969 national conference had been selected for debate. Its purpose was to break the BBC's monopoly on radio broadcasting in Britain, allowing private enterprise stations (known as "pirates" in those days,) to compete in music and light entertainment. The telegram from London was followed by a telephone call from the British ambassador in Teheran. The Conservative party leader and future Prime Minister, Ted Heath had asked him to convey his personal request that I should "make myself available to formally move the motion" and—a typical Heath'ism— "explain what good this will do"!

"When and where?" I asked.

"Day after tomorrow," said the voice from Teheran. "In the Promenade Ballroom. In Llandudno, in north Wales."

It never occurred to me to do anything else than jump at the opportunity to get my Motion approved. Getting from the coast of the Caspian to the coast of north Wales in less than forty-eight hours proved to be less easy. I made the 200-mile drive to Teheran over narrow switchback roads in just over seven hours, caught an overnight flight to Istanbul, and connected there with the next day's BA flight to Heathrow. This was followed by a taxi ride to a mainline railway station and a five hour train journey to Liverpool, where a Conservative party agent met and drove me through the Mersey tunnel and the villages and towns of pre-freeway north Wales. Arriving in Llandudino barely an hour before I was due to take my place at the podium, Ted Heath's only comment when I gave him the tin of caviar I had brought back for him was, "I hope it's black not red." None of my colleagues was in the least interested in where I had been or come from. They had their own fish to fry and none of them was sturgeon.

My speech was well received and the motion passed unanimously. There followed a large number of radio and TV interviews after which I flew back to Teheran, via Cyprus. Two years later Ted Heath as prime minister introduced a bill in Parliament to end the BBC's radio monopoly. Paul Bryan, the postmaster general, took charge of the legislation leaving me to celebrate the launching of free enterprise radio in Britain over dinner with Janet Milford Haven, Homayoun Mazandi and the visiting Iranian ambassador to Washington, Ardeshir Zahedi.

We ate caviar and drank vodka at the Iranian embassy.

PARTY AT PERSEPOLIS

Once a king declares that day is night,
Be sure to marvel at the moon's bright light.
　　　　　— quoted by Asadollah Alam from a
　　　　　medieval Persian poem

T he most spectacular and as it turned out, most damaging to the monarchy event in Iran in the 1970s was a magnificent if contrived celebration of the 2,500th anniversary of the founding of the Persian empire by Cyrus the Great. This took place amid the ruins of Persepolis, the great palace destroyed in 330BC by the Greeks, and brought together several dozen of the world's kings, queens, presidents and prime ministers, plus hundreds of diplomats, business men, bankers, arms salesmen and scores of internationally famous writers, painters, film and stage celebrities. Among the Iranians present were close to a thousand politicians, bureaucrats, academics and public-sector company chairmen, backed up by eight thousand troops.

I had visited Persepolis on my first trip to Iran and was delighted to receive the gilt edged card that invited me to return there for the Shah's great party on October 12, 1971. The invitation was personal and included a note from a court official reminding me that the ceremony would also mark the thirtieth anniversary of the Shah's accession to the throne. I was keen to attend but as a lowly under secretary was informed by the prime minister's office that my place was in London. The British delegation would be led by "bigger fish," among them the Queen's husband, the Duke of Edinburgh, and their daughter, Princess Anne. Representing the United States was the vice president, Spiro Agnew and half a dozen U.S. Congressmen. Agnew,

*Shah and family arrive in Persepolis for world's most magnificent party. Celebrating 2,500
years of Persian monarchy, the extravaganza played into hands of his critics.*

who was tainted by unproven charges of financial impropriety, would
shortly be forced to resign.

The Shah met his guests as they flew into a specially built new airfield at Shiraz. Among them were President Podgorny of the U.S.S.R.,
Marshal Tito of Yugoslavia, the presidents of Austria, India, Italy,
Poland, Pakistan, Tunisia, Turkey and West Germany, and half a
dozen others from the African and Soviet bloc countries. Also present
in resplendent uniforms were the Emperor of Ethiopia, Haile Selassie,
the kings and queens of Belgium, Denmark and Jordan, the king of
Morocco, Norway, Nepal and Thailand and the emirs of all the Arab
Gulf States. The smaller the country, I was told, the larger the retinues
of retainers and family members.

It was the largest—and most expensive—party ever thrown in the
Middle East, matching anything one sees at royal processions in London
or New Year's Day parades in New York. Glued to the BBC's television
coverage, I watched from London as a caste of several thousand actors,

singers and soldiers put on a pageant of Iranian history with bare chested Medes, Persians in helmets and breast plates, clouds of horsemen and chariots. Overhead, air force jets painted the sky in the green, white and red colors of the Iranian flag. According to a program which I obtained from the Iranian embassy, there were reproductions of the siege of Babylon and the crushing of a Roman legion by Parthian cavalry and camels. One of the pageants re-enacted the Iranian conquest of northern India, another a charge by armored infantrymen playing the part of Darius's 10,000 immortals.

The climax came when the Shah, chest glittering with medals, climbed onto a stage at the foot of Cyrus the Great's mausoleum, still intact after twenty centuries. In English as well as Persian he proclaimed:

Great Cyrus, king of Kings.
Founder of the oldest Empire on earth.
I, the Shah of Iran and its people
Salute you and address you
Rest in peace, Cyrus; for we shall keep watch
Forever. Over your glorious heritage.

I had mixed feelings about this. The Shah was clearly trying to evoke his people's pride in their glorious heritage. Less convincing was his attempt to identify himself with Cyrus. I could not help comparing his performance with that of Richard Burton in *Anthony & Cleopatra,* though Queen Farah wore her diamonds more discreetly than Elizabeth Taylor.

Later, I learned from those who attended the gala dinner in Persepolis that the banquet was far more French than Iranian. The guests were seated according to royal protocol, Spiro Agnew and the presidents of Russia and India placed far below the Emperor of Ethiopia and the Queens of Denmark and Belgium. More men than women being present, the Duke of Edinburgh, Prince Bernhard, Crown Prince of the Netherlands and the Polish president all sat next to each other. Asked why there were no ladies between them, the Duke of Edinburgh is reported to have replied, "They must think that some of us are male queens!"[1]

All the food and wine was flown in from Maxim's in Paris and served by two hundred waiters from Potel et Chabot. The dishes included quail's eggs and lobster mousse, lamb glazed in French brandy, peacock stuffed with foie gras and salade Alexander Dumas The desert champagne sorbet was followed by a cake baked in France that weighed more than one hundred pounds. The evening then concluded with "son et lumiére" in the ruins of the palace of Darius, the commentary, written in French, having to be translated into Persian and English.

For Mohammed Reza Shah, the party of Persepolis was the high point of his thirty-eight-year-long reign. He planned it to mark the tenth anniversary of the launching of the "white revolution" whose reforms undoubtedly helped drag Iran into the modern world.

When he came to the throne as a youngster, life expectancy in Iran averaged thirty years, infant mortality was among the highest in the world. Barely one man in fifty was literate. Few women went to go to school. Contrast that with the condition of most, though not all, Iranians at the time of the Persepolis party. Living standards were higher, there were more and better schools and hospitals and greater opportunities for Iranians to buy a small car and travel. Except for Israel and Lebanon, Iran was the only country in the Middle East where women could drive, vote and take jobs in business and government.

Iran too was emerging as a major regional player and not only in the Middle East. With oil prices soaring and foreign investment flooding in, Teheran had become a Mecca for Japanese and Korean as well as American and European businessmen. Following Britain's military withdrawal from the Persian Gulf, the Nixon administration saw Iran as a bastion against Communism and America's principal military ally in the Persian Gulf.

The Shah's party at Persepolis was meant to underline this. He wanted to showcase the emergence of his country onto the world stage as well as the progress it was achieving as a result of his reforms. Internationally, he may have succeeded. But this was also one of history's greatest ego-trips. Power, wealth and flattery had gone to the head of the man who had never himself won an election, fought a war, invented a new product or launched an original idea. The Shah was starting to believe that what he wanted to happen would happen. I was reminded of a couplet in a poem quoted by Asadollah Alam,

Once a king declares that day is night,
Be sure to marvel at the moon's bright light.

Outside the court circle, the party at Persepolis was *de trop.* By its ostentation and huge cost (estimated at $200 million), it offended more Iranians than it impressed. The mullahs represented it as a French and American take-over. Even Ardeshir Zahedi, a lover of French food, refused to attend and demanded to know why at a party celebrating 2,500 years of Persian culture, not one of the dishes served was a traditional Iranian kebab.

Politically it was a disaster. Reformers calculated how many schools and clinics could have been built with the oil revenues squandered to produce a Hollywood style extravaganza. The Shah was accused of confusing Darius the Great with the producer, Darryl Zanuck, of Metro Goldwyn Mayer.

Watching the closing ceremonies on television, I could not help comparing the glitz with the dignity and timelessness of the great silent pillars of Persepolis among which I had wandered alone. "Magnifique," I wrote in my diary, "Wish I had been there. But too much hubris, too much make believe."

Later I added a postscript: "I wonder if the Shah will live to regret Farah's francophilia!"

RADARS AND TRAILERS

*Capitulations reduce the Iranians to a level lower
than an American dog.*
— Ayatollah Khamenei

Three years after the Shah's Persepolis extravaganza, the Conservative government of 1970–74 fell in Britain and I returned to the opposition benches in Parliament. As one of my party's front bench spokesmen on industry, my contacts with businesses multiplied and I was invited by a number of large companies to assist in promoting exports to among other countries Iran, where higher oil prices and the Shah's purchases of defense equipment offered numerous sales opportunities.

My contacts in Teheran included a new Minister of Court, Asadollah Alam, who previously had served as prime minister. He invited me to his home and recounted an extraordinary story. One of the deputy prime ministers of the Soviet Union who had recently visited Iran asked the Shah if there had been an increase in the number of sturgeon caught on the Iranian side of the Caspian.

"Why do you ask," said the Shah.

"Because some damn Englishman told me that pollution on the Russian side has sent the sturgeon to live on the Iranian side."

"Were you that Englishman?" Alam asked as I sat with him on the patio of his home.

I could not deny it.

While serving as an under secretary in the U.K.'s Department of the Environment, I had visited Moscow to work out an Anglo-Soviet exchange of scientific and technical know-how, and while there had been taken to see a giant sewage works handling effluent from the steel and chemical plants that ended up in the head streams of the river Volga. Comparing this with the river Thames where London's advanced sewage systems were improving the water quality to a point where salmon and trout were reappearing, I rashly commented that the Russians, by fouling the Volga, would drive the sturgeon in its delta to migrate across the Caspian in search of cleaner water. "They're off to live with the Shah of Iran," I quipped.

"You were correct," said Alam reaching under his chair. He picked up a silver pail containing a kilo of caviar and handed it to me. "Please accept this Persian caviar; it tastes better than the Russian variety."

Alam was the principal channel through which the U.S. and British ambassadors kept in touch with the Shah. More than once he hinted that the diplomats were more concerned with helping their business-men win contracts than reporting on political developments. Alam had been "badly burned" as he put it, when the U.S. embassy con-veyed a message from the Pentagon insisting that the American military personnel now flooding into Iran to help train the Shah's armed forces, must be immune from prosecution in the Iranian courts. "Capitulations," as these extra-territorial privileges for foreigners were known had been abolished in Iran in the 1920s on grounds that they exhalted foreigners and demeaned Iranians. To get the Majlis to approve the U.S. demand in the teeth of public resentment Alam, at the Shah's insistence, had ram-rodded a bill through his cabinet but left it to his successor Amir Hoyveda to carry through the legislation. This was achieved by a process that deceived the public and both houses of the legislature. Government ministers told downright lies, for instance that the Americans' wives and children were not covered by the immunity, when, in fact, every member of the Iranian cabinet knew perfectly well that they were.

In protest, an ayatollah from Qom, Ruhollah Khomeini, of whom I knew nothing at the time, denounced the bill as "reducing the

Iranian people to a level lower in law than an American dog." Khomenei, then young and untested, was arrested and later exiled. Alam in our conversation passed this off as a "storm in a tea-cup" but complained that it had provoked riots at Teheran University whose students accused the Shah of "selling Iran to the Americans." Mosques and religious schools henceforth reverberated with charges that Khomenei had been "sacrificed on an altar of American arrogance."

A youthful Ayatollah Khomeini condemned U.S. serviceman's privileges in Iran. His arrest and exile made him a hero.

It was his protest against capitulations and the whiff of martyrdom that stuck to Khomeini as a result of his arrest and exile that first made the ayatollah a hero in the eyes of millions of Iranians.

Through it all the American mission concentrated on selling high performance fighter aircraft, helicopters and short range missiles to the Iranian air force. Boeing pressed 747s on IranAir. Westinghouse signed further contracts for work on the nuclear power station that the Shah had mentioned to me. American uniforms, accents and large cars filled Teheran's boulevards, better hotels, restaurants and shops.

The Europeans were less conspicuous but no less vigorous in promoting their exports to Iran. From Germany, France and Japan came tens of thousands of automobiles and trucks that turned central Teheran into a massive hooting traffic jam. The Brits supplied heavy tanks, naval equipment and an assembly line to mass produce one of the most uncomfortable cars I've ever ridden in, the Iranian-built Peykan.

Representing the Brits defense firms was one of the most remarkable characters of the era. Shapoor Reporter was the son of an Anglo-Indian Parsi whose mother was alleged to have suckled the

Author (left) with 1975 British Ambassador to Iran, Sir Anthony Parsons, business leader John Cuckney and wife, and Lady Parsons on the steps of the embassy. The diplomats focused more on trade than politics.

Shah when he and Shapoor were milk babies. Shapoor worked as a British middleman. I never had anything to do with his business activities but enjoyed his anecdotes about the Shah's compulsive need to have sex in unusual places, for instance in his helicopter which Shapoor insisted was a practice that President Kennedy also indulged in. Shapoor Reporter's commissions, which he kept in accounts at Grindlays Bank in London, made him a very rich man. Acquitted of taking bribes at a sensational trial in England, he was knighted in 1975 for his services to U.K. exports.

A British company named Plessey Radar meanwhile was invited to bid on a project to install radar towers along Iran's frontiers to give advance warning of air attacks. Philco-Ford, a U.S. company built several of these radars on the northern frontier facing Russia, but the Shah presciently insisted that four more should be built on the border with Iraq. The chairman of Plessey asked me to advise on the prospects of the British government's offering export credit guarantees to underwrite his company's bid and on my next visit to Iran I discussed this with the British embassy. The officials as always were helpful but thought the Shah was "paranoiac" in visualizing an attack by Iraq.

Plessey's bid on the radars never got beyond the design stage while the Shah remained on the throne. The entire project was then canceled by the Islamic regime. As a result, the Iranians had no warning of the air and missile attacks that preceded the 1980 invasion launched by Saddam

City of Yazd

Hussein. Neither the CIA nor British intelligence anticipated this—but the Shah, to his credit, did.

Another Anglo-American venture in Iran in which I played a part involved a trailer truck assembly plant that was to be built at Ahwaz in the south of the country. This made good sense since most of Iran's home grown food is produced in the rain belt along the Caspian Sea and in widely spread oases that are equally remote from the main centers of population. Every summer, large quantities of fruit and dairy products went bad between farm and markets. The solution was to ship the food in refrigerated long distance trucks.

Enter Crane Fruehauf, a half American, half British firm with three plants building trailers and containers in Norfolk, bordering my constituency.

The Crane Company located a large flat area of land outside Ahwaz on which it proposed to build a trailer assembly line. With its vice chairman and later chairman, Angus Murray, I flew to Ahwaz, inspected the site (which was ideal) and began the search for an Iranian partner on whom we could rely for site clearance, civil engineering and the recruitment of local labor. The partner would share in the marketing of the trailers within Iran.

The first group we interviewed included some top-level Iranian industrialists but they proved to be unsuitable. One of them was connected with the secret police agency, SAVAK. Our second trawl for a partner turned up trumps. Akbar Lari was a rising young entrepreneur with an engineering degree from New York University. Born in Yazd where the Lari family's spacious adobe-walled compound is cooled by the tall ventilating towers that are the most conspicuous features of this dust-dry desert city, Akbar's firm was engaged in industrial plant construction and large scale community development projects in many parts of Iran.

Meeting him at the Hilton Hotel in Teheran, Angus Murray and I liked Akbar and he liked us. His record as a builder was impressive, his bank references impeccable. Akbar was a man we could trust.

All the necessary paperwork for a joint venture was completed and signed. A Scottish engineer was appointed as CEO and Akbar's company prepared to start work on a new site north of Ahwaz.

Then the roof fell in. Back in Detroit, both the chairman and the CEO of the giant Fruehauf Corporation, co-owner and 50 percent shareholder in Crane, were convicted of conspiracy to defraud the U.S. Internal Revenue Service. Fruehauf was found guilty of boosting its sales in North America by omitting to collect the taxes due on its trailers' wheels, thereby holding down its prices below those of its competitors. This was a serious offense. Both these prominent businessmen were sentenced to jail.

For the British directors of Crane this posed an awkward dilemma. U.K. law forbids anyone convicted of a felony to serve on a public company's board. But the Americans refused to resign. They wanted to take control of Crane's venture in Iran. The publicity surrounding their removal from the board of a British company might also lead to demands that they should resign their directorships of a number of U.S. companies, including the Bank of Detroit.

Searching for a way out of this dilemma, I flew to Detroit and consulted a number of other senior American businessmen. The outcome was not a happy one. On legal advice, Cranes directors insisted that the two Americans must step down, pending a review of their sentence by a U.S. appeals court. The chairman of Fruehauf's response when I conveyed this to him was brutal, "I'll have your guts for garters, buddy boy."

Using its shareholders' money, Fruehauf Corporation went into the U.K. market and bought up enough shares to obtain a majority of votes on the Crane board. The cost of this to Fruehauf's shareholders was out of all proportion to the asset value of the British company. A lot of U.K. shareholders reaped an unexpected windfall. But in the end, the two Americans, both of whom were required to serve custodial sentences when their appeals were rejected, got their way with Crane Fruehauf Ltd. Once they were in control, they voted Angus Murray and me off the board, and took over the Iranian project.

Akbar Lari meanwhile had faithfully carried out his undertakings. Now he was left high and dry as Fruehauf, alarmed by rumors that the Shah's government was in trouble, hummed and hawed over whether to construct the plant north of Ahwaz. Six months before the revolution, the Americans unilaterally backed out of the joint venture and planned to build the plant in Saudi Arabia. The only compensation they paid to Akbar was for his out of pocket expenses.

For me there was one consolation. Akbar and I stayed in touch. When the mullahs took over Iran, his company was confiscated. All his assets were lost, but Akbar returned to America and started a second career. By 2005, he was one of the most successful property developers in Manhattan, and chairman of a company that after 9/11 was chosen to build the FBI's most modern and secure new office building. He is one of the many Iranians who have helped enrich America, and I have no better friend.

IRANIAN WHEELER-DEALERS

To be first in the Middle East is not enough.
We must raise Iran to the level of a world power.
— Shah of Iran, March 1974

The Shah reached the apogee of international acclaim in the mid-1970s. Flush with cash and ready to lend or invest it to enhance his own and his country's reputation, he and the fashionably-gowned queen were invited to visit nearly all the world's great capitals. Skiing in the Swiss Alps, staying as honored guests in the palaces of kings, queens and presidents, the Pahlavis were celebrities, and they loved it. Iran dazzled the commentators.

The Shah and Ardeshir Zahedi in Swiss ski resort; arriving as a guest of the Queen at Buckingham Palace

At London dinner parties with politicians and economists, guests were asked to write on the back of their place-cards the names of the nations most likely to be "on top of the world" by the end of the century. Nearly all included Iran in the top ten; some agreed with the Shah that his country was well on the way to becoming the world's fifth or sixth largest economy!

There was never any chance of that. Yet the Shah had much to boast about. Iran's GDP per head had risen from barely $160 in 1963 to well over $1,000 by the mid-1970s. Iran was the world's second largest oil exporter shipping 270 million tons of crude from the world's largest tanker port on Kharg Island. The rial, its national currency, held steady against the dollar for fifteen years. Reserves of foreign currency exceeded those of the Netherlands, Belgium, Italy and Spain combined. Millions of Iranians benefited from their country's bonanza. Schools, clinics and hospitals sprouted up in every large town. Twenty new universities and one hundred and thirty-five colleges of further education opened their doors to more than 200,000 students, nearly all of them on state scholarships.

The rural areas still lagged behind. Most of Iran's peasants were, as they still are, dirt poor. Iranian women marrying in their early teens were amongst the world's most prolific, raising families that swelled the population at a rate that far exceeded the increase in food production. Unable to find work on the land, millions moved to the cities, swelling the proportion of urban dwellers from less than 30 percent in the 1960s to 50 percent in the late 1970s. Urbanization and youth unemployment remain Iran's biggest social and economic problems.

Yet in most of the villages I visited in the mid-1970s there were conspicuous signs of improvement. High dams brought hydro-electric power and irrigation for the farmers. Better seeds and a huge increase in the number of tractors and mechanical harvesters boosted the yields of rice, sugar and cereals. These improvements reflected the White Revolution's land reforms. Where once most peasants were sharecroppers at the mercy of feudal landowners and monasteries, the Shah's forcible breakup of the large estates (including his own) gave nine out of ten of Iran's farm workers ownership of their own small farms.

High dam at Karaj: power and water for Teheran

The author of the Land Reform Act that made these changes possible was a former Iranian boy scout named Hassan Arsanjani, who like me, had switched from journalism to politics. Arsanjani was a showman. To underline his accomplishments, he would bus thousands of the new owner occupies peasants into the center of Teheran where he harangued them—and their former landlords—on the merits of the dry farming methods he had seen on visits to an Israeli *kibbutz* (collective farm) close by the one on the Lake of Galilee where my step-daughter Philippa was later to work as a *sabra*. I visited one of Arsanjani's showcase owner-occupier farms near the Shapoor I dam that the Shah had opened in the mountains above a city named Mahabad. Commending its neat fences and well-tended crops, I asked my guide to translate into Persian an old English farmers saying, "The best muck is the farmers own foot." He replied in passable English, learned at an agricultural college in Scotland with a verse from the poet, Walter Scott:

> *Breathes there a mon with soul so dead*
> *Who to himself hath not said,*
> *This is mine ain, my native sod.*

Arsanjani's land reform act was one of the lasting achievements of the Shah's White Revolution. Between 1960 and 1972, the share of owner-occupied farmland in Iran rose from 26 to 78 percent. But in Teheran, as in Washington, no good deed went unpunished. Arsanjani's fiery tongue and well-publicized love affairs upset the Shah and led to his dismissal and appointment to be ambassador to Italy. There Arsanjani married a buxom Italian wife and received a crate full of wedding presents from the Israeli government which applauded his support for its policies in Palestine. Returning to Teheran, he made a fortune as a lawyer defending some of Iran's most notorious business leaders. He died suddenly, some said of poisoning, at the age of forty-seven.

◆◆◆

The Shah, as I had discovered on my earlier trips, had a curiously split-minded approach to economic development. Like his father he knew that Iran was still basically a third world country—with oil. He had a vaguely Marxist notion that the commanding heights of the economy must remain in the hands of the state. At the same time, he believed in the words of another and greater monarch, Louis XIV of France, *"l'e-tat c'est moi"* (the state is me!) The government must therefore own and manage Iran's railroads, banks, utilities, power generation, and above all, the oil and gas industry which generated half its income. Yet for the rest, the Shah was a free-booter, an admirer of the rip-roaring private enterprise that made America boom while the Soviet Union stagnated. Iran in the 1970s was therefore a mix of two business cultures, both of them running to extremes: a monopolistic state sector that held the country to ransom, and a buccaneering free market sector where in the idiom of the day, it was literally true to say that "anything goes."

In this climate, the Iranians' penchant for paper shuffling thrived uneasily alongside their formidable talent for trade and business. Bureaucracy ruled, yet the streets of suburban Teheran filled rapidly with the big cars, big houses and big egos of unregulated private success.

I met several of Iran's new wheeler-dealers on flying visits to Teheran. One was Habib Sabet, chairman of a conglomerate whose fingers reached into furniture, trucks and buses, Pepsi cola bottling plants, pharmaceuticals and the 1960's equivalent of the French circus, Cirque du Soleil, which on the spur of the moment Sabet had imported from Paris. He was already an old man when I met him but still a bundle of the wise-cracking New York-style energy that had led him in his twenties to use the yellow pages of the Manhattan telephone directory to make cold calls on two hundred of the largest U.S. corporations, offering his services as a sales agent in Iran. Sabet's effrontery paid off. By the late 1960s his Sabet Group held the Iranian franchises for Revlon makeup, Union

Top: Habib Sabet; Bottom: Ali Rezai

Carbide batteries, Nabisco confectionery, RCA television sets and Whirlpool washing machines, as well as representing Volkswagen and Standard & Chartered Bank.

Through my former *Newsweek* colleague, Joe Mazandi, who had left the newsmagazine to become, among other things, one of the Shah's Mercedes dealers, I learned that Habib Sabet had began his business life with three strikes against him—he was poor, had no connections and was a devout member of the persecuted Bahai faith. Like Emil Toyota, founder of Japan and the world's most successful automobile business, he started building and repairing bicycles in his garage, before moving on to cars and founding a truck and bus line that carried freight and passengers from Teheran to Baghdad and Beirut.

When TV came to Teheran, the Sabet Group provided both the sets and the programs, most of them American. *Fortune* magazine estimated that by 1974, Habib Sabet owned "10 percent of practically everything in Iran." He lived in a newly-built palace modeled on the Petit Trianon in Versailles which he filled with some original and many replica items of French eighteenth century furniture. His New York office was not far from the one I had occupied as a *Time* magazine writer in Rockefeller Plaza.

The Sabet brothers were by no means unique. Another family, the Rezais, owned an even larger commercial group based on theaters, tobacco and mining. Ali and Mahmoud Rezai, two of four talented brothers from Sabzevar, in northeast Iran, parlayed their shares in cash from the sale of their father's estate to create a string of shops and offices from which for ten lucrative years they controlled an ever larger proportion of Iran's tobacco monopoly (until the Shah nationalized it). The Rezais had backed the Shah against Mohammed Mosaddegh and ever since had paid their dues to his twin sister, Princess Ashraf's Pahlavi foundation. Their contacts at the court paid dividends. By 1975, their businesses had a turnover of $300 million per year and employed 8,000 Iranian workers and four hundred expatriate managers and technicians. Ali concentrated on a steel mill that the Shah was eager to build using U.S. and British technology. When both countries embassies spurned this as an "industrial folly," the Iranians turned to the Russians, the arrival of whose 600 technicians the U.S. then condemned as KGB spying.

Mahmoud Rezai meanwhile had purchased a concession to mine chromium deposits in the Khorasan desert from a university teacher. These turned out to be many times larger than he or the teacher in their wildest dreams had imagined. The Rezais reaped a substantial profit which they employed to acquire the rights to mine the world's richest copper deposit outside Chile, at Sarcheshmeh in southern Iran. Selection Trust, the Anglo-South African mining company invested $400 million at Sarcheshmeh and gave the Rezai brothers a lifetime guarantee of 30 percent of the profits. Mahmoud and Ali became multi-billionaires.

AMERICAN'S IRANIAN U-TURNS

The United States admires the efforts being made by Iran and her sovereign, to strengthen democracy and make human rights respected.
— President Jimmy Carter,
December 1977

The Shah of Iran was always more interested in foreign policy and defense than he was in domestic affairs. Encouraged by the U.S. and Britain, he shopped the world for the latest combat aircraft, warships and armored fighting vehicles. Iran's defense expenditure in the mid 1970s exceeded that of every other country save the U.S., Russia, Britain, France and Germany. Arms salesmen occupied the best hotels in Teheran, selling weapons as if they were toys.

The Shah, wherever he traveled, was dined, wined and flattered as Iran's procurer-in-chief of defense equipment. In London I attended a banquet given by the government in his honor at Lancaster House, and the British Secretary of Defense, Lord Carrington, organized a top secret briefing in Whitehall with the chiefs of staff. One of them was an Army general described by Carrington as "a cavalryman with a full-skirted tunic and bowed cavalry legs sufficiently wide apart for a horse to be inserted between them." During the briefing, on a new class of armored fighting vehicle the British hoped to sell to Iran, the Shah interrupted.

"Tell me, General, how fast do those vehicles go?"

The general, a master of foxhounds, explained in fruity tones, "about the huntin' pace of the Beaufort (one of England's most famous fox hunts), Your Imperial Majesty."[1]

Flying on to Washington, the Shah was received by President Nixon as America's number one ally in the Middle East region. There was no mention of Israel or Saudi Arabia in the president's speech. The White House overruled State Department doubts about Iran's need for or ability to deploy, the latest air superiority fighters that the Shah insisted on buying. Henry Kissinger was quoted as saying, "Whatever he wants and can pay for, the Shah of Iran can have."

Ardeshir Zahedi by now had returned to Washington for a second tour as ambassador of Iran. One of his achievements was to rebuild the Iranian embassy on Massachusetts Avenue as a showcase for Persian architecture and pictures, complete with cupola, tiled paths and foun-

tains. Visiting Washington in the course of a series of lectures I gave to audiences in the South and the West, I was one of the first guests to stay there overnight. Ardeshir was in his element. Only the British ambassador had easier access than he did to the White House and the top floor of the State Department where Henry Kissinger's door seemed always open to him.

Ambassador Zahedi in the mid-1970s was one of the U.S. capital's most sought after diplomats. Sally Quinn who wrote the "must read" hostess's guide, *Adventurous Entertaining*, described him as the city's "most gracious host and most eligible bachelor." I looked through the embassy visitor's book. The signatures included

Top: Shah in Washington with Henry Kissinger (left) and Ardeshir Zahedi (right). "Whatever the Shah can pay for he can have," said Kissinger. Bottom: Nixon and Zahedi. The president regarded Iran as America's No. 1 ally in the Middle East.

those of Richard Nixon, Gerald Ford and at least half the members of the United States Senate. More florid were the messages from actors such as Dean Martin and David Niven with whom Ardeshir in his youth had crashed a racing car, and from Barbara Walters, Liza Minnelli, Elizabeth Taylor and Jacqueline Kennedy Onassis. As JFK's First Lady, Jackie had made a point of snubbing the Shah; now as a ship owner's lady she had become more partial to Iran.

It was all too good to last.

When the Watergate scandal brought down Richard Nixon, Iran and Ardeshir Zahedi were two of the biggest losers in Washington. President Ford at first maintained the "special relationship" between his administration and Iran, but the election of Jimmy Carter brought with him to the White House a new caste of youthful Democrats for whom the Shah was one of the "bad guys." The United States proceeded to make not one but two of those abrupt U-turns in its foreign policy that America's friends as well as enemies find so difficult to keep up with.

President Carter in his election campaign had promised to make "human rights" the test of the value of his allies. Democrats in Congress and the U.S. media thereupon turned the spotlight on Iran's human rights record—the lack of parliamentary dissent, the subservience of its businessmen, the excesses attributed to SAVAK, its secret police organization. The new administration let it be known that America's relations with the Shah henceforth would be "cooler." Ambassador Zahedi no longer was able to pick up the phone and speak to the Secretary of State. Zahedi returned to Teheran. Politically, though not economically, the U.S. distanced itself from Iran.

Until the second U-turn.

Two days after Christmas 1977, one of the "flying command post" aircraft at the American air base at Mildenhall in my constituency took off on a special mission on behalf of POTUS, the secret service acronym used to identify the president of the United States. Jimmy Carter was crossing the Atlantic and the U.S. third air force in Britain was under orders to keep the skies clear for Air Force One. That New Years Eve, I attended a party in the Officers Mess at Mildenhall and

President Carter welcomed the Shah and Farah Diba (far left) to Washington but U.S. relations with Iran cooled.

learned, to my surprise, that Carter had landed in Teheran.

Asked why, the U.S. embassy in London downplayed the president's visit. He was on his way to India and had stopped in Iran for only a few hours. He would not stay overnight. It was nothing more than a courtesy call reciprocating the Shah's visit to Washington. Mr. Carter would take the opportunity to press Iran to improve its human rights record.

That night the president appeared on the Shah's arm at a state dinner in the Niavaran Palace. He danced with Farah Diba while Rosalyn Carter waltzed with the Shah. The text of the speech that Jimmy Carter's advisors had prepared for him was innocuous, even boring, but the president jazzed it up. Expressions of surprise appeared on the faces of his American officials as he said, "No other country is closer to America in the matter of our military security and there is no other leader to whom I feel deeper gratitude or greater personal affection than I do to your Imperial Majesty. Iran owes it existence as an island of peace and stability in one of the world's most troubled regions, to Your Majesty's abilities as head of state and to the respect and admiration accorded to you by your people."

Tributes of this kind are the currency of heads of state banquets but Carter's departure from his script went further than his natural effusiveness. Not only for the Iranians, but for the western diplomats and media present, his words appeared to mark the Carter administration's second U-turn on Iran. The Shah was back in favor. Iran no longer was in the Democrats' doghouse!

Underlining this, the president said in his peroration that the United States admired "the efforts being made by Iran and her sovereign, to strengthen democracy and make human rights respected."

The Shah was delighted. One of those present wrote, "He beamed without restraint. No other head of state—and certainly no other American president—had ever shown him such cordiality, or (why not say it?) such flattery!"[2]

Instead of flying on to Delhi as scheduled, the Carters stayed the night at Niavaran palace, where a surprise guest, King Hussein of Jordan joined them. Carter regaled the two kings with stories about his peanut farm in Georgia. From King Hussein's brother, Crown Prince Hassan, I subsequently learned that the Shah had been fascinated by the president's description of his U.S. Navy experiences with nuclear submarines. The Shah hoped to equip his expanding Iranian navy with nuclear powered submarines but Mr. Carter advised him to be careful with the changing currents and shifting sands of the Persian Gulf.

Prince Hassan's comment was that the U.S.-Iranian partnership was vulnerable to the changing currents of partisan politics in Washington. Time and events were soon to prove that the Shah's personal relationship with Jimmy Carter was also built on shifting sands.

AN AMBASSADOR POISONED, A PRIME MINISTER SACRIFICED

Perhaps we ought to slow down. Is is possible that we are moving too fast, upsetting too many people, undertaking too many different things on too many different fronts at the same time.
— Amir Abbas Hoveyda,
Prime Minister of Iran

hen Margaret Thatcher succeeded Ted Heath in 1976 as leader of the Conservative Party, she appointed me as a spokesman on foreign affairs. One of my jobs was to help draft her speeches, another to brief her on international issues on which, in her early years, she was a long way from possessing the background and authority she was later to acquire as prime minister. Iran was a country that Margaret wanted to know more about. I therefore arranged to take her to the Iranian embassy in London to meet a newly arrived ambassador, Amir Teymour Kalali.

I had met Amir Teymour in Teheran shortly after he returned from his assignment as Iranian ambassador to India, where rumor had it that he had drunk too many pink gins and run up gambling debts. Displeased with his performance in New Delhi, the Shah had reassigned Amir Teymour to what Iranian diplomats then regarded as "outer darkness," the embassy in Moscow. When Teymour heard from the Minister of Court that I had visited Russia several times, he asked me to share my impressions of life in the Soviet capital. I told him to take plenty of warm clothes and thought no more about this until in 1978, when Amir Teymour was promoted to be Iran's ambassador to London.

On his arrival I phoned the embassy and was invited to lunch. Amir Teymour complained that he had been badly treated in Moscow, not so much by his Soviet hosts as by his own Foreign Office officials in Teheran who had failed to reply to his telegrams and rarely had taken his advice. "Someone in the Shah's family is out to get me," he said.

A month or so later, the Shah's twin sister, Princess Ashraf was due to stay at the embassy during one of her frequent shopping sprees in London. To kill two birds with one stone, I rearranged Mrs. Thatcher's appointment at the embassy so as to include the princess as well as the ambassador. Arriving punctually at 10:30AM, I rang the door bell but no one answered. It took three or four minutes to get any response. Eventually, an official admitted us and we were shown into the drawing room and asked to wait until Her Royal Highness was ready. Coffee would then be served.

That and the delays at the door was not the kind of treatment that Margaret Thatcher expected. As the minutes passed, she became concerned about her next appointment. Suddenly there appeared at the head of the stairs a figure in a long black dress. It was Ashraf looking like a witch. "I am terribly sorry," she said, "The ambassador has committed suicide."

Amir Teymour's body had been found that morning in a small flat into which he had moved overnight. He had poisoned himself.

Briefing cancelled, condolences exchanged, Mrs. Thatcher departed and I stayed on in effort to discover what had led the ambassador to kill himself. It was a murky story. Since arriving in London, Amir Teymour had again started gambling. He was also drinking heavily. Ashraf had conveyed to him that his appointment to London was therefore being rescinded. He would be replaced with a young man named Parviz Radj who on my previous visit to Teheran had been one of the secretaries to the prime minister, Amir Abbas Hoveyda. Still in his late thirties, Radj was a good looking and capable official but very much Amir Teymour's junior. He was also alleged to be one of Ashraf's young admirers.

Humiliated, Amir Teymour had taken his own life!

Not long afterward, Margaret Thatcher, still opposition leader in Britain, accepted an invitation from the Shah to visit Teheran. I drafted a good deal of the speech she made to the Iran-British Chamber of Commerce. Like President Carter, she was impressed by the Shah's hospitality and eager to drum up business for British defense firms in Iran.

Her words as delivered were more guarded then Carter's but, in retrospect, they too were over the top:

> *As a person who hopes soon to lead another great nation, I value this opportunity to learn the views of the Shahanshah. Surely, he is one of the world's most far-sighted statesmen, whose experience is unrivaled . . . He is leading Iran through a twentieth century renaissance . . . transforming an ancient land in a single generation from one of the world's poorest countries into one of its leading military and industrial powers.*

It was my fault that this language was over optimistic. I had failed to recognize that the Iranian economy was overheating and underestimated the depth and breadth of opposition to the Shah that was building up in Iran.

On her return from Teheran, Mrs. Thatcher told me that she had been surprised by the high levels of security surrounding the Shah. On visits to his troops or religious shrines, he invariably traveled by helicopter rather than through the streets where his car would be subject to attack. Margaret also gave me one of a number of tins of caviar that Prime Minister Hoveyda had given her. "I would like it if you will accept one as a thank you for all the work you did on this speech," she wrote.

The Shah received Hoyveda as he read proclamation honoring Ardeshir Zahedi as foreign minister (left)

I do not think that I deserved either her thanks or the caviar—but six months later I too had an opportunity for a further and fuller meeting with Hoveyda.

Ushered into his darkened office I was greeted by the prime minister in French. Only when an aide reminded him that I was a British MP did he revert to heavily accented English. Hoveyda had put on weight. A large, round faced fellow with an orchid in his lapel and a pipe with which he gestured to emphasize his points, he opened our conversation with a recitation of his own and his family's wide experience in international affairs. His father was a diplomat in Damascus and Beirut, where Hoveyda grew up speaking French. He was a student in France when Paris fell to the Germans in 1940, spent three years in Stuttgart when Germany was recovering from World War II, then served in Geneva and briefly in Turkey as an official of the Iranian Foreign Office. His wife, he added, gave him a fresh orchid for his buttonhole every morning. He showed me her picture and said she spoke "English English" as a result of her education at a boarding school in Sussex whose head mistress was the daughter of my former grammar school headmaster. "I speak 'American English,'" said Hoveyda, a graduate in accounting from UCLA in California.

Hoveyda spoke in glowing terms about the Shah despite the monarch's tendency to rely more on the advice of Ardeshir Zahedi than on that of his prime minister. To my comment that the party at Persepolis had been "over the top," he replied that it was a measure of "His Imperial Majesty's determination to restore Iran to its rightful place as one of the world's first civilizations." Under questioning, Hoveyda acknowledged that all was not well with the economic miracle. Success, he said, was proving to be its own worst enemy. Illustrating this, he said that so many ships were arriving with imports of consumer goods as well as industrial and military equipment that Iranian ports could not handle them. Shortages were developing. Goods were not being delivered because the roads to the ports were inadequate and there were not enough Iranian truck drivers. Four hundred Korean drivers had been hired to help clear the congestion.

I asked Hoveyda about inflation. He prefaced his reply by saying, "I do not know if His Majesty would approve of my saying this," and went on to observe, "Perhaps we ought to slow down. It is possible that we are moving too fast, upsetting too many people, and undertaking too many things on too many different fronts at the same time."

Hoveyda's judgment proved to be correct. By the late 1970s Iran was in the grip of runaway inflation. Despite its huge oil revenues, the government was overspending and over-borrowing to cover its deficits. The bazaaris (street traders) of Teheran and the other big cities complained that their profits were disappearing while members of the Shah's family indulged in conspicuous extravagance. The Shah's private charity, the Pahlavi Foundation was described to me as a "drainpipe" down which revenues from the oil industry disappeared into the personal accounts and homes in France and America of his sister, cousins and aunts. At the interface of government and business, corruption was becoming a way of life. General Nematollah Nassiri, who had just been replaced as the head of SAVAK and appointed as ambassador to Pakistan, was accused of having authorized the torture of writers, actors and other critics of the regime. His successor General Nasser Moghadam was condemned as "not much better."

During our interview, my longest and last meeting with Hoveyda, I asked what steps his government and the Shah were taking to respond to these criticisms. He replied that the Shah's reforms were bringing free votes in local elections, abolition of censorship and independence

The Shah's twin sister, Princess Ashraf indulged her expensive tastes

for the courts of law and the Majlis but when I asked for evidence that this was happening, he had none to offer.

Hoveyda also claimed that in response to widespread criticism of the royal family's extravagance, he had suggested a "code of conduct" forbidding the Shah's relatives to accept fees from foreign companies or to behave in public in a manner "distasteful to Iran's social customs." There was no need for the prime minister to name names. Influence peddling by the Shah's daughters and their husbands was rife in 1970s Teheran.

Princess Ashraf was widely regarded as the most conspicuous offender. She had long since shed the black veil she wore when I took Margaret Thatcher to meet her in London. She was a lady of expensive tastes who spent money like water. Typical of her excesses was Ashraf's demand for $350,000 to cover her expenses during her six week appointment to be Iran's representative at a UNESCO conference in Geneva. The prime minister objected but after much wrangling in the cabinet, the princess got the money and was reported to have spent a large part of it to pay one of her collection of young men to accompany her.

The Shah was well aware and often critical of his relatives venality, but unable or unwilling to check it. The Pahlavis' conspicuous extravagance undoubtedly was one of the factors that enabled the Islamic Revolution to sweep them away. Meanwhile, as the economy deteriorated, the political situation took a turn for the worse. Whenever the authorities eased their grip on local councils and the media, there was an upsurge of criticism of the government's incompetence. Political unrest turned to violence. Housewives and civil servants joined students and members of the clergy in noisy street processions that led to clashes with the police many of whom supported the demonstrators. For this, the Shah blamed Hoveyda. He had loyally served as prime minister for thirteen years, typically working fourteen hour days and taking his prime ministerial papers and bodyguards home with him every night. His devotion to the Shah cost Hoveyda his marriage. When Laila sued for divorce he did not resist. "She didn't divorce me, she divorced the prime minister," Hoveyda told his friends and Laila agreed. She still continued to send him a fresh orchid for his button-hole every day.[1]

In July 1977, Hoveyda took his ex-wife for a much needed vacation in the Greek islands where he lounged on the beach and read French paperback detective novels. Returning to Iran, he learned that a new U.S. ambassador, William H. Sullivan had presented the Shah with a list of criticisms of the country's over-ambitious industrialization program. This urged him to slow down the pace of economic growth which was fueling inflation and forcing the central bank—which until recently had lent large sums to foreign clients—to borrow heavily from America and Japan.

That is precisely what Hoveyda himself had been worrying about when I met him earlier that year. But since no one, least of all the international lending institutions dared to put the blame on the Shah, it was Hoveyda as prime minister who became the target of a fusillade of attacks by economists, businessmen and editorial writers. Unlike most Iranian politicians, he had not made a fortune in politics. He did make enemies in the court, whose excesses he sought to curtail and in the Majlis where jealous rivals accused him of being a "lackey of the British." Hoveyda was also blamed for "tricking" the Majlis into passing the hated Capitulations bill to grant U.S. military personnel and their families immunity from the Iranian courts for offenses committed in Iran. "Lick-spittle of the Americans" was a label attached to his name by the gossips of Teheran's coffee shops who also falsely linked his name with belly dancers, call girls and pederasts.

On return from his Greek vacation, Hoveyda flew to the Caspian where the Shah too was reading detective novels. He offered his resignation which the Shah immediately accepted. Hoveyda was moved sideways, to the position of minister of court, but he never recovered his influence nor his self confidence. Twice I tried to see him through the good offices of his former aide, Ambassador Parviz Raji, but Hoveyda was unavailable. His fate was a cruel one. He was arrested by the Shah on trumped up charges of disloyalty in the final weeks before the Islamic revolution, then denounced again by Khomeini for being too loyal to the Shah! His trial and judicial murder by the self-styled hanging judge of the Islamic regime are described on pages 103–104.

BLACK FRIDAY

If the trumpet give an uncertain sound,
who shall prepare himself to the battle?
— Corinthians X1V c 55,
New Testament Bible

I once asked my boss British Prime Minister Harold Macmillan what he thought were the most decisive factors in politics and government, "Events, dear boy, events." replied Macmillan.

Events turned decisively against the Shah in 1978–79. Asadollah Alam, his closest—and shrewdest—confidant died of cancer. A terrible fire that may well have been the work of an arsonist broke out in a cinema in Abadan killing 177 people, many of them children, because the exit doors were locked. The Shah and his wife at the same time were attending a fireworks display celebrating the twenty-third anniversary of the fall of Mosaddegh. When they failed to visit the site of the disaster, Iran's bazaars and mosques rang with the cry, "While an entire city wept there was dancing and fireworks at the court."

As discontent spread and challenges to his authority multiplied, the Shah sought to place the blame for the court's misjudgments on his advisers, his ministers, the Brits and the Americans, on anyone except himself. Following the sacking and arrest of Hoveyda, the Shah appointed as head of the government an unimaginative technocrat, Jamshid Amouzegar who served as prime minister for fourteen months. Amouzegar pressed for "deceleration" in the speed of Iran's unsustainable economic growth which was fueling double digit inflation but the Shah refused and instead went on a borrowing spree to pay for it. The balance of payments turned from a surplus of $2 billion in 1974 to a deficit three times higher in 1978. The only significant cut in public expenditure was an overdue reduction in subsidies to the mosques and religious schools. Some of these, I was told, were paid from secret funds made available by the U.S. embassy "to keep the mullahs quiet!"

Amouzegar's successor was an even less inspiring prime minister, the septuagenarian president of the senate, Jafar Sharif Emami. It did not help that he was head of the Pahlavi Foundation which invested the Shah and his family's money in hotels and casinos in Iran and high rise buildings in New York. Sharif Emami was a disaster. On the Shah's behalf, he announced and then abandoned proposals for political reform, ordered the army to prepare plans to impose martial law, then counter-manded them. The Shah by this time was suffering from the onset of cancer. His physician Professor Safavian, subsequently disclosed that he told his royal patient, "The country is in critical condition . . . It's like a raging sea and the people . . . are waiting for the captain of the ship to take things firmly in hand and state our course."

"Yes, yes, yes," replied the Shah, but when he sought advice from the prime minister as to how best to do this, Sharif Emami's comment was, "No one is taking any notice of me. I do not know what to do."[1]

Not so the Shah's fiercest opponent, Ayatollah Ruhollah Khomeini. From Najaf in Iraq to which he had been exiled following his attack on the Capitulations bill granting immunity to U.S. servicemen, Khomeini railed against the twin pillars of the white revolution—land reform (which entailed the break up of the mullah's estates) and the emancipation of women (which Khomeini denounced as "sacrile-gious.") The Shah pressured Saddam Hussein to expel Khomeini from Iraq. This was a grievous error. The Ayatollah went to Kuwait and thence to Paris, a vastly more popular media center, acquiring in the process the mantle of "persecuted refugee" and an international plat-form from which to hurl his imprecations at the Shah to an ever wider audience of European and before long American admirers. Unwisely, the royals hit back by planting an article in the Teheran press claiming that

Khomeini was the son of an Indian street dancer, an agent for foreign intelligence services with the sexual morals of a catamite. True or false, these allegations outraged the Shiite clergy, to whom attacks on their aya-tollahs were the next thing to attacks on Allah. The protest riots that broke out in Iran's religious centers were not unlike the ones that flared up in 2005 in protest against a Danish newspaper's cartoons of the prophet Mohammed. Nothing did more to elevate the then relatively obscure Khomeini to national and international prominence.

My hopes for Iran at that time were pinned on a far more influential religious figure, Kazem Shariat-madari, the Grand Ayatollah of Qom. Diplomats whose judgment I trusted described him as "sensible and practical . . . positive about the monarchy . . . not at all anti Western." Shariat-madari disliked and distrusted his former Qom inmate Khomeini. Though deploring the "imported immorality" of the court (he objected, for example to Queen Farah being photographed dancing with Jimmy Carter), Shariat-madari wanted no part in revolutionary Islam. Like his Iraqi co-religionary, Ayatollah Sistani, another product of the "quietist" school of Qom who later was to counsel the Shiites to avoid bloodshed in Iraq, Shariat-madari preached that Shiism is not all about martyrdom. Of its founder he once famously remarked, "Imam Hossein was not a Che Guevara."

In a series of coded messages conveyed through Houchang Nahavandi, who acted as a go-between, Shariat-madari told the Shah that the situation in Iran was deteriorating rapidly. In particular, he warned that the conduct of the Princess Ashraf was handing ammuni-tion to the Shah's bitterest enemies. A cassette containing a mass of detailed facts, with dates, places and names of witnesses to Ashraf's excesses, was sent from Qom to the Shah. This included some clear cut advice from the Ayatollah, "The time has come for radical deci-sions. If the Shah fails to take clear decisions within the next few weeks, he will soon lose everything.[2]

Events then took charge in the form of a street riot in Qom that led the police to shoot a theology student and chase some of the demonstrators into the ayatollah's private residence. Shariat-madari closed the Grand Mosque but the local SAVAK commander ordered it to be reopened, provoking further demonstrations and a clash with the army whose troops opened fire. Scores more students were killed and hundreds wounded. The fat was now in the fire. From Paris Khomeini unleashed a barrage of condemnations of the Pahlavis' "blasphemy and self adulation." The international media, led by the BBC, began treating this still relatively minor league cleric as the "voice of Iranian freedom." Khomeini's militancy trumped Shariat-madari's moderation.

On September 8, 1978, I heard a BBC bulletin that reported, before the event took place, that hundreds of thousands of demonstrators were about to converge on government buildings in Jaleh Square in the center of Teheran. The mob and a battalion of troops collided in the streets. Excited journalists reported that "thousands of innocent Iranians had been killed." The correct numbers were bad enough: 191 died, hundreds were wounded. Seventy of the dead were police and soldiers, shot by gunmen in the crowd. Some of these gunmen were reported to be members of Jascha Arafat's Palestinian El Fatah movement.

Black Friday as this massacre came to be known was the first nail in Mohammed Reza Shah's coffin. According to a friend in Teheran to whom I spoke by telephone, he was devastated by TV pictures of the demonstrators shouting "Death to the Pahlavis." Houchang Nahavandi who was with him wrote.

"Burying his head in his hands, the Shah kept repeating. 'What have I done to them . . . what have I done to them?'" His hold on power was broken. His dream was smashed. His love for his country betrayed."[3]

COULD THE MONARCHY
HAVE BEEN SAVED?

In these troubled times for Iran,
it may be that your time has come.
— Letter to Ardeshir Zahedi,
Ambassador of Iran

Most of the Iranians I knew believed that there still was enough time after Black Friday to avoid a revolution. The monarchy was still popular among the mass of rural people. The army, police and most of Iran's bureaucrats were loyal.

Pressure mounted for the Shah to declare martial law and appoint a military government which would enforce law and order and begin a "national dialogue," offering concessions to his critics from a position of strength. The chiefs of staff crafted a plan, Operation Kach to take control of Teheran and intern 400 of the opposition leaders at a camp in the Baluchistan desert. The Shah meanwhile would move temporarily to a military base. "Anywhere among your troops your Majesty will be safe," they assured him.

But the Shah was a broken reed. He did not know which way to turn. Like Sharif Emami, he confused his troops by giving them contradictory orders. "Uphold the law . . . but no blood must be shed . . . Maintain public order . . . but no wounded and no dead . . . "

As the crisis mounted I kept in close touch with Ardeshir Zahedi. He was commuting between his embassy in Washington and the palace in Teheran. Some of the letters that passed between us illustrate the growing concern I felt about the lack of a firm hand on the tiller.

House of Commons, London, 4th October 1978.
E.G. to A.Z.:
What a ghastly time the Shah is having. The earthquake was terrible. Coming on top of the riots and the dangerous situation in Afghanistan, it must have imposed a severe strain on the entire government—including you.

Embassy of Iran, Washington, 12th October 1978.
A.Z. to E.G.:
Since I saw you here, I have been to Iran and back. While with His Majesty, we talked about you. I hope to see you again soon.

House of Commons, London, 4th December 1978
E.G. to A.Z.:
The best hope for the future is surely for the army to hold the ring while order is restored and enough breathing space is gained to get the economy moving forward again. But military rule can surely not last for more than a year or so. Voltaire was right when he said: "You can do anything with bayonets, accept sit on them!"

By this time, I had concluded that the Shah was no longer capable of making the tough decisions that were needed to save Iran from being forced into a choice between the surging Islamic extremists, whipped into frenzy by Khomeini's broadcasts from Paris, and a military dictatorship—provided the Army could agree on a dictator!

Both alternatives were appalling. There had to be a better way.

My preference was for a speedy and irreversible change from Iran's imperial regime to a constitutional and accountable monarchy, like that in the U.K. A suggestion along these lines already had been made to the Shah by a quixotic character named Mozafr Baghai Kermani who I first met when he accompanied Mohammed Mosaddegh to

New York and offered to help *Time* magazine with the cover story I wrote about him. Baghai on the strength of his oratorical and writing skills had several times offered to serve as prime minister and found it hard to understand why the Shah and many others did not share his own estimation of his talents.

Baghai taught ethics at Teheran University before launching into a political career in which for over thirty years he flirted with the Tudeh Communist party, then formed the Toilers, a party of his own, which named Baghai "the Leader." With his silver tongue and flair for dramatic gestures, he was unquestionably a celebrity in Iran in the 1960s and '70s, in modern American terms, a cross between Bill O'Reilly and Reverend Jesse Jackson. Shortly after the Black Friday riots, Baghai once again volunteered to become prime minister. Invited to meet the Shah, he put the chances of a religious takeover at 70 percent and of the monarchy's survival at only 10 percent with the Shah and 20 percent if he abdicated in favor of his seventeen-year-old son Crown Prince Reza.

I elaborated on this proposal in a letter to Ambassador Zahedi, which I copied to the Minister of Court:

> *There can be no more difficult task than to convince the Shah to safeguard the throne by himself preparing to vacate it—but this is what seems to me to be the best way forward. The Shah's contribution should be to draw up an Instrument of Succession whereby the Crown prince will ascend the throne with a council of state to advise him until he is of age.*

Reinforcements came from the *London Times,* whose editor shared my views. In a *leader* (as *Times* editorials were called), he advised the Shah to "Surrender his prerogatives not through formal abdication, but by transferring them gradually but visibly to a council of the realm which will hold them in trust until the crown prince reaches his majority. In that way both the politicians and the armed forces might become accustomed to a monarchy which is genuinely constitutional."

This was a "very British" suggestion whose provenance might well have doomed it but from Teheran came this reply:

> A.Z. to E.G.
> *I have brought your proposal to the attention of His Imperial Majesty and will naturally follow up and let you know the outcome.*
> (Handwritten postscript):
> *While with His Majesty, we talked a lot about you and send you warmest regards.*

Talk and warm regards were not enough. To have any chance of succeeding at what clearly was the eleventh hour, the proposal for a

transition from an imperial to a constitutional monarchy with the Crown Prince succeeding his father, required an Iranian champion with two indispensable qualities—an ability to win the Shah and his wife's consent to abdication and the authority and nerve to carry the necessary legislation through the Majlis, and sell the Crown Prince to the public.

There was only one candidate who I believed might be able to do this. Thirty-seven years earlier General Fazlollah Zahedi had saved the monarchy and Iran from chaos and a Communist takeover. Could his son, Ardeshir Zahedi, now rescue his country from civil war or Islamic revolution?

Ardeshir Zahedi confers with the Shah. The ambassador was tough, decisive, pro-Western and had the support of the army.

Ardeshir was not an ideal candidate. Among Iran's left-wing nationalists the Zahedi name was synonymous with the removal of their hero, Mosaddegh. The mullahs identified him with the Shah's indifference to *sharia* law and the White Revolution's reforms of women's rights and land ownership. Many of the Teheran intellectuals with whom I had discussed alternatives to the hapless Sharif Emami also turned thumbs down on grounds that Ardeshir might have handled some of the Pahlavi family's vast wealth in America. Nor were the Americans and Brits enamored of a Zahedi candidacy. For all his embrace of the American way of life, Ardeshir had vocally criticized U.S. policy in the Persian Gulf and the Middle East. To the British Foreign Office he had also been an irritant, notably over Bahrain and the islands in the Persian Gulf.

Discussing the possibilities with colleagues in London and Washington, I recalled the objections to the Brits choice of Margaret Thatcher three years earlier ("too radical . . . talks to much") and of Winston Churchill in 1940 ("too impetuous . . . too many enemies"). Ardeshir Zahedi was not a Thatcher and certainly not a Churchill—but in Iran's circumstances, he seemed to me to offer three advantages. He was tough, decisive and could count on support from the Army. He was pro western. Above all, he was an Iranian patriot—and he was there.

On December 20, I sent a further message to Ardeshir:

Hope the Army will be able to restore public order and pave the way for the return to normal life: but sooner or later a new and stronger prime minister must emerge—and you know to whom I (and many of my friends) are looking! No one else has as much stature and authority in the civilian field as you do. No one else has your wide experience or so many powerful friends in the Western world. In these troubled times for Iran, it may be that your hour has come!

Alas, it was too late. The Shah was a sick man. Having micro-managed his government, the armed forces, the police and the public sector of the economy, all the lines of decision-making led to his door; but the Shah was now incapable of making the crucial moves that might have saved the monarchy. Three more powerful and in the end decisive forces meanwhile had turned against him. The mullahs and Iran's rural clergy adopted Khomeini's claim that the court was "ungodly." The international media, notably the BBC, the *New York Times* and *Le Monde* depicted Iran as a police state. And crucially, the Carter administration in Washington concluded that the Shah was finished. The White House therefore sent one of America's top soldiers, NATO deputy Commander Gen. Robert Huyser to urge the American-trained Iranian army not to support any further efforts to keep the Shah in office. Iran's top soldiers stayed loyal to their commander in chief and many Americans, notably Gen. Al Haig, himself a former NATO commander and soon to become secretary of state in Ronald Reagan's cabinet were outraged by Huyser's efforts. But the sands were now running out. Religious demonstrators ruled the streets in Isfahan and Shiraz. Riots erupted in Tabriz. Strikes brought public services in Ahwaz, Kerman and Mashad to a halt.

It was all over by the middle of January, 1980. With Teheran in chaos, rival mobs clashed in the streets, some carrying placards that said in English, "God Save the King." Others, the vast majority, said in Persian, "Down with the Shah."

REAPING THE WHIRLWIND

Shall I tell you your greatest mistake, Reza?
You loved Iran more than you loved Iranians.
— Hassan, King of Morocco

T he Shah left Iran piloting his own aircraft on January 16, 1979. His first destination was Egypt where he planned to stay a few weeks before heading for the United States where his sisters owned homes in New York and California. As he waited in Cairo for clearance to fly on to America, I wrote an analysis for my colleagues in Parliament of why after thirty-seven years of peace, rising prosperity and greatly increased international respect for Iran, the Shah had lost his throne and the U.K. and U.S. their strongest ally in the Middle East.

> *It was our pressure that led the Shah to overestimate the Soviet threat and spend far too large a share of Iran's income on the sophisticated weapons of which we were the main suppliers. It was the Pentagon's demands that the U.S. military in Iran should be immune to Iranian law that lent credibility to the charge that he was a puppet on an American string. Many of us condemned him for not moving fast enough to "liberalize" yet what did most to undermine him were the reforms he pushed through that struck at the base of the Moslem clergy's power—women's rights and land reform.*

Time and change have given me no reason to change that assessment but the Shah's own personal failings are clearer to me now than they were when he was in office. Where he erred—as we all did—was in failing to listen to the charges echoing from the mosques and schoolrooms, that Iran's oil wealth was being squandered, its culture and religion devalued by the import of other peoples' values. Corruption, too, played a larger part than I realized in disenchanting the intelligentsia and the Iranian middle class. Above all the Shah became the creature of his own illusions. So eager was he to restore Iran's ancient grandeur and propel it onto the world stage, that he lost touch with what was happening at the grassroots in his own back yard.

David Rockefeller, chairman of Chase Bank who was to prove one of his most loyal friends, wisely observed, "His Majesty seemed to think that because he believed something it was automatically a fact. The term hubris occurred to me as I sat listening to his startling vision of an imperial Iran reclaiming the ancient domain of the Mades and the Persians."

But it was King Hassan of Morocco who offered what for me was the most perceptive judgment. Speaking directly to the Shah when the

dethroned Pahlavis were his guests in Rabat, the King said, "Shall I tell you, your greatest mistake Reza? You loved Iran more than you loved the Iranians."

Khomeini on his return to Iran was greeted by a crowd of three million, hailing him as the Redeemer

Shortly after the Shah left Teheran, the Ayatollah Khomeini was received on his return to Iran by a crowd of three million people beating their breasts as they hailed him as the Great Redeemer. Within a week, the trials began, the executions and killings multiplied, as they did in the bloody days that followed the French and Bolshevik revolutions. Despite the Iranian armed forces declaring their "neutrality" and staying in their barracks, hundreds of senior army officers were summarily tried and shot. Their corpses were displayed for all to see, entombed in the steel drawers of Teheran's overflowing morgue.

For me, the most obscene of the Revolution's trials was that of the former Prime Minister, Amir Abbas Hoveyda. The judge was Sadegh Khalkhali, one of Ayatollah Khomeini's enforcers, whose previous contributions to jurisprudence included such gems as "the Christian bible is a book of nonsense and shameful lies," and "the Jews are a criminal race." There was no jury, no

Corpses of four army generals executed in Teheran; Hoyveda in jail cell

defense attorney, no right of appeal, and the proceedings took place in secret after midnight. The indictment which was entirely political and religious accused Hoveyda of:

> *Being an enemy of God . . . Corruptor of the Earth . . . Forming Cabinets that were puppets of the United States and England . . . Turning over underground resources of oil, copper and uranium to foreigners . . . Expanding the influence of American imperialism . . . Paying national revenues from oil to the Shah and Farah (and) borrowing money at high interest, and enslaving conditions . . . Ruining agriculture and forests . . . Participation in terrorizing the justice seeking people . . . Spreading cultural and ethical corruption . . . and Granting capitulatory rights to Americans.[3]*

The trial was a farce. Hoveyda had been found guilty and sentenced before the proceedings began. Pictures of him cringing in his cell and later of his corpse sprawled on the floor of the yard outside the court where he was shot in the neck by the son-in-law of the Ayatollah Khomeini, appeared on the front pages of the Teheran newspapers. His death was slow and painful. Only when the prime minister begged one of the revolutionary guards to "finish me off" was he dispatched with a bullet to the head. He is buried in an unmarked plot, somewhere outside Teheran.

The day after the news of Hoveyda's execution was made known I convened a meeting of the British Iranian committee of the House of Commons. We had two questions on the agenda. Why did the Shah fall? And what happens next?

Lord Carrington, who had become foreign secretary, told us, as he later wrote in his memoirs,[4] that "the Shah had faults, like most of us—vanity, touchiness, a certain (probably necessary) ruthlessness and a propensity greater than his ability to listen to sycophants who concealed the truth from him. But of his aim, in which he had a considerable measure of success, to improve the condition of the people of Iran there can be no doubt, and no doubt either of his intelligence and dedication."

My tribute was shorter.

> *The Shah's failings we all know. Perhaps like Aesop's frog, he tried to puff himself up to a size too big for Iran. But the history books, I predict will speak more kindly of him than we do today. He did a great deal to help his people and a lot to help us too.*

The committee then turned to the future. The British, French and American governments already had come to terms with Khomeini's emergence as the new source of power, and were looking to his Islamic acolytes to safeguard their political and economic interest in Iran. The Carter administration in particular, believed that Khomeini as he had promised, would retreat to his monastery at Qom and leave the governance of Iran to sensible, non-religious men like Prime Minister Bazargan, who had hastened the Shah to exit and flung open the door to the mullahs. The White House too was wallowing in self admiration following the first Camp David talks between the Israelis and the Palestinians. If Jimmy Carter could get them to shake hands, why wouldn't he be able to salvage something from the ruins of U.S. policy in Iran?

Summarizing the view from Washington, one of the shrewdest observers wrote: "Khomeini after all had no love for the godless Soviets, Iran still needed western markets, and if a conservative Islamic monarchy like that of the Saudis could enjoy excellent relations with (the United States) why not a revolutionary Islamic republic?"[5]

My British-Iranian parliamentary group was less optimistic. Our verdict on the new Islamic dispensation was based on a verse from the Book of Hosea in the Old Testament of the Christian bible:

The Iranians have sown the wind
They will reap the whirlwind.

THE FLYING DUTCHMAN

What are you guys going to advise if they overrun
our embassy and take our diplomats captive?
— President Jimmy Carter's question
to his cabinet

The Shah of Iran's wanderings that followed his flight from Iran led Henry Kissinger to call him "The flying Dutchman." Shunted from country to country his experiences were chronicled in detail by William Shawcross in his book, *The Shah's Last Ride*. They reflected badly on both the country of my birth and the country of my adoption.

His first stop was in Egypt where he was welcomed as a still reigning monarch with bands, red carpets, and an honor guard. He spent five days at Aswan with President Anwar Sadat, who twice had visited the Pahlavis in Iran. The Shah and Sadat prayed together and cruised through the islands in the Nile, the Shah no doubt recalling the honeymoon he spent there with his first wife, Princess Fawzia, daughter of King Farouk, the last of the Egyptian monarchs. Farouk had been deposed in 1952 with the help of the same CIA agent, Kermit Roosevelt, who a year later had assisted in the removal of Mohammad Mosaddegh and the Shah's return to the throne in Iran.

Madam Jehan Sadat, the Egyptian president's wife already was a fast friend of Farah Diba. With the Pahlavis' future uncertain, her pledge that they could always count on protection and a home in Egypt was a promise that Farah noted in her diary and in less then eighteen months would redeem. It was, she wrote, "a source of enormous comfort. A friend in need is a friend indeed."[1]

While in Aswan, the Pahlavis received an invitation to visit Morocco as the guests of King Hassan, another potentate to whom the Shah in his heyday had lent large sums of money. Morocco was on route to America, where the Pahlavis were planning to settle, so they accepted Hassan's invitation and flew to Marrakesh, where Farah

The Shah and Farah Diba reunited with family in Morocco

had always wanted to stay at the famous Mammounian Inn. There Winston Churchill often came to paint. The regular guests included the 1970's big names of haute couture, among them Pierre Balmain, Yvez Saint Laurent and Pierre Cardin.

It was in Morocco that the Pahlavis' plans were abruptly turned upside down. Both the United States and Britain now backed out of their pledges to grant the Shah and his family asylum.

Before they left Iran, speaking on behalf of President Carter, the American ambassador, William Sullivan had suggested that a good place for the Shah to stay would be at the Palm Springs home of Walter Annenberg, a former U.S. envoy to London. Annenberg was a strong supporter of the Shah's most important American ally, Richard Nixon. The State Department confirmed this in a message to the U.S. Embassy in Morocco, a copy of which was passed on to the Pahlavis when they arrived in Rabat:

> *We have assured the Shah publicly as well as in private messages that he will be welcome in the United States should he decide to come here. There should be no doubt whatsoever as to our willingness to receive and to provide him with appropriate protection.*

Britain's assurances were no less explicit. On behalf of the Labour Government, the British ambassador to Iran had indicated that the Shah would be welcome to use Stilemans, the spacious country home he owned in England, not far from Windsor Palace. Margaret Thatcher, then leader of the opposition said, "I would be ashamed of the British if we could not give the Shah refuge."[2]

Within weeks these commitments were worthless.

The United States went back on its pledge to admit the Shah to America because the Carter White House became fearful that the Pahlavis' presence in America would wreck its attempts to find a *modus vivendi* with the revolutionary regime in Iran. American companies were still buying oil from Iran and selling it military equipment and so were the Brits. Both countries believed—or hoped—that Ayatollah Khomeini would quietly fade away, leaving the prime minister Bani Sadr to go on running the government of Iran. The revolution would run out of steam, life would return to normal. Too bad about the Shah but he was now just a nuisance. Keep him out of sight and all would be well!

This was a gross misreading of the situation in Iran. For the Ayatollah and the revolutionaries, the Shah was a thief and a tyrant who must be brought back to Iran for trial and execution. For them it was as if Louis XVI, King of France, had escaped from the French revolution. They wanted the Pahlavis to be trundled through the streets to face the guillotine.

The Brits got cold feet about accepting the Shah when in the confusion that gripped Teheran following the return of Ayatollah Khomeini, a mob of his followers invaded the grounds of the American embassy on February 14, 1981. This first occupation, hardly reported and largely forgotten by Americans, lasted only a few hours. A naturalized U.S. citizen, Ebrahim Yazdi, mobilized pro American students at Teheran university, marched with them to the embassy and after much confused shouting and fist fights ejected the attackers. The Iranian government apologized. Ayatollah Khomeini sent a deputation of mullahs to express his regrets and relief that no Americans had been hurt in an action that he insisted had been "entirely contrary in his wishes." Ebrahim Yazdi went on to become the revolutionary regime's first foreign minister.

But the Brits were not reassured. The Foreign Office persuaded Margaret Thatcher, who by now had become prime minister, that if the Shah went to his home at Stilemans, the British embassy in Teheran might be seized and the ambassador and his staff taken hostage. These anxieties were shared with the Iran desk of the State Department but the White House was preoccupied with more pressing matters. President Carter was at Camp David trying to resolve the dispute over Palestine. It therefore fell to Secretary of State Cyrus Vance to once again switch the signals the U.S. was sending to the Shah of Iran.

Vance sent Richard Parker, the American envoy to Morocco, to see the Pahlavis in their suite at the Mammounian. He gave them the bad news: the United States no longer would find it convenient for the Shah to go to America. "There would be demonstrations, lawsuits to find his money, problems with security, even subpoenas by the United States Congress, some of whose members were more sympathetic to the new revolutionary regime in Iran than they were to its ousted monarch."[3]

The Shah, according to Parker "took it like a man!" He said that Mexico would suit him better than the United States, but while waiting for its president, Lopez Portillo, to give his consent, he felt sure that King Hassan would not mind the Pahlavis staying in Rabat for a few weeks longer. The Shah's assumption was wrong—though only later did I discover from Crown Prince Reza why allowing the royals to remain in Morocco would also prove "inconvenient" to King Hassan (see pages 154-155).

It came therefore as a surprise when the Reuters correspondent at the House of Commons asked me on March 27, 1979 if I had any comment on the Shah of Iran's departure from Morocco and arrival in the Bahamas. Not for the first time the media knew more than I did.

By good fortune I had a contact in the Bahamas where from time to time I had stayed at Prospect Ridge, one of the large colonial houses

The Shah and family, on the beach at Paradise Island, Bahamas

overlooking the harbor at Nassau. Bill Ormerod, former head of British Information Services in New York had just enjoyed three strokes of good fortune: he inherited from an admirer a fortune that allowed him to retire in comfort from the foreign service; he was knighted by the Queen and henceforth went by the name of Sir Berkeley Ormerod; and he married a wealthy widow Maude Martineau, the cousin of one of my constituents. I telephoned Ormerod in Nassau who knew nothing about the Shah's arrival but quickly discovered that Ardeshir Zahedi and David Rockefeller had persuaded the Bahamas prime minister, Linden Pindling, to let the Pahlavis move from Morocco to one of Nassau's most elegant suburbs. There on Paradise Island, the Shah had gone to ground in a villa belonging to the Ocean Club Casino, a beachfront property owned by a U.S. company, Resorts International.

I had no contact with the Shah while he was on Paradise Island, but I heard a lot of stories and read a dozen articles about the elaborate security arrangements that the Bahamas police insisted on to protect him. The most serious threat came from the Palestinian leader Jascha Arafat who following the Islamic revolution, had flown to Teheran with a gang of his El Fatah fighters and seized the Israeli Embassy. Arafat was reported to have promised Ayatollah Khomeini that his Palestinian warriors, some of whom had played a part in the attacks on the Iranian police that forced the Shah to flee, would now "capture and bring him to justice" or "kill him in the attempt." British intelligence officers passed on these threats to the Bahamas. The chief of security in Nassau doubled the Shah's protection squad. "We know that Arafat doesn't fool around,"⁴ he said.

Guarded by the Nassau police and thirty private security men hired by Chase Manhattan Bank, the Pahlavis' sojourn in the Bahamas did not live up to the promise of Paradise Island. Tourists and paparazzi with zoom lenses, dogged their footsteps when they walked on the beach. They were forbidden to cross the causeway that joins the island to Nassau. The news from Teheran to which the Shah listened on his short way radio told of the torture and execution of scores of his former ministers and army officers. The Shah locked himself in his room and spent days in prayer, alone.

An unexpected figure then arrived from London, disguised in a pair of dark glasses and a false name, Edward Wilson. This was Sir Dennis Wright, the former British ambassador to Teheran with whom I had stayed and played tennis on numerous occasions. Dennis Wright was now a director of Shell Oil Company. Disenchanted by the Pahlavis' conduct during the later years of the Shah's rule, he had helped to persuade Mrs. Thatcher to change her mind about offering them asylum at Stilemans in England.

Sir Dennis, aka Mr. Wilson, gave the Shah the British cabinet's decision over a cup of tea at the Ocean Club. "Her Majesty's government cannot offer asylum to you or your family," he said, then added, "as an old friend," that he hoped the Shah would "understand and accept this." The Shah had no choice but to accept though he later was to comment that it was hard to understand why the British would think it to be in their interest to "give in to terrorists."[5]

The British decision inevitably made Prime Minister Pindling nervous about the Pahlavis' presence in the Bahamas. Pindling and his associates had done well out of the Shah's stay in Nassau, charging huge sums for the services of the police, much of which ended up in the prime minister's political coffers. But Pindling now let it be known that the Bahamas no longer were prepared to accommodate the Iranians. The Shah's visa which expired in ten days time, would not be renewed.

Where would the Shah go next? His preference was Cuernavaca in Mexico but the Mexican Foreign Office objected that this would expose their country to risks that the United States and Britain were not prepared to assume. Help came from Ardeshir Zahedi who had lost his post as ambassador and had been named as a target for assassination by the Islamic regime but still was able to mobilize an impressive lobby of his friends in Washington to go to the aid of the Shah. Henry Kissinger weighed in, as well as John McCloy, former chairman of the World Bank and senior partner of one of Wall Street's most powerful law firms. My previous work as a *Time* and *Newsweek* editor had brought me into contact with both these American heavyweights so it did not surprise me when the Mexican president overrode his officials' objections and allowed the Pahlavis to move into the Villa Des Roses, an elegant walled home at the end of an easily guarded cul-de-sac in Cuernavaca.

Farah Diba enjoyed Cuernavaca. She tended the garden and went swimming on the private beach. But the Shah was a very sick man. The cancer that had been diagnosed by his doctors in Teheran was advancing into his liver and spleen.

The most renowned lymphomatic surgeon of the day was Benjamin H. Kean who had a private practice on Park Avenue in New York. Asked to attend the Shah, Kean assembled a team of American oncologists, chemotherapists and splenectomy specialists and flew to Mexico to

examine his royal patient. Kean recommended that the Shah should be transferred to New York hospital. But would the United States admit him?

The State Department advised against. Anything which suggested that the U.S. was favorably disposed to the Shah would wreck its attempts to come to terms with the revolutionary regime in Iran. Street mobs in Teheran, urged on by Islamic extremists,

President Carter with cabinet officials wrestled over whether to admit the Shah to the United States. When he did, the American embassy in Teheran was ovrrun and its diplomats seized

more than likely would attack the U.S. embassy. Secretary of State Cyrus Vance supported his officials but the National Security Advisor Zbigniew Brzezinski disagreed. The U.S. should not be bullied by a "third rate regime." Hamilton Jordan, the White House Chief of Staff was worried about the political implications. If the Shah died in Mexico, President Carter would get the blame for refusing to admit a sick man for treatment in America.

"What are you guys going to advise if they overrun our embassy and take our diplomats hostage?" Jimmy Carter asked. It was a question that was to haunt him for the rest of his presidency, but the cabinet records show that no one had an answer.

Brzezinski and Vance eventually sank their differences and came down in favor of admitting the Shah "on humanitarian grounds." Dr. Kean was given permission to fly the patient and his wife to New York for urgent medical treatment—after which they must return to Mexico.

The strange story of how the Shah was subsequently smuggled into New York hospital under the sobriquet of Mr. David Newsome, the name of the State Department's undersecretary for political affairs, has been widely and luridly reported. So have the details of the ferocious reaction in Iran where Khomeini declared that by receiving the Shah the Americans had proved that they were plotting to forcibly restore him to the throne. The Ayatollah called for action by theological students, "to expand with all their might attacks against the United States to force the return to Iran of the deposed and criminal traitor." Two days later, as Jimmy Carter had feared, demonstrators scaled the walls of the U.S. embassy in Teheran, and seized the Americans who were working there.

So began one of the most bitter and prolonged struggles in modern diplomatic history. At the time we could not know this, indeed when I heard the news in London and called the *chargé d'affaires* at the Iranian

The Shah, a sick man, was given permission to have an operation in New York hospital following a plea by Ardeshir Zahedi (right)

embassy I was told that "the people's anger against America is deep and justified," but that Iran would "honor its obligations." Its dipomats should be "free to carry out their duties unhindered."

The *chargé's* response reflected what the Iranian government wanted and hoped would happen. A new Prime Minister Mehdi Bazargan and foreign minister Ibrahim Yazdi, for several weeks had secretly been in contact with the United States. Both sides were hoping to resume normal diplomatic relations. Brzezinski secretly met Yazdi in Algiers on November 1. A deal to free the hostages in return for the U.S. releasing the Iranian assets it had frozen appeared to be on the horizon. But the mullahs had different ideas. It was Khomeini, not Bazargan whose commands were now law in Iran. Instead of condemning the students' seizure of the U.S. embassy, Khamenei gave it his blessing. The police made no effort to interfere. Bazargan and Yazdi resigned and day by day the captured Americans were displayed on the world's TV screens, some manacled, others blindfolded, all terrified by the possibility that their captors would carry out their threat to behead them.

The Shah by this time had been hustled out of New York hospital. He expected to fly back to Cuernavaca in Mexico, as President Portillo had promised he would be welcome to do. But the militants occupation of the U.S. embassy in Teheran led President Portillos to change his mind. Why should he admit the Shah and risk the seizure of the Mexican embassy in Iran? Why should Mexican soil be used to "pull Uncle Sam's chestnuts out of the fire?"

ESCAPE FROM PANAMA

*The way our government behaved in this situation will be recorded
as one of the black pages of American history.*
— Richard Nixon, thirty-seventh
President of the United States

The seizure of the U.S. hostages in Teheran ushered in a clash between the United States and Iran and ever since has poisoned relations between them. For fourteen months, the television brought Iranian mobs into America's living rooms, setting fire to the Stars and Stripes, yelling abuse, intensifying fears for the lives of the fifty-four hostages, the most senior of them being Bruce Laingen, the author of the preface of this book. These pictures wrote the *London Sunday Times* "served as a daily turn of the thumb screw for an America inchoate with rage and impotence."

I several times visited Washington while the fate of the hostages was making front page news. The administration's response was a preview of the U.S. reaction, a quarter century later, to reports that Iran was building nuclear weapons. Carter's cabinet split wide open. Zbigniew Brzezinski urged military action. Secretary of State Cyrus Vance argued for patience and diplomacy. President Carter tried—and failed—to do a deal with the Islamic regime's first puppet prime minister, Bani Sadr.

The most sordid option contemplated by the United States was to swap the dying Shah for release of the American hostages. I found it hard to believe that Jimmy Carter would stoop so low—and he did not. Others in the White House did, and U.S. senators like Edward Kennedy urged them on. The evidence is compelling. It accumulated in my files in the course of visits I paid to Panama to see my son, who in the late 1970s served his apprenticeship as a merchant banker in the Panama headquarters of the Bank of London South America and subsequently when I was a member of the Foreign Affairs Committee of the House of Commons.

Following his surgery at New York Hospital, the Shah had hoped to convalesce with his sister, Princess Shams, at her apartment in Manhattan, but this was vetoed by his White House minders. With Iranian mobs assembling outside the American embassy in Teheran, the State Department still hoped to avoid an attack on the mission by getting the Shah out of sight and out of America *toute suite*. FBI and CIA agents rushed the sick man out of New York Hospital before the scars of the operation to remove his gallbladder had properly healed. Under orders from President Carter, who fourteen months earlier had expressed his "deep gratitude and great personal affection" for the Shah (see page 81), they bundled him and his wife into an Air Force plane that flew them to Lackland Air Force base in Texas, where at first they were lodged in a room with barred and shuttered windows and a door with no handle on the inside.

At Lackland, U.S. diplomats pressured the Shah to "volunteer" to give himself up to the mullahs and return to Iran for trial. His response was, "I've been called many things in my time, but imbecile is not one of them." The United States then asked Panama to offer the Pahlavis temporary asylum. The advantages of Panama was that while there, the Shah would still effectively be under U.S. control and therefore available to be traded for the American hostages in the event that President Carter changed his mind and agreed to do this. General Omar Torillos, the strong man of Panama also felt that he owed Jimmy Carter a favor in return for the President's pushing through the U.S. Senate the agreement to restore the Panama Canal to Panamanian sovereignty.

The go-between was Ambler Moss, a Virginia millionaire and distant relative of Nancy Astor, the first woman member of the British

Parliament. Moss, as Carter's ambassador to Panama, was an admirer of Torillos, a figure made famous by Graham Greene's novel, *Getting to Know the General*. Ambassador Moss advised that President Carter should personally ask Torillos to admit the Shah to Panama.

Panama's caudillo, Omar Torillos gave asylum to the Shah but angled to exchange him for the return of U.S. hostages in Iran

Why not send Hamilton Jordan, the White House chief of staff to see him on behalf of the president? Jordan, after all, had got to know and drink with Torillos during the negotiations that led up to the signing of the Canal's Zone treaty.

The sequence of events that followed was confirmed by Hamilton Jordan in his book titled, *Crisis*:[1]

- Jordan flew in disguise to Howard Air Force Base in Panama and drove with Ambassador Moss to see Torillos. Drink in hand, Torillos rose to greet him. "Buenos Noches Papa General," said Jordan. They embraced and began to drink the local brew, balboa.

- Jordan recalled that he was nervous. He was not accustomed to being a diplomat. Instead they talked about sex. Torillos said that his idea of security was to keep constantly on the move, "Sometimes I wake up and don't know where I am." "Or who you're with," interrupted Jordan. They all laughed.

- As Jordan explained Carter's problem with the Shah, Torillos lit one of the large cigars his friend Fidel Castro had sent him, and leaned back in his chair . . . When he eventually said yes to the Shah's being given asylum in Panama, Jordan says that he wanted to shout with joy.

• Although it was the middle of the night Jordan at once called Carter. "Mr. President sorry to wake you," he said. "I'm with our friend down south and he's willing to accept that gift." "Thank God," said Carter and personally thanked Torillos in Spanish.

Flying to Texas, Jordan next day called on the Shah at Lackland AFB. With him was Lloyd Cutler, the White House Council who had hurried down from Washington. The Shah was sitting on a vinyl sofa wearing a blue air force dressing gown with a U.S.A logo on the back. Air force doctors who had taken blood samples reported that his health was deteriorating. The operation in New York had not removed the cancer. His spleen should be taken out as soon as possible.

The Shah was not amused by the prospect of moving to Panama. His wife had heard "bad things" about Omar Torillos. Only under pressure did the royal couple agree to move to Panama. Hamilton Jordan promised that he could be treated by his own doctors in the U.S. Army hospital in the Canal Zone, and that a suitable house could be found where he and his family would be safe from the "hit men" who the CIA reported had been dispatched from Teheran with orders to kill them. Lloyd Cutler added that the Pahlavis could return to the United States if the Shah's surgeons decided that the medical treatment he received in Panama was inadequate. President Carter then telephoned and wished the Pahlavis well.[2]

There are several conflicting versions of the events that followed the Lackland agreement as it became known. Many of them were reported to me by bewildered Panamanians in the Canal Administration. What is not in doubt is that on December 12th, Hamilton Jordan returned to Panama, where he and Ambassador Moss located a secure house for the Pahlavis on the island of Contadora, thirty miles offshore in the Pacific. Owned by one of Torillos' associates, Puntadora had an airstrip from which the Shah could quickly be helicoptered to the U.S. military hospital at Gorgas in the Canal Zone.

Panama City. the Shah's condition continued to worsen

The State Department told Ambassador Moss that the Shah would arrive on December 15. Moss needed to confirm the still secret arrangements with the government of Panama. Torillos could not be found. Almost certainly he was with one of his mistresses. Moss called the figurehead president, a lawyer named Aristides Royo, who knew nothing of Torillos' plans to admit the Shah to his country. Royo's response, as Moss recorded it was, "It sounds pretty crazy to me, but if that's what Trojillos wants, what can I say?"

"Thank you Aristides, you are a gentlemen," said the U.S. ambassador.

Moss then spoke to the State Department's Operation Center in Washington. He was asked the question he was dreading: "Now Mr. Ambassador, is everything ready?"

For the first time in his life, Moss told William Shawcross, "I lied to my government. Those bureaucrats in Washington would never have understood if I told them, nothing has been done, Omar's drunk in his bed."

Instead Moss said, "Yes, everything's fine. Send him down."[3]

It proved to be a close run thing. Torillos was in no condition to meet the Shah when he arrived in Panama. Instead the Pahlavis were greeted by a man named Chuchu, a professor of Marxist philosophy at Panama University, and companion of the novelist Graham Greene. During the Pahlavis' stay in Panama, Chuchu, whose real name was Jose De Jesus Martinez was Torillos' contact man with the Pahlavis. At one point he tried to cheer up the Shah by saying that Torillos liked

Persian art. This was a complete fantasy. A year or so later, when they were at the British Museum together, Chuchu pointed to a piece of Persian pottery and said to Torillos, "That is what I told the Shah you liked so much."[4]

To guard the Pahlavis on Contadora Island, Torillos provided squads of his national guardsmen. Their commander was the head of Panamanian intelligence, Colonel Manuel Noriega, a sinister figure who the United States was subsequently to depose when he succeeded Torillos as Caudillo of Panama. Noriega was a double agent working for both CIA and Cuban Intelligence. He was also the "facilitator" of a shady network of agents who handled the shipments and laundered the profits of the Caribbean's fastest growing industry, narcotics trafficking.

Noriega's men guarded the Shah by frisking visitors to Contadora Island and loitering around his house in jeans and T-shirts. They set up an anti-aircraft gun behind the house and planted sonar devices in the seabed to deter James Bond-like attacks by frogmen. Panama made no charge for these precautions but the Shah had to pay for the Noriega men's meals at a cost of $21,000 per month. When Farah Diba complained, Chuchu replied that the Panamanians were being asked to lay their lives on the line for her family. "Why shouldn't they eat decently?" he asked.

The Shah's cancer grew worse during his stay in Panama. Two teams of physicians, one French, one American squabbled over how best to treat him. As his condition deteriorated, the Iranian regime's new foreign minister, Sadegh Ghotbzadeh sent agents to Panama to seek the Shah's extradition. One of these men was a French lawyer, Christian Bourguet, the other an Argentine, Hector Villalon. The Carter White House and the CIA by this time were trying hard to establish a back channel to Teheran that might help to free the hostages. Hamilton Jordan urged the president to work through this strange pair.

Jordan and the U.S. assistant secretary for Near Eastern and South Asian Affairs flew by Concorde to London, traveling under false names to meet them. Meeting Bourguet, fresh off the plane from Teheran, Jordan asked how the hostages could be freed. The Frenchmen minced no words. "You must return the Shah to Iran." After some discussion, he amended this to, "The Shah returned or the Shah dead. Nothing can be done until the problem that caused the American hostages to be seized is made to disappear."

Jordan in his book, *Crisis*, confirms that he went on from London to Paris, where he secretly met a high placed Iranian whose name he promised not to reveal. This man suggested that Shah should be given a lethal injection while in the U.S. hospital in Panama. This would make it look as if he had died of natural causes.

"You're kidding," said Jordan, shocked.

"I am very serious Mr. Jordan," came the reply, "I am only asking you to do what the CIA did to thousands of innocent Iranians over the past thirty years."

Jordan says that he responded, "That's impossible. Totally out of the question."

Subsequently, his interlocutor in Paris was revealed to be Sadegh Ghotbzadeh, the Iranian Foreign Minister.[5]

It was at this point that reports in the Teheran press claimed that the Shah would shortly be sent back to Iran. A special cage was constructed in which to parade the former ruler through the streets. This was wild speculation. A warrant for the Shah's arrest and request for extradition had indeed arrived in Panama from the Iranian foreign minister. But, political crimes were not extraditable under Panamanian law. Nor, since there was no capital punishment in Panama, could anyone be removed from its jurisdiction to countries like Iran where he might be executed. Torillos told the Pahlavis that they were in no danger. They were not reassured. They knew that Torillos would not allow the Shah to return to the United States, where his reappearance more than likely would provoke Iran's revolutionary guards into even more drastic action against the American hostages. This in turn would scupper Jimmy Carter's prospects for reelection. The Shah also knew that Torillos would do anything to help Jimmy Carter to defeat Ronald Reagan, the most likely Republican candidate to oppose him at the next U.S. presidential election. Reagan had denounced Torillos' proudest achievement, the U.S. Panama canal treaty.

Farah Diba suspected the worst. Torillos, she believed, would not hesitate to "sell" the Shah to the ayatollahs in exchange for U.S. hostages. He had also propositioned her several times, suggesting that she should "act nice" to him. Farah telephoned to Egypt and spoke to her friend, Jehan Sadat, wife of President Anwar.

"Our situation is desperate," said Farah.

"Why, Farah? Why?"

Farah Diba replied that it was hard to discuss this over the telephone. "But we must leave Panama immediately. There are ominous reports."

It was at this point that President Sadat of Egypt intervened. Told of Farah Diba's plea to his wife for help, he offered to send his own airplane to collect the Pahlavis and ordered the Koubbeneh Palace in Cairo to be prepared as their residence for the rest of the Shah's life. This upset the White House. Once the Shah left Panama, he would no longer be available to be exchanged for the hostages. What followed was more like a French farce than serious foreign policy. Hamilton Jordan set off for Panama, to head off the Pahlavis. One after the other, two separate air force planes the White House had commandeered for his flight developed engine trouble on route and had to divert to New Orleans. Lloyd Cutler instead met the Shah and urged him to abdicate, but the Queen interrupted and said to her husband in Persian, which Cutler's aide understood, "Don't you dare abdicate. Think of our son and our people."

Back in the White House, President Carter telephoned Anwar Sadat in Cairo, warning him that Egypt would face the wrath of the Ayatollahs and isolation in the entire Muslim world if he gave safe haven to the Shah. In his memoirs, Carter says that the Shah's life was not in danger in Panama and that he was selfish in not considering, as Carter did, the adverse effects that his presence in Cairo would have on Sadat. But the Egyptian President did not agree. He was a man of honor. His reply to Carter was, "Jimmy, don't worry about Egypt. Worry about your hostages."

The Shah did not want to wait for Sadat's plane which lacked the range to fly direct from Egypt to Panama. Instead he took off for Cairo in a DC8 his aides hired from a Taiwanese company, Evergreen International. But the drama was not yet over. From Iran came a message to Torillos from foreign minister Ghotbzadeh, sent through his French go-between, Christian Bourguet. This said that the hostages would still be released if the Shah could be prevented from reaching Egypt. Torillos called his pal, the American ambassador, Ambler Moss. Maybe the Shah's DC8, which had to stop at the Azores to take on extra fuel, could be held there for forty-eight hours while the U.S. checked up on Ghotbzadeh's offer.

Moss contacted Hamilton Jordan, who by now was on his way back to Washington. Jordan phoned the U.S. Secretary of Defense, Harold Brown, who agreed that the Shah's plane could be held for a limited amount of time in the Azores. And so it was, for several hours, while the Shah was greeted by U.S. and Portuguese officials and his wife, as she revealed later, paced up and down the tarmac, desperately worried that they were trapped.

But Ghotbzadeh could not deliver the hostages. The militant students in Teheran refused to give them up and Bani Sadr, the Iranian prime minister rejected Ghotbzadeh's request that force be used to extract them.

Torillos slammed down the phone and uttered an expletive after his final call to Iran. To Moss, the ambassador, he said, "Ambler, forget the whole thing. I told Ghotbzadeh to go to hell. It's over."[6]

Only then did the U.S. government allow the Shah's plane to be released from the Azores!

◆◆◆

When the Shah's plane touched down in Cairo, Anwar Sadat and his wife were at the airport to welcome him. "Thank God, you are safe," said Sadat. Later, Jehan Sadat wrote that she had been shocked by the Shah's appearance. "He was mortally ill, so thin that his suit seemed two sizes too big for him. Looking at him, I was struck by the callousness of the Americans. Thank God that my husband had the courage to treat the Shah with humanity."[7]

Mohammed Reza Pahlavi died on July 27, 1980 and was buried at a grand state funeral attended by three million Egyptians and their president. Conspicuously absent were representatives of the governments with which for thirty-seven years he had been most closely allied. The only Arab nation represented was Morocco. Israel sent its first ambassador to Egypt. The United States was represented by its ambassador; Britain made do with the deputy chief of its embassy in Cairo. The only distinguished American present was Richard Nixon who spoke for large numbers of his countrymen when he said, "The way our government has behaved in this situation will be recorded as one of the black pages of American history."

Marching behind the catafalque in Cairo, Richard Nixon was the only distinguished American to attend the Shah's funeral

THE CORPSES OF EAGLE CLAW

The Lady would never exploit an American military disaster to score political points against any president of the United States.
— British MP on Margaret
Thatchers' approach

The Shah's death brought another abrupt change in Washington. Deprived of the former ruler as a bargaining chip, President Carter abandoned his efforts to win the release of the U.S. hostages by diplomatic means. The U.S. would now "lance the boil" by covert military action.

No one knew anything about this outside the White House and the Delta force commandos who ever since the Embassy was seized had been practicing a rescue attempt, but on Sunday morning April 27, I got a strange telephone call from the chairman of my local Conservative Party in England. The previous night, his daughter's boyfriend who worked for a local undertaker had brought her home in one of the company's hearses. Asked why, the young man explained that early the next morning he and all the other undertakers he knew had been asked to present themselves at the USAF base at Lakenheath for a highly confidential assignment. Intrigued, the girl's father asked if I knew anything about this. Had an airplane crashed or had there been an explosion at the airbase?

The following day, I learned that a long range U.S. aircraft had flown into Lakenheath with a large number of corpses aboard. Many were so badly burned that they were unrecognizable. The bodies had been taken to the base mortuary but since no U.S. staff morticians were available to prepare the cadavers for burial, the commander and his RAF adviser had been authorized to call on my constituents for help.

This information was given to me on the basis that I would treat it as "top secret," and so I did until the following morning when I learned something that worried me even more. Each wrapped in a burial sheet and placed in a standard Airforce coffin, the corpses had been transported in air force trucks from Lakenheath, to the USAF base at Mildenhall, from which a long-range U.S. aircraft had flown them to America.

"Who were these guys?" I asked.

The Lakenheath commander did not know or would not say.

"Did you get a coroner's certificate before removing them from U.K. jurisdiction?"

This question floored him because he knew, as I knew, that no corpse can lawfully be removed from the U.K. (or any other civilized country) without the cause of death being certified and a coroner being satisfied that no crime has been committed.

Unable, unusually, to get any answers from Third Air force, I arranged to see the Home Secretary at the House of Commons. As we met, the BBC reported that a U.S. attempt to rescue the hostages had failed, incurring heavy casualties.

Operation Eagle Claw had been launched the previous Thursday at dusk Iranian time. Six Hercules C 130 transports carrying Delta force commandos and extra fuel had flown to an uninhabited spot in the desert about 250 miles south of Teheran. There, they were to rendezvous with six Sea Stallion helicopters launched from the aircraft carrier U.S.S *Theodore Roosevelt*. Re-fuelled from the C 130s, the helicopters would fly on to Desert Two, a mountain hideout close to the Iranian capital from which a convoy of trucks, procured by CIA agents and disguised with Iranian army markings would drive the commandos to the U.S. embassy. One group would overpower the guards, another collect the hostages. Four more U.S. helicopters would then pick them up and take them to an abandoned airstrip south of Teheran where U.S. transport aircraft would be waiting to fly them out of Iran.

It was a bold and risky plan, meticulously rehearsed eight times in the California desert before the president gave the word "go." And it might well have succeeded if sandstorms and mechanical problems had not forced three of the original Sea Stallions to abandon the mission. Tragedy then struck when, as President Carter signaled that Eagle Claw should be aborted, another helicopter preparing to leave collided with a C 130 and the two aircraft exploded in flames. The bodies of three U.S. marines and five U.S. airmen left behind in the charred wreckage were picked up by the Iranians and put on display for the hostages to see in the Embassy compound, while the rest of the casualties were flown back to Egypt and thence as we now realized to England.

But here is the rub. When President Carter announced the number of casualties suffered by the troops who took part in the Eagle Claw, he told Congress, that nine had been killed. Yet according to the Suffolk undertakers who worked at Lakenheath that Sunday morning, the number of charred corpses they handled, and the number of coffins that were trucked to Mildenhall, was double that number.

Had Carter misled Congress? He already was in trouble. With the 1978 presidential election campaign in high gear, the Republicans accused him of micro-managing the raid, losing his nerve, destroying all further chance of rescuing the hostages, and holding up the U.S. to ridicule. Suppose it had also been made known that the number of corpses flown into and out of

Wreckage of U.S. aircraft and Jimmy Carter's hopes in Iranian desert. Sadegh Khalkhai, the regime's "hanging judge" gloated over the dead bodies

England was higher than the president acknowledged? The Republican candidate, Ronald Reagan, could only have benefited from the additional discomfiture that this revelation would have heaped upon Carter.

I discussed this with William Whitelaw who as British Home Secretary was as disturbed as I was by the removal of dead bodies from England without a coroner's certificate. We both surmised that the most likely explanation of the difference between the official U.S. death count and the number of corpses I was told had arrived at Lakenheath, was that President Carter in his statement had referred only to the *American* dead. The other corpses were probably those of Iranians who assisted in Eagle Claw whose presence the CIA wanted to withhold so as to protect whatever remained of its network of collaborators in Iran.

I asked Willie Whitelaw to share this with the prime minister. Mrs Thatcher had been deeply upset by the failure of the raid. Watching President Carter explaining what had happened she said later, "I felt America's wound as if it were our own." Like me, she was nevertheless hoping that Ronald Reagan would be the next president, though as always, she was meticulous in avoiding any comment that might be construed as interference in the American election. Told of the incident at Lakenheath, Margaret Thatcher made inquiries, but I never learned what response she got from the British ambassador in Washington. What I did learn from Ian Gow MP, at that time her closest confidant, was proof of the value she placed on the old fashioned virtue of honor in dealing with the White House.

"Making a fuss about this might have helped Reagan and helped us politically," said Gow when we discussed it. But the Lady—that's how he referred to Margaret Thatcher—"would never exploit an American military disaster to score points against any president of the United States!"

RESCUE AT THE LONDON EMBASSY

The hardness of reality compels me thus to act.
— Virgil, *Aeneid*, Book I, 563–4

The revolutionary Islamic regime in Teheran had been in office for less than eighteen months when Saddam Hussein launched a surprise attack on Iran. The Iranian armed forces had been demoralized by the mullahs' execution of scores of their top commanders. The Iraqi dictator ordered his air force to bomb Teheran, his army to seize the Iranian oilfields and his small boat navy to interdict the movement of tankers carrying oil from Kharg Island.

Saddam hoped to seize—or destroy—the Iranian oilfields and win control of both sides of the Shatt el Arab waterway, Iraq's only outlet to the sea. He was also motivated by a desire to punish Iran for its longstanding support for the Kurds in northern Iraq and its new leader, Ayatollah Khomeini, for his religious evangelism among the oppressed majority Shiites in central and southern Iraq.

At first all went well for the Iraqis. They had the advantage of surprise. The U.S., Britain and France had also halted the supply of western military equipment to the Islamic regime in Teheran.

In the south, the Iraqi armed forces crossed the Shatt el Arab, ferried their tanks across the Karun River and captured Khorramshar. Six days of ferocious fighting cost the invaders twenty four thousand and the defenders twenty eight thousand casualties. Abadan was severely bombed and most of the refinery destroyed but the Iranians' fierce resistance saved the city.

On the central front, Saddam's infantry pushed through the mountains to seize several Iranian towns and bombard the city of Dezful, a key transport hub in the northern Iranian oilfields. But the Iranians after the first shock, recovered and fought back. Imbued with the Shiite zeal for self sacrifice and martyrdom, tens of thousands of Revolutionary Guards hurled themselves against the advancing Iraqis tanks in *kamikaze*-like waves that forced the invaders back onto their own soil. There followed a bloody stalemate of World War I proportions. Little noticed in America or Europe, the fighting went on for the next seven years, causing as many as 800,000 casualties of which more than half were Iranian.

During these war years (1980–87) I continued to be chairman of the British Iranian parliamentary group. Our relations with the representatives of the Islamic regime who took over the Iranian embassy in London ranged from cold to cool until, as a new *chargé d'affaires* was settling in, a terrorist drama brought us, temporarily, closer together.

On April 30, 1980, hooded gunmen attacked the policeman on duty at the Iranian Embassy on Princes Gate in West London and forced their way inside. Iranian Arabs trained in Iraq and bitterly opposed to the new Shiite regime in Teheran, these terrorists belonged to an organization calling itself "the Group of the Martyrs." Seizing the Iranian staff and one policeman as hostages, they passed out a list of ninety-one prisoners they wanted the Iranian government to set free, and demanded that an airplane be made available to fly the gunmen out of Britain. Otherwise, they would blow up the embassy and kill the twenty-one hostages.

My thoughts went back to Black September's attack on the Israeli athletes at the Olympic Games in Munich which I had attended as minister of sport in the British government. On no account must the mistakes made by the Germans be repeated in London.

William Whitelaw immediately activated COBRA, the special emergency unit in the British cabinet office. Scotland Yard took charge of operations. The Police Federation whose interests I looked after in Parliament, asked me to pay special attention to the situation of police constable Trevor Locke, the captured London bobby. Contact with the gunmen was established by means of a specially laid telephone line, but there was never any possibility that the Brits would yield to the terrorists' demands.

Hooded gunmen attack policeman on duty at Iranian Embassy in West London and force their way inside

Negotiations continued for five days while the police and the Special Air Service (SAS) made preparations for an assault. The challenge was to storm the embassy, capture or kill the gunmen and still save the lives of the hostages. Given the split second timing involved some never-before-attempted counter-terrorist methods were used. One involved the diversion of airplanes heading for London airport, raising the noise levels over the embassy while police lasers made microscopic holes in the walls. Through these holes silver wires with miniature TV eyes were inserted. These helped the troops distinguish the body shapes of the terrorists who could be shot from the hostages they were to rescue.

I was in the crowd outside the embassy when the police concluded that the terrorists were getting jumpy and might soon start killing the hostages. The SAS was ready to go in, some dropping down onto the roof from helicopters, others swinging on ropes through the windows; but their assault was bound to involve a serious risk of the hostages, as well as the gunmen being killed. Willie Whitelaw telephoned the prime minister who was driving back to London from Chequers. She had her car pull into a lay-bye as he outlined the decision she must make. If the troops went in and a gun battle broke out, the chances of casualties was high. If they did not, the terrorists might in any case kill the hostages, more than likely starting with the policeman. Either way, the government would be blamed for the loss of innocent lives.

The Home Secretary later told me how Margaret Thatcher responded. She had unhappy memories of the Iranian embassy, reaching back to our meeting there when Ambassador Amir Teymour Kalali killed himself. (see pages 83–85) But there was none of the micro-management displayed by President Carter during the far more difficult operation the U.S. had undertaken to free the American hostages.

The prime minister was determined that Britain should never appear to be a soft touch for terrorists. After a pause of twenty seconds, she spoke two words. "Go in" and put the phone down.

The SAS assault took place after dark but in full glare of the TV cameras. Two helicopters swooped down. Commandos repelled down the ropes. There was a crash of breaking glass, stun grenades and gunfire. Within four minutes, it was over. Four of the gunmen were killed, none escaped, and there were no SAS casualties. Every one of the hostages were rescued, including PC Trevor Locke who I later was to meet when the London branch board of the Police Federation gave him an award. His comment was laconic. *"It was just in time!"*

SCUDS AND CHEMICAL WEAPONS

Before entering the minefields, the children wrap themselves in blankets and then roll on the ground. The blankets keep their body parts together when the mines explode so we can carry them to their martyrs' graves.

— War correspondent's description of Iranian boy soldiers

Not long after the SAS smashed the terrorist attack on his embassy, the Iranian *chargé d'affaires* in London, Sadatian came to see me at the House of Commons. He was haggling with the Foreign Office about the costs of repairing the Embassy which had suffered extensive damage during the rescue operation. He also demanded to know why Britain was not supporting Iran in its war with Iraq. Citing the U.N. charter, he said that all members of the Security Council were duty bound to go to the aid of the victims of aggression. In reply, I stuck to the British and U.S. line that both sides were at fault. The U.K. must therefore stay neutral. But we wanted an end to the war. That was why we supported the U.N.'s ban on the sale of arms to either party.

I was never comfortable with this. And the reality, I soon learned, was more cynical. A British military historian, John Keay put it well when he wrote. "The best the west could hope for was that neither side should gain a decisive advantage and eventually both would lose." But if that was the approach of both the U.S. and Britain when Saddam Hussein attacked Iran, opinion began to change as the Iraqi onslaught faltered and the Iranians, especially in the south, went over to the offensive and began to get the upper hand. U.S. intelligence suggested that an Iranian breakthrough to Basra, the second city in Iraq was imminent.

In spring 1982, after a four week nonstop battle, the Iranians recaptured Khorammshar and took 22,000 Iraqi prisoners. Saddam Hussein who came close to being captured when his convoy ran into an Iranian armored unit as it crossed the border into Iraq, announced that his mission had been accomplished and that he was ready to negotiate a ceasefire. The Iranian response was the same as the one the United States offered to Japan in World War II when the tide turned in the Pacific—"unconditional surrender," with the addition, in Iraq's case, that the Iranians also required Saddam's head on a platter.

It was at this point that I began to hear some disturbing stories from friends in Washington about an American "change of direction." The Reagan administration was said to be worried that Iran would win the war that Iraq had started, and that this would unleash the Islamic regime's "dogs of war" against the Arab monarchies of Kuwait, Saudi Arabia and the U.A.E. on whose oil America depended. There were rumors that turned out to be true that a "senior official" from the U.S. Department of Defense had visited Baghdad and that the talking points prepared by the State Department for his meeting with Saddam Hussein included a statement that was to appear in a secret U.S. National Security

Decision (Directive 114 of November 26, 1983). This said that the president would regard a "major reversal of Iraq's fortunes as a strategic defeat for the West. The United States would therefore take whatever steps were "necessary and legal" to prevent Iraq from being defeated and occupied.

It took some time to ferret out the name of the "senior U.S. official," who conveyed this encouraging news to Iraq. He was Donald Rumsfeld, later U.S. secretary of defense until the the Democrats' victory in the 2006 midterm elections forced him out.

Donald H. Rumsfield; he ran the U.S. war against Iraq but earlier helped Saddam Hussein fight against Iran

By the time the House of Commons recessed for Christmas 1983, the United States had ceased to be "neutral" in the Iran-Iraq War. Instead it was tilting sharply towards Iraq, supplying Saddam Hussein's forces with satellite intelligence on the Iranians' dispositions and credits to buy weapons. America, not for the first time, had adopted the Arab mantra that "the enemy of my enemy is my friend."

Visiting Iran or Iraq at the height of their war was all but impossible. Only in December 1985, returning from a visit to India, did I get my first look at revolutionary Islamic Iran. The fighting with Iraq had died down and both sides seemed exhausted. I therefore traveled on an Indian Airline's flight from Delhi to Paris which made twice weekly stops in Teheran. This made it possible to spend three wintry days in the Iranian capital where David Reddaway, the British *chargé d'affaires*, met me at the airport and overcame the not unreasonable reluctance of the immigration officials to admit me without a visa.

Teheran looked grubby and war-battered. The streets were full of snow speckled with grit from the city's power stations. Stalled trucks caused a traffic jam that took two hours to clear (normal, I was told in mid winter). In the foyer of my hotel, once the gleaming Hilton, now the shabby Adana, a huge sign read "DEATH TO SADDAM HUSSEIN." Another said, "BEWARE GREAT SATAN, AMERICA."

Upstairs, the bath water was the color and temperature of warm tea. The telephone did not work. On the portable shortwave radio, on which I rely when traveling to keep up with the news, the BBC and VOA were drowned out by local stations blasting out Moslem prayers.

Lacking introductions, the most I was able to achieve in three days were briefings by E.U. diplomats and cold calls on the Iranian Foreign Office and the Majlis. Driving from the Adana one of the hubcaps on my ancient taxi flew off on one of the freeways. The driver, a wild- eyed

Azerbaijani with black beard and sideburns, insisted on reversing 300 yards into the rush hour stampede to retrieve it. Terrifying!

The Iranian Foreign Office arranged a meeting with a senior economist at the ministry of finance. A graduate of Harvard University's former campus in Teheran, this man estimated that in addition to the terrible human losses, the war had cost Iran a quarter of its capital assets and a third of its national income every year for the past five years. Battle damage in Khuzestan and Iraqi bombing of Teheran and other Iranian cities had caused $800 billion of material damage. He calculated Iran's loss of oil and gas exports, he calculated was close to $2 trillion.

My chief concern was to discover how and why the Iranians, shorn of the professional army and airforce I had watched the Shah build up with weapons from the U.S. and Britain, had been able to turn the tide of battle against Saddam Hussein. There were two main explanations that any U.S. strategist contemplating an attack on Iran would do well to bear in mind. First geography. Iran is three times larger than Iraq. Except for Abadan and the southern oilfields, the Iraqi airforce had to penetrate many hundreds of miles into Iran to hit "high quality" military targets. The Iranian airforce, by contrast, had to travel less than a hundred miles to reach all major targets in Iraq. Second, and critically important, Saddam's invasion aroused a mighty storm of patriotic zeal and anger among Iranians of all political persuasions. Without exception, the diplomats I met were convinced that the war had done what the mullahs could never have achieved on their own, the identification of the Islamic revolution with the nationalism of the Iranian people.

Ayatollah Khomeini called the Iraqi invasion a "divine blessing" because it provided him with the perfect opportunity to Islamize the Iranian response. Khamenei conjoined patriotism and religion by calling on Iran's young people to seek everlasting life by dying in the sacred cause of saving Iran from Satan. Behind the Revolutionary Guards who fought fanatically against the better-armed and trained Iraqis, were millions of Iranian teenagers, some as young as twelve years of age. These kids volunteered to earn their places in "Paradise" by joining the Basiji Mostazafan, literally a "mobilization of the oppressed."

The Hitler Youth had nothing on the Basiji. Most of them came from the countryside and were often illiterate. When their training was done, each boy received a blood-red headband that designated him a volunteer for martyrdom. Before going into battle he was given a plastic key, imported from Taiwan, to be hung around his neck and used after his death, to open the gates of heaven.

The Basijis' chief tactic was the human wave attack, whereby barely armed teenagers would move continuously towards the enemy in perfectly straight rows. It did not matter whether they fell to enemy fire or detonated the mines

Following Saddam Hussein's onslaught, Iranians fought back, suffered heavy casualties, especially among teenage Basiji, martyred in human wave attacks

with their bodies: Once a path to the Iraqi forces had been opened up, Iranian commanders would send in their more valuable Revolutionary Guard troops.

By the spring of 1983, some 450,000 Basiji had been sent to the front. After three months, those who survived were sent back to their schools or workplaces. Writing in the semi-official daily newspaper *Ettelaat*, an Iranian war correspondent reported while I was in Teheran:

> *We had fourteen, fifteen and sixteen year olds. They went into the minefields. Their eyes saw nothing. Their ears heard nothing. And then, a few moments later, one saw clouds of dust. When the dust had settled again, there was nothing more to be seen of them. Somewhere, widely scattered in the landscape, there lay scraps of burnt flesh and pieces of bone.*

The most convincing evidence I saw of the war's impact was given to me by one of the Majlis members, representing a district in Khuzestan, who gave me a graphic account of the injuries caused by the Iraqis' chemical weapons. Thousands of Iranian soldiers had been burned to death. I asked for proof of this and he showed me hundreds of photographs taken on the battlefields. The next day I visited the British embassy compound in the hills above the city. David Reddaway's wife and newly born daughter had moved there to reduce the risk of being killed by air attacks. Walking with Reddaway in the snow-covered gardens we came upon a crater, deep and wide enough to hold several of his Range Rover cars.

"*What caused this?*"

"*An Iraqi scud,*" he replied. "*Two hundred of them are thought to have landed in greater Teheran.*"

"*Were any of your people injured?*"

"*No one was here at the time.*"

"*What did HMG (Her Majesty's Government) do about it?*"

"*Not very much, I fear.*"

I thought long and hard about that crater on my way back to England. Not only was it proof that Iraq was using missiles with a longer range than that permitted under the Missile Control convention which Saddam Hussein had signed; it was also a gross violation of the diplomatic security guaranteed to embassies under the Vienna Convention. Back in London, I asked for details of the protest that the U.K. must surely have made to Iraq and of the compensation that I assumed, it had demanded. The answer was a Foreign Office fudge:

Protest? "Of course."

Compensation? "Still being considered."

Was Parliament informed? "Until now, no one has asked."

Not long after this exchange I received from the Iranian embassy copies of the photographs of chemical casualties that I had been shown by the Majlis member. There were thirty of them, in color, taken in the burns unit of an army field hospital in Khuzestan. Some showed young soldiers whose faces and chests were covered in blisters the size of soup plates, others whose eyeballs had burst. Bags of flesh hung down from incinerated torsos.

This wasn't my first experience of third degree burns. In World War II and during the IRA's attacks in Northern Ireland, I had seen some terrible things. Those pictures from Iran were nevertheless my first exposure to the realities of chemical warfare. Together with the evidence that Saddam Hussein possessed and had not hesitated to use missiles of the kind that landed in the British embassy garden in Teheran, they were among the reasons why I subsequently backed the 2004 decision of President Bush and Tony Blair to remove Saddam before he got his hands on still more terrible WMDs.

OLLIE NORTH'S IRANIAN FOLLIES

About Operation Enterprise, Churchill's phrase seems apt—
"a riddle wrapped in a mystery, inside an enigma."
— Reverend Terry Waite,
prisoner for 1,763 days

y enquiries into the Scud attacks on Teheran and the arms
embargos imposed on both sides at the outset of the Iran-
Iraq war led me into deep waters. During the course of the
war Washington had tilted sharply, and London only slightly less so,
towards Saddam Hussein. The Americans, for example underwrote
loans for the Iraqis, provided them with spare parts for their warplanes and satellite-based intelligence about Iran's defenses.

The U.S. approach if not admirable was understandable. The State
Department having dumped the Shah had tried but failed to come to
terms with the Islamic regime in Teheran. Memories of the show trials
and executions that followed still were raw in Washington. Khomeini's
revolution had torn a hole in the U.S. strategy of blocking the Soviet
Union's thrust towards the Persian Gulf and the Indian Ocean. Soviet
troops had invaded Afghanistan.

The hostages crisis and the humiliating failure of President Carter's
attempt to rescue them turned the knife in American wounds.
President Reagan now faced a new kind of Middle East horror. In
April 1983 a suicide bomber blew himself up at the U.S. embassy in
Beirut, killing sixty three of its employees, among them seventeen
Americans. This outrage was blamed on Palestinian and Hezbollah
terrorists both of whom got help from Iran. Six months later, 241 U.S.
marines died when their barracks near Beirut airfield were blown to

bits by another truck bomber. Reagan's response in the words of a cynical Brit was to "deny the enemy any further triumphs by redeploying the marines off shore."

The U.S. retaliated by sending the battleship New Jersey to steam up and down the coast of Lebanon bombarding villages along the skyline where the CIA guessed (but could not be sure) the bombers' accomplices might be lurking. I did not admire this indiscriminate collective punishment which previewed the tactics employed by Israel in its counter-attack on Hezbollah in South Lebanon in 2006. Writing in the *Security Gazette,* widely read by the British police and security services, I quoted an American expert, Saul Landau, of the Institute of Policy Studies in Washington:

> *When the guns of the New Jersey blow away a Lebanese village, hitting at people who can't get back at you, terrorism is sometimes the only response they can make. These people are going to get back at us the only way they can.*[1]

Sure enough, Arab guerrillas, predecessors of Hezbollah, "got back" at soft U.S. targets. Two of the victims were individuals, William Buckley, the CIA's Beirut station chief who died in captivity under torture, and Terry Anderson, an Associated Press reporter who I had met in Beirut. Anderson was captured on March 1985 and held for seven years.

Hostage taking proved to be a profitable tactic for the terrorists. The response in Reagan's America was a backstage political somersault. For close to a year the United States, while still professing its neutrality in the Iran-Iraq conflict, though actually leaning towards Iraq, simultaneously became a secret armorer of the country the president had called *"Murder Incorporated"*—Iran!

I got a first faint inkling of this in spring 1985 when I was walking out of the Foreign Office in London after a talk with Douglas Hurd, the British Secretary of State. Waiting in his ante room was a huge man with a beard, Rev. Terry Waite, an aide to the Archbishop of

Canterbury. Waite who was later to become my constituent had won international acclaim by helping to free British hostages held captive in Libya. He and I had a good deal in common, both being the sons of police officers, brought up in the northwest of England, head boys of our respective grammar schools and both addicted to world travel. Standing six foot seven inches tall and weighing 300 lbs. Terry Waite had briefly served in the Grenadier Guards and now represented the Archbishop as head of the Anglican church's international communities in which capacity he had met U.S. presidents and the heads of state of many Asian and African countries. While in Africa, Waite arranged the first meeting between the Archbishop of Canterbury and Pope John Paul in the capital city of Ghana. Informed of this by telephone, the head of the Catholic Church in England congratulated Waite, "Well done. But I do not understand why they had to meet in a car." "Not a car," Rev. Waite replied. "The capital of Ghana is Accra!"[2]

Shortly after I saw him in the Foreign Secretary's waiting room, Terry Waite set off on his most hazardous and ill-fated mission, to win the release of a group of Western hostages held by terrorists in Lebanon. Among them were four Americans, one of them, Terry Anderson. That explained the presence of the square jawed American I had also seen in the Foreign Office. He was Lt. Colonel Oliver North, United States Marine Corps.

I knew nothing of North at that time and thought no more about this brief encounter with Waite until a report in a Beirut newspaper set the world agog with the strange story of Operation Enterprise.

Colonel North had undertaken to rescue seven American hostages held in Lebanon by Hezbollah terrorists. To contact them he used two very different approaches, through the "front door" in Beirut, using Terry Waite as a volunteer, and through the "back door" in Teheran where North himself undertook a cloak and dagger mission to meet a group of high-placed Iranians described by U.S. intelligence as "moderates."

North's demarche, though approved by the CIA and National Security Council, on the face of it was a strange departure from U.S. policy. Since the hostage crisis, Washington had cut off all contacts with Iran. President Reagan had described the ayatollahs as "the strangest collection of misfits, loony Tunes and squalid animals since the advent of the Third Reich." Yet the White House in the hope of winning the release of the U.S. hostages secretly authorized North's outlandish proposal to exchange them for anti tank missiles that the Iranian army needed for its offensive against Iraq!

Scores of books and TV programs have since related the details of this tragic-comedy which made America look simultaneously duplicitous and naïve. One of the most carefully researched accounts was written by Harold Evans, former editor of the *London Sunday Times,* who moved to the U.S. when his wife, Tina became editor of the *New Yorker.* Evans wrote:

"The deal was that "moderates" in Iran would arrange the release of four of the seven Americans being held by pro-Iranian Shiites in Beirut. The missiles were sent on August 20. No hostage was released. This was to be the pattern over fifteen months, the Iranians consistent in their bad faith, the Americans steadfast in their credulity."[3]

North and his boss Bud McFarlane, the U.S. National Security advisor had put their trust in an Iranian arms dealer named Manuchehr Ghorbanifar. Traveling on false Irish passports with phony names, they flew to Teheran armed with Ghorbanifar's promise that three "moderate mullahs" would meet them to negotiate the hostages' release. As gifts for their hosts, North had packed a set of matching pistols and a birthday cake in his luggage. The Americans were kept waiting at the airport by a group of young revolutionary guards. No high powered Iranians showed up but the guards unwrapped North's birthday cake and gobbled it up!

Discussions with low-level Iranians continued for several days. The most the Iranians offered was to help retain the release of two hostages.

Returning to Washington, McFarlane reported that no moderates were to be found. He advised the White House to break off dealing but the president was not ready to do this. Determined to help the hostages, Mr. Reagan inscribed a Bible for North to take to another bargaining session with the Iranians in Frankfurt.

As news of this U.S. dickering with Iran reached me in London, I did not know whether to laugh or to cry. My chief concern was for Reverend Waite who some how had got mixed up in Colonel North's activities. Waite had visited Teheran in 1981 but openly, as the archbishop's envoy. After weeks of painful haggling he had negotiated the release of seven British and American Christian missionaries. Told of Colonel North's secret overture when Waite flew with one of these Christian pastors to the U.S. Air Force base at Wiesbaden in Germany, the clergyman was thunderstruck. "This was a total shock. I felt a sickness rising in my stomach. Up to this point Oliver North . . . despite his secretiveness . . . had [always] seemed utterly dedicated to the cause of the hostages. But if arms had been traded, that would be nothing short of disastrous."[4]

Reverend Waite telephoned the White House. Eventually he spoke to Colonel North.

> *What is going on? We're getting very strange reports about a visit you made to Iran.*
>
> *He attempted to reassure me. Everything would be okay. I replaced the phone with a deep sense of foreboding. This is bad news—very bad. Every instinct I had told me it would not be okay.*

Nor was it for Terry Waite.

Taken to meet Terry Anderson and his fellow captives in Beirut, the Englishman was handcuffed and thrown into a cell by Hezbollah gunmen who demanded information about Oliver North's activities. When Waite said, correctly, that he had none, he was stretched out on a bench with two cushions placed over his head. One of his captors squatted on the cushions while another beat the soles of his bare feet with a long thin cane. This stripped off the skin and much of the flesh leaving Waite unable to stand.

Terry Waite coming home after being held prisoner in Beirut for 1,763 days

During the weeks and months that followed Terry Waite was chained and blindfolded. He was imprisoned for the next four years and six months, a total of 1,763 days. Part of this time he spent in a eight foot by ten foot cell underneath the urinal in a Beirut bar.

Oliver North meanwhile completed America's secret exchange of "missiles for hostages." It was a one-sided deal. The Iranians got the missiles, delivered from Israel stocks which the U.S. secretly replenished, but only three of the original U.S. hostages were released. Seven more Americans were kidnapped.

It was five years before I next set eyes on Terry Waite. He was older, wiser and ninety pounds lighter in weight. Only after his release did he learn that Ollie North had another motive for his eagerness to trade with Iran. This was the "neat idea" of charging the Iranians six times the cost of the missiles and diverting the profits to the Contras, a right-wing military group bent on overthrowing the Sandinista government of Nicaragua.

Appearing before the U.S. Senate, which had forbidden all aid to the Contras, North revealed that Operation Enterprise had worked through dummy companies with Swiss bank accounts, their own airplanes, pilots, a ship and a lissome secretary named Fawn Hall, who helped the colonel shred the incriminating papers. He became a national hero when he answered a Senator's question by saying, "I'm not in the

Oliver North appearing before the U.S. Senate

habit of questioning my superior. I saluted smartly and charged up the hill."

Ollie North went on to run, unsuccessfully, for the U.S. Senate and has since made a career as a military TV broadcaster. Terry Waite became a "fellow commoner," a fancy name for a non-tenured resident professor at his college at Cambridge University. He bought a house in my constituency in Suffolk. To my knowledge, he has never made any public criticism of the Reagan administration's strange attempt to rescue the hostages from Lebanon by selling missiles to Iran. Of this Operation Enterprise, he wrote: "The Iranians, at war with Iraq, needed weapons. The hostages provided the leverage to get weapons from America."[5] Of Oliver North, he said only: "Churchill's phrase about Russia seems apt, 'a riddle wrapped in a mystery, inside an enigma.'"

President Reagan meanwhile was forced to disclose his role in the Iran-Contra affair. Having repeatedly denied that the U.S. was dealing with Iran, he now appeared on TV and said: "I told the American people I did not trade arms for hostages. My heart and my best intentions tell me that is true, but the facts and the evidence tell me that it is not."

This admission came as a shock to Mr. Reagan' staunchest ally in Britain. Pressed to tell Parliament what she knew about the U.S. "arms for hostages" trade that contradicted the "No deals with terrorists" strategy her government had adopted, Margaret Thatcher refused to make any public comment. But privately, she confided, "No one could get away with that in England. But in America Ronnie will."

And he did!

SANCTIONS HAVE FAILED

*Iran is turning its face to the North. One day there will be a
central Asian Common Market with Iran as a member.*
— Hamid Reza Assefi, spokesman,
Iran Foreign Ministry

Before leaving Parliament in 1990 I paid one more visit to revolutionary Iran, this time traveling with a visa provided by the Islamic government's mission in London. It was a humiliating time for Iran and the mullahs. The war with Iraq which two years earlier the resurgent Iranians had looked like winning, petered out as Khomeini accepted a U.N.-brokered cease fire which the Ayatollah described as "like drinking a poisoned chalice." The cost to Iran had been dreadful: one-third of a million killed and three times that number wounded; a huge reduction in its gross domestic product as output fell by 40 percent; and a corresponding increase in poverty and unemployment. Not long afterwards Ayatollah Khomeini died of a heart attack precipitating a tsunami of lamentations. His funeral was

marked by a grotesque incident when the pallbearers opened his coffin to allow the breast-beating mourners one last glimpse of the Redeemer. His naked corpse slid out into the arms of the horrified crowd.

The Ayatollah's religious successor, Sayed Ali Khamenei, responded to the national mood of disenchantment over Iran's

*Khomeini's death in 1989 precipitated
a tsunami of grief. His pallbearers
tipped his corpse into the crowd of mourners.*

economic and military failures by easing up on some of the Revolution's more intrusive religious strictures. A briefing paper I read en route from London to Teheran quoted a report on these measures in the *New York Times*:

> *To ease public discontent, rigid structures both big and small were relaxed. Revolutionary* komitehs *that monitored compliance with Islamic regulations were reined in. Night-time road blocks were eased. Iran's movie industry moved from themes of war and revolution to love and adventure. The bazaaris, merchant class, won guarantees that foreign trade would not be nationalized. Chess, once forbidden as a form of gambling, was again permitted. And pale nail polish became permissible.*

This time I was met in Teheran by officials from the Iranian Foreign Office who took me for a drive around the city. A great deal of new construction was underway in the northern suburbs. The downtown shops were poorly stocked by western standards. With the exception of traditional Iranian glass and leather work, their goods were of inferior quality. Fresh fruit, chicken and lamb, were abundant and seemed to be cheap. I saw no beggars—only black market currency dealers.

To the south in the huge sprouting suburbs, there was massive overcrowding, primitive sanitation and crowds of unemployed young men at every intersection. The streets were filled with those piles of uncollected garbage that threaten the public health of growing cities as far apart as Mexico, Cairo and Bombay.

I paid a call on the empty shell of the bolted and barred U.S. embassy. It was plastered with anti-American graffiti and guarded against further mob violence by Iranian troops who marched in and out through a gate at which scruffy looking Revolutionary Guards invited me to visit a propaganda shop labeled "Center for U.S. espionage den's documents."

The shelves were filled with brass-bound volumes of U.S. documents, some marked SECRET that the invading students had retrieved from the embassy's shredders. Hundreds of thousands of scraps of paper had been re-assembled and pasted together, making these papers available for visitors to study at a charge of one dollar for half a day's reading. Business at the shop, like that at the embassy, seemed to be non-existent. The German, French and Japanese embassies by contrast were buzzing with activity, reflecting their undiminished trade with Iran. The British embassy was more run down. Relations between the U.K. and Iran were strained by the row over the Ayatollah's death threat to a British immigrant author, Salman Rushdie, the writer of a book entitled *Satanic Verses* that Khomeini had judged to be insulting to Allah.

U.S. embassy in Teheran where diplomats were held captive, by 1990s was an empty shell where Revolutionary Guards sold copies of documents marked "Secret" pieced together from shredders

At the Majlis I met Hossein Sobhaninia, elected representative for Nayshaboor, a district close to Iran's northwest border with Azerbaijan. A bearded cleric in turban and gown, he seemed open-minded when I asked for his views on abortion and trading on the Sabbath. Sobhaninia explained that conflicts in the Majlis between the strict orthodoxy of the Muslim ayatollahs and the "more liberal" policies that he favored were referred for settlement to a Guardianship Council made up of clerics and lawyers appointed by the spiritual leader, Ayatollah Khomeini. When this fails the conflict goes to a further body, the quaintly (and accurately) named Expediency Council, whose decisions are final.

Sobhaninia introduced me to a colleague in a black turban, black-rimmed spectacles and what I took to be a welcoming grin. We talked through an interpreter for only a few minutes and the only point I registered was that this man, another ayatollah, was unhappy about the rising unemployment and thought the revolution would be judged by its success or failure in tackling Iran's economic problems which he blamed in ascending order on the Shah, the Brits, the Iraqis, the Russians and the Americans—but not at all on the Iranians themselves.

It was a mistake on my part not to listen more carefully to this man in black turban and thick spectacles. He was the Speaker of the Majlis, Ali Akbar Hashemi, re-named Rafsanjani in accordance with the Islamic tradition for his hometown Rafsanjan. Within a year Ayatollah Rafsanjani would be elected president of Iran. He served two terms (1989–1997) as head of the government and ran again in 2005 when he was defeated by the present leader, Mahmoud Ahmadi-nejad. As chairman of the Expediency Council, Rafsanjani remains a powerful figure in Iran, prominently associated with its nuclear program.

The most striking feature of my conversations in Teheran was the absence of rancor against the United States on the part of the government officials I met. What a change there has been since then. Like their clerical masters, the bureaucrats made no bones about their hostility towards Israel, their desire to see U.S. forces withdraw from the Persian Gulf and Iran's ambition to become the dominant regional power. In return, I pointed out that the West could not be expected to bury the hatchet with any country that lends support to terrorism. Yet despite our disagreement, there was in 1990, an underlying feeling of friendliness toward the United States and a vestigial respect for Britain. Many of Iran's top officials were graduates of U.S. and U.K.

schools and universities. Not one of them parroted the mullahs' stock phrases about my two countries being the "source of all Iran's problems" or the "Great Arrogance" or the "Great Satan."

At the Ministry of Industry I was invited to subject a group of senior officials to a no holds barred interrogation about Iran's 1989-93 five year plan. When I asked how this was to be paid for, they said that with the war ended Iran had a strong trade surplus; its reserves were at a record high; inward investment was sharply increasing. China, they said, before long would become one of Iran's chief trade partners. A French, Russian and Malaysian consortium was investing $2 billion in oil and gas developments that the U.S. had forbidden American companies to touch.

At the National Iranian Oil Company, Dr. H. Ghanimi Fard, a graduate (MBA) of Santa Clara College in California, outlined plans to increase oil output to four million barrels a day and add two new refineries to the war damaged Abadan oil complex, still (he said) the largest in the world. These projections were unrealistic. Thanks in part to U.S. sanctions, NIOC's plans to open up new fields have been thwarted and older ones suffer from declining output due to a lack of gas re-injection technology. By 1996, Iran's oil production was still no more than 3.9 mbd. More realistic was Ghanimi Fard's forecast that Iran would become a major supplier of gas and LPG to India and China. With confirmed reserves of 940 trillion cubic feet, 15 percent of the world's known supply, NIOC had won contracts to ship vast quantities of gas by refrigerated tankers to Europe and via pipelines now being built to Pakistan, India and still in the planning stages, to China.

Most revealing and, in one respect, encouraging were my talks in Tehran with the Under Secretary of State, Hamid Raza Assefi at the Foreign Ministry. We started with the fatwa against Salman Rushdie. "No U.K. government," I told him, "can accept a foreign head of state's ordering the murder of a British citizen." His reply suggested a basis for the settlement that was eventually reached. "The Ayatollah's decree that the author of the *Satanic Verses* deserves the punishment prescribed by the Koran is a religious command. But it is not the business or the intention of the Iranian government to enforce it."

I asked Assefi, who is now (2006) the official spokesman of the Iranian Foreign Office, about Iran's relations with its ancient enemy Russia. There was a gleam in his eye when he said that Iran is "turning its face to the North." Not so much to Russia as to the former Soviet republics of central Asia, which are bound, he said, by economic as well as religious and cultural ties to their Islamic neighbors, Turkey and Iran. Assefi had recently visited Armenia, Kazakhstan and Turkmenistan. For these landlocked countries he said, Iran offers swifter and shorter routes to the oceans than the Russian railway system. Cross frontier trade was therefore growing fast. Barbed wire defenses along Iran's northern border were being dismantled. One day, said Assefi, "there will be a central Asian common market with Iran as a member."

I reported on this trip to the World Affairs Councils of America as well as to my colleagues in London. Before long, I would resign from Parliament to become president of the WAC chapter in Orange County, California. Americans then as now were intensely suspicious of Iran but eager to know more about it. I therefore pulled no punches in the article I wrote for the Sunday edition of the *Orange County Register.*

> *The Iranian middle class is fed up with the austerity and sheer joylessness of a puritanical theocracy that has turned their TV sets, newspapers and theaters into a dreary monotone. Younger women deeply resent their subordination and the graceless headgear and veils they are forced to wear to hide their eyes and mouths. (Penalty for disobedience; a public lashing.)*
>
> *In their homes, many Iranians defy the regime's commandments. But when a group of students recently threw a party in a private house, with cheek-to-cheek dancing and*

liquor, the Islamic police raided the party: Three young men got away in a car but the host was fined 12 million rials (about $8,000) and sentenced to forty lashes.

The main threat to the regime is economic. Unemployment is rising, living standards falling. The main reasons for this have less to do with the Iranian government than with the terrible damage done by the Iran-Iraq war and the rapid growth of population (for every three Iranians on my last visit to Tehran, there are nearer five today). But the discontent is palpable. "You can't eat theology," a Tehran shopkeeper said. "Nor should we have to put up with a diet of sermons and lectures on television," said his wife.

That said, I did not think then, nor do I now, that economic sanctions against Iran would bring a change of regime. To the contrary, in a paper I shared with colleagues in London and Washington I said:

- *The U.S. embargo on Iran has failed, just as surely as it did against China. U.S. sanctions still provide the most rabid anti Americans in Iran with their most popular card. As in Cuba, they help the regime to switch the blame for its failures onto the United States.*

- *The Iranian economy, though suffering from inflation and high unemployment, in most respects is healthier under U.S. sanctions than those of many developing countries to which the U.S. gives much of its aid, e.g. Egypt.*

- *The U.S. boycott on contacts with Iran has isolated Washington more than Teheran. When the U.S. first imposed sanctions, the Islamic Republic's friends could be counted on the fingers of one hand; today, despite the sanctions—perhaps because of them—Iran has close links with Russia, China, India, Indonesia and Brazil.*

REZA PAHLAVI

Where do you want to go?
— Don Aggar, former U.S. Assistant
Secretary of Transportation

Before retiring from the British House of Commons, I paid a visit to the young man who as crown prince of Iran I vainly had hoped might play a part in the shift to a constitutional monarchy, before the roof fell in on the Shah.

Reza Pahlavi had recently completed his training as a fighter pilot in America. I met him as he was "contemplating his future," as he put it in a spacious villa surrounded by date palms and jacaranda trees overlooking the surf on the faraway coast of Morocco, south of Casablanca. It was many years since I had seen his picture in the Shah's office, as a child in Farah Diba's arms. Now in his late twenties, Reza was slim and good looking in a well-cut Saville row pinstriped suit as he offered drinks on his patio, followed by lunch with *loup de mer* (small mouth bass) and over iced Pouilly Fuisse. As a host, he was, like most Persians, superb—but it was his retrospective narrative of his father's sojourn in Morocco when he was expecting to go to America that still lingers most hauntingly in my mind.

Looking back across the years Reza Pahlavi quietly confirmed that the rulers of Saudi Arabia, Jordan and Pakistan had all been asked by the U.S. to give the Shah asylum. All refused. South Africa still subject to apartheid, and Paraguay ruled by South America's most detested dictator agreed to admit him but the Shah rejected both. The pressure then increased when his host King Hassan was advised that the 1979 Arab League summit that Morocco was scheduled to chair might be wrecked by Islamic extremists if the Pahlavis remained in his country. The chief of France's intelligence service, Comte de Marenches, visited Rabat to advise Hassan that the Pahlavis' presence could endanger Morocco. He warned that the ayatollahs had sent kidnappers to seize Hassan's family and bargain them for the return of the Shah to face trial and execution in Iran.

Reza Pahlavi's recollections of these maneuverings intrigued me because they involved an American lobbyist and a former U.S. senator with whose lavish facilities in the U.S. capitol the *New York Times* had contrasted my more spartan circumstances in the House of Commons when both of us were first elected to office. The lobbyist was Don Aggar, who served as assistant secretary of transportation under Lyndon Johnson. His colleague was Charles Goodell, Republican senator for New York 1964–70. Agger and Goodell who earned fat fees to represent Morocco in Washington had been summoned to Rabat to advise King Hassan on how to "get the Shah's butt outa there," as Agger described their mission. Reza Pahlavi's account of what happened next is confirmed in the narrative of *The Shah's Last Ride* by William Shawcross:

> Goodell tried to cheer up the Shah. He too, had lost an election, he had felt very bad when the people of New York rejected him, and he could empathize with how the Shah felt.
>
> Agger was more direct: "Your aircraft has been arranged for Friday. Where do you want to go?"

The Shah and his family left Morocco in King Hassan's Boeing 747, taking with them 368 pieces of luggage. Their flying Dutchman-like wanderings in North America are outlined on pages 109–119. As Reza Pahlavi recounted their experiences over the painful year when the Shah's health deteriorated and his parents were shuttled from the

Bahamas to Mexico, the United States, Panama, and eventually to his father's death in Cairo, he took a green handkerchief out of the top pocket of his jacket and wiped his eyes.

Only then did we get down to the main purpose of my visit to Casablanca. What role, if any, could Reza Pahlavi play in the future of Iran?

He didn't have any clear answers. Instead he handed me a sheaf of speech notes written for him by the sons of former courtiers in his father's court. I was not impressed.

Back in London, I discussed Reza's prospects with my colleagues in Parliament and officials at the U.S. embassy. Their instinct, like mine, was to write him off. Some thought he would be assassinated by one of the contract killer squads sent abroad by the Islamic regime to wipe out the Shah's family and courtiers in the bloodthirsty early years of the Revolution.

Yet as the Ayatollah's regime in Teheran descended into the darkness of kangaroo trials, mass executions of army officers and the stoning to death of women caught outdoors without their veils, I changed my mind. There was no realistic prospect of the Pahlavis returning to the Peacock throne. Islam henceforth would play a commanding role in any future government of Iran. Yet there needed to be an alternative to the theocratic tyranny that was enveloping the Iranian people. And though Reza Pahlavi in the 1990s could be no more than one of the voices saying this, I believed that his name and his father's memory could attract audiences that no other figure could command, inside as well as outside Iran. I therefore urged the British Foreign Secretary, Douglas Hurd to let Reza Shah travel to London to address a dinner that I would organize under the auspices of the British–Iranian parliamentary group.

The Foreign Office was not happy about this. But the British government in those halcyon days before 9/11 was not about to exclude the guest of a Member of Parliament who vouched for his bona fides and guaranteed that he would leave after making his speech. As a venue, I hired Fishmongers Hall, the home of one of London's most prestigious livery companies. Three hundred politicians, businessmen, bankers and cultural leaders came to hear what the "young Shah" had to say and paid more than enough for their tickets to cover my expenses. Reza Pahlavi said all the right things. Disclaiming any ambition to return to Iran as Shah ("those days have gone," he said), he avoided recriminations and spoke with fetching modesty. He affirmed his intention to "dedicate my life to ensuring that the Iranians shall not forever remain victims of adverse policies imposed by cruel dictators at home and skeptical governments abroad."

Reza Pahlavi subsequently transferred his base from Casablanca to an estate in Virginia and a house in the suburbs of Washington. He jumped at my invitation to speak in 1990 to the World Affairs Council of Orange County, California at the Richard Nixon birthplace and Presidential Library, and again in 1992 at a Republican Party breakfast. His modesty and quiet good humor made a strong impression on these mainly conservative audiences. We agreed to stay in touch as events in Iran developed and we have done so.

THEY CAME NOT EMPTY-HANDED

Seeking a refuge from the cruel battering of fortune we have come.
— Hafez, Iranian poet (1320–1390)

My Iranian connections multiplied in the early 1990s when Betty and I took up residence in the United States upon my retirement from the House of Commons. To my new job as president of the World Affairs Council of Orange County, California, we drove across the continent in a Range Rover given to Betty by my New York friend, Akbar Lari as a belated wedding present, following our marriage three years earlier. Akbar by now had flourished as a house builder in Long Island. Among his friends were numerous other Iranians I had met over the years, one of them, Ahmad Teherani, the Shah's former ambassador to South Africa.

Akbar Lari in 2003 was named one of America's outstanding immigrants and honored by the mayor of New York at a ceremony at Ellis Island. When I took Betty to see this, we saw a picture of a some words scrawled in chalk by some unknown immigrant on the base of the Statue of Liberty which aptly summarized what Akbar and an estimated two million other Iranian immigrants have contributed to America:

We came not empty-handed here, we brought a rich inheritance.

En route to California we stopped in New Orleans where I was a fraternal delegate, a fancy name for foreign guest, at the 1990 convention of the Republican party which nominated the first

Akbar Lari: Outstanding immigrant

George Bush as its candidate for president. Al Haig who I had met when he was NATO Supreme Commander gave us lunch with Bob and Elizabeth Dole. They were waiting to hear who Bush would choose to run with him as vice president, Senator Dole himself being one possibility. A butler brought a message to the table. "He's picked Dan Quayle," said Bob Dole, naming the youthful Republican from his next door state of Missouri. This was a surprise and no doubt a disappointment to Dole but within seconds he was back on form. "Quayle kept him (meaning George Bush) waiting for an answer," he said. "Before committing himself he wanted to have a shave. His first!"

I mention this because another aspiring politician we met, I think at this GOP convention, was a young Iranian Rob Sobhani with a much heavier afternoon shadow than Dan Qayle's. Sobhani ran for election as a Republican candidate for U.S. Senate in Rhode Island and like another Iranian candidate, Goli Ameri who ran for Congress in Oregon, failed to win a majority, though one day I suspect they both will. Their candidatures underlined a point that Ambassador Bruce Laingen confirms in the preface of this book—that thanks to its Iranian immigrants, the United States is now the world's second largest Persian-speaking nation.

The largest concentration of these Iranian Americans, not less than 800,000, is to be found in the greater Los Angeles area. Another quarter million live in the sprawling cities that dot the coastal plain between the mountains and the ocean where Betty and I now have our home in Orange County.

Most of these Iranian immigrants lost everything when the Islamic revolution tore down the Shah's regime. On their arrival in the United States, many of them at first were exposed to a generalized hostility towards Iran that had been generated among Americans by the hostages crisis. Yet few new arrivals have brought with them as much business and professional talent and intellectual capital as the Iranians. Drawn to California by the warm sunshine and snow-capped mountains that remind them of home, most are entrepreneurs and technicians, builders, dentists, doctors especially gynecologists, plus a sprinkling of craftsmen and taxi drivers. Their average earnings are higher, the proportion of their children who excel at school is greater than that of most other immigrant groups. Two- thirds of them are graduates, many with advanced degrees from universities in Britain, France and Germany.

I made a point of reaching out to Orange County's Iranians on behalf of the World Affairs Council. Prominent among them were Bijan Rafiekian, grandson of a Cossack-Iranian brigadier, who had shortened his name to Kian and was now serving as director of the State of California's Office of Foreign Investment, and Ali Razi, a construction engineer educated at Imperial College, London, whose successful family business had been confiscated by the Islamic regime. Ali, in California, like Akbar Lari in New York, had quickly built up a second career as a home builder and community developer. By 2005, he was putting up more houses than any other builder in the Inland Empire, the rapidly expanding area of Riverside County, west of Los Angeles.

Soon after I arrived, Ali Razi invited me to join the board of his private company, Stratham Associates as an adviser on international business. Together we traveled to Tokyo, Seoul, Hong Kong and Taipei, in search of Asian investors. Stratham's projects were good ones but the times were unpropitious. High interest rates and a temporary but sharp downturn in the U.S. economy in the early 1990s

were compounded in California by fires, floods and an earthquake that shattered one of the freeways in Los Angeles. The result was scare headlines that left the Asian bankers we met reluctant to invest in a market where rents were falling and some of whose high rise offices were described as "see through buildings" because their space stood empty and unfurnished. Two years later, California was booming. Property

Ali Razi, builder, philanthropist

prices soared and kept on rising at a pace that doubled and redoubled land values. Lines of would be investors beat a path to Ali's door, offering loans that Stratham no longer needed but which, five years earlier, we had invited them to make—and they refused!

Ali Razi was named Builder of the Year by the Inland Empire's chapter of the Building Industries of America and now sponsors an annual lecture on Iranian culture at the Los Angeles County museum. He and Bijan Kian, together with Fred Ameri, an Iranian civil engineer who arrived in America with nothing but two suitcases helped me to recruit a cross section of Orange County's Iranians into the World Affairs Council. They applauded and attended in large numbers when I organized programs on U.S.-Iranian relations and quoted one of my favorite verses from the great poet Hafez's "Ode to Thorns and Roses," which translated into English says:

If this spinning world in a day or two
Does not bring fortune's gifts to you
Remember, life has many turns
No two of which bring the same return.
Despair not.

One of the biggest crowds attended a meeting in 1990 at the Richard Nixon Presidential Library in Yorba Linda when my guest was Reza Pahlavi with whom I had stayed in contact since we met in Morocco. Now living on an estate in Maryland where with his family he keeps constantly in touch with large numbers of Iran's compulsive e-mailers and bloggers, Reza's life was, and still may be, at risk from Islamic fanatics, though the Iranian government no longer regards him as target.

As relations between America and Iran turned sharply worse after the U.S.-led invasion of Iraq and the collision between the United States and Iran over its nuclear power projects, Reza became a much sought after guest of honor among Iranian-Americans in greater Los Angeles, where whole swatches of the city, reaching from Encino to Westwood and Beverly Hills are now known as "Irangeles." There, the sons and daughters of the Iranian diaspora for the most part have inherited their parents' hatred of the ayatollahs. Southern California has twenty local Farsi language TV stations, two daily Farsi newspapers and ten weekly and monthly magazines, most of them vitriolic in their comments on the Islamic regime. NITV, a privately financed shortwave broadcaster pumps the news and views of the diaspora into Iran twenty four hours a day.

President Bush's 2006 decision to increase from $10 million to $85 million U.S. expenditure on propaganda broadcasts to Iran and covert support for its opposition causes gave the activists among these Iranian Americans "a sudden prospect of relevance," as the *Los Angeles Times* described it. "They touted contacts with the White House, Pentagon, State Department, and CIA . . . (and) bragged about recruiting people back home in Iran to gather information on its internal opposition and the Islamic nuclear program."

By early summer 2006, many of these Iranians were convinced by the tough talk in Washington that it was only a matter of time before the Bush administration would move forcibly against the Islamic regime. The timing was ripe, they argued. "The mullahs by their corruption, oppression and incompetence have turned the vast majority of Iranians decisively against them," I was told. "Dissidents are everywhere, in the universities, workplaces and the conventional armed forces." Before the end of the year, one of the diaspora leaders assured me, the people of Iran would rise against the hated regime.

Then came the Bush U-turn. In June 2006, John D. Bolton, American ambassador to the U.N., announced that the regime in Iran that he so often had condemned as the number one danger to world peace, "no longer needed worry about staying in power —as long as it ceases to reach for nuclear weapons." Secretary of State Condoleeza Rice wrapped up this change of front in layers of diplomatese, but her message was the same: the U.S. no longer would refuse to talk to the Iranian leaders who only two days earlier she had called the "global bankroller of terrorism." The United States therefore joined with the E.U., Russia and China in offering Iran a package of benefits that would assist in its development of nuclear power to generate electricity, provided Iran dropped any pretension to build atomic weapons. By so doing, it pulled the rug out from under those members of the diaspora who until now had assumed that the president, the vice president and the U.S. secretaries of State and Defense meant what they said about isolating Iran until there was a change of regime!

I asked Reza Pahlavi how he felt about the change of front in Washington. His response displayed a diplomatically grown-up capacity to have things both ways. First, he welcomed the switch in U.S. policy on grounds that it ruled out U.S. military action against Iran. Like me, he regarded this as unwise and guaranteed to drive the Iranian people back into the arms of the regime that they—and we—wanted to change. Secondly and less convincingly, Reza argued that U.S. involvement in talks with Iran would smoke out the mullahs, revealing that they are in fact determined to acquire atomic weapons. This in turn would demonstrate that the regime's earlier protestations that it had no intention of building a nuclear bomb were false, underlining its untrustworthiness as a partner in any negotiated settlement.

Only time and events will reveal whether this forecast is well-founded. In the meantime Reza Pahlavi planned in summer 2006 to call together the diverse fractions of the Iranian diaspora in America to form a united front. I asked for what purpose, and he answered:

To go to the aid of the oppressed people of Iran by flood-ing the country with cash and volunteers to help its opposition parties and by a blitzkrieg of international propaganda against the ayatollahs.

Reza recommended a combination of "external pressure"against individual members of the Iranian government, including a ban on travel and seizure of the "dummy corporations" in which they hide their overseas assets, and "internal resistance" based on marches, mass demonstrations and refusal to pay taxes. Within Iran, he claimed, elements of the Revolutionary Guards were turning against the ayatollahs. They and large numbers of underpaid officials were ready (he said), to support French-style strikes by transport and municipal workers that could bring the country to a standstill. Backing them up there would be "massive civil disobedience of the kind that has changed governments from Argentine to Ukraine." I asked him:

> *Are you in contact with some of the revolutionary guard commanders?*
>
> *Absolutely. The guards keep saying that they are under utilized, that they have a role to play but are left in no man's land.*
>
> *How soon might an internal rebellion take place?*

Reza Pahlavi replied that he was not calling for violence or civil war but that Iranians were so fed up with the regime that they might well rise up against it in 2006–7.

That struck me as optimistic. Economic conditions in Iran were deteriorating. Living standards were falling. Discontent was widespread, especially in the cities where unemployment is not less than 12–15 percent and young people resent the suffocating religiosity and corruption of the regime. Yet nothing had done more to assist Ahmadinejad's appeal to Iranians deep-seated suspicions of foreigners than the impression that the U.S. was determined to close down Iran's nuclear power program, which nearly all its people regard as a badge of their nation's scientific and technical progress. Washington's support for Israel's massive counter-attacks on Lebanese towns and villages, using American-built planes and missiles that killed hundreds of civilians, among them scores of children, has also dissipated the high regard that most Iranians once had for the United States. Broadcast sixteen hours a day by Iranian and Arab TV stations, pictures of the victims of the Israelis' disproportionate response to Hezbollah's rocket attacks made it easier for the regime to not only revile Israel but to present America as the enemy of both Iran as a nation and Islam as their creed.

It is possible that the Iranian diaspora in America, together with its colleagues in London and Paris, one day may play a part in bringing about regime change in Teheran. Given the frequent visits that some of these exiles now make to their homeland, they almost certainly know more about what is happening on the ground in Iran than the U.S. government which has no representation in Teheran.

That said the example of Ahmad Chelabi, the Iraqi exile who helped to spur the U.S. invasion of Iraq with his discredited intelligence about Saddam Hussein's WMDs, is not helpful to their cause. Reza Pahlavi in particular cannot afford to be tarred with the same brush as Chelabi.

Reza's future is obscure. Juan Carlos I, son of the Spanish monarch, who lost his throne in 1938, now reigns in Spain as its popular and not unpowerful king. Another ex-monarch I knew, Simeon of Bulgaria found a new lease of life when he returned to Bulgaria as prime minister. But Iran is now Islam country. Allah alone knows if Reza Pahlavi has a role to play there.

ORANGE COUNTY OPENS A DIALOGUE

A California dinner without wine and women? Preposterous.
— President, Orange County World
Affairs Council

A political earthquake occurred in Iran in spring 1987. An unknown cleric emerged from the shadows to challenge the Islamic establishment's choice to succeed Ali Akbar Rafsanjani as the Islamic Republic's fourth president. Mohammad Khatami was the mullah who smiled. He had been purged from his post as Minister of Culture and Islamic guidance because of his tolerance for diversity; now, after a twelve day campaign and a record turnout, Khatami won a landslide victory with 70 percent of the vote.

The smiling mullah appeared to espouse the same things as George W. Bush and Tony Blair ten years later advocated for Iraq (and Iran): "democracy and the rule of law." By this he meant more freedom and less interference by the mullahs in the Islamic people's lives. "Voting for Khatami was like falling in love," a political scientist at Teheran University told Robin Wright of the *New York Times*.[1]

In his inaugural address to the Majlis, the new president said:

An Islamic government must be one that considers itself to be the servant of the people, not their master. A government's authority is not realized by coercion or arbitrariness, but by legal acts, by respect for right and encouraging people's participation in decision making. People must believe that they have the right to determine their own destiny and that there are limits to government.

Those words were music in my ears.

The Majlis had never heard anything like it.

Nor, since the Shah's days, had Iranians seen anything like Khatami's western style outreach to the public. On his first day as president, he ate with his fellow workers in the office cafeteria. On Clean Air day, February 1998, he and his wife rode buses instead of his presidential limo. Later, he was seen on TV removing his turban and clerical gown and lying down to donate blood to a hospital. He even did a radio talk show. "Go ahead caller, President Khatami is on the line," said the Teheran Radio announcer.[2]

Iran's reforming president, Mohammad Khatami addresses the Y2000 Millennial Conference of the United Nations. "The Middle East should be nuclear-free," he said.

I woke up to the significance of Khatami's emergence when Christiana Amanpour interviewed him for CNN. The new president asserted Iran's right to create, but not to export, its own form of Islamic government and condemned what he described as U.S. efforts to reverse this. He also suggested that the West's support of the Shah, the seizure of the American embassy and the shooting down of an Iranian airliner by the U.S. cruiser Vincennes were now "events of the past." It was time to "crack the wall of mistrust" that had built up between America and Iran.[3]

Did Khatami mean it, and could he deliver? I had asked the same questions about Mikhail Gorbachov when he came to the House of Commons and later met Margaret Thatcher who decided that this was a man with whom she could do business. Could Khatami be a Persian Gorbachov? I put the thought aside but it kept reverberating in my mind when two years later, at the 2000 Millennial Conference of the

U.N., Khatami went to the same rostrum where once I had watched Mohammed Mosaddegh in action.

Addressing the Y2000 Millennial meeting of the United Nations, Khatami proposed a "dialogue of civilizations" instead of the cold war between the West and Islam. On Afghanistan where hundreds of Iranian traders and diplomats had been killed by the Taliban, he pledged to work with the U.S. and the E.U. to "halt the deadly business of smuggling narcotics." On terrorism, he reminded the General Assembly that fanatical bombers had killed an Iranian president and more than two hundred government officials, including ten cabinet ministers and twenty-seven elected members of the Majlis. Iran would therefore "vigorously combat all forms of terrorism including state terrorism." That was nine months before 9/11.

Turning to WMDs, Khatami recalled the chemical weapons attacks, some of whose results I had seen for myself that Saddam Hussein had launched against Iran (see pages 129–130). He pledged Iran's support for international efforts to outlaw and destroy all forms of WMDs and made a special point of saying that Iran wanted the Middle East to become "a zone free of all weapons of mass destruction."

I read and reread the text of Khatami's speech underlining his words about a nuclear free Middle East. I wondered if U.S. officials in Washington had listened to him. Concern about Iranian support for Hezbollah in Lebanon already haunted the White House. Memories of the hostages crisis were still painful. But the State Department acknowledged that the new president's overtures were "worth exploring." I therefore wrote to Khatami inviting him to send a representative to Orange County to explain in greater detail what he meant by a "dialogue of civilizations."

Nothing happened until, six months later, I received a strange telephone call. A heavily accented voice said, "My ambassador has instruction from Teheran to accept your invitation. Please tell me how to arrange this."

The voice was that of the number two man at the Iranian mission to the U.N. In order to come to Orange County, Ambassador Nejad Hosseinian would need a State Department permit to travel outside the twenty-five mile limit around the U.N. to which the U.S. confines the envoys of governments it does not recognize. To get this was not easy. Permits required the personal authority of Secretary of State and this, I was told, automatically would be refused. Not since the U.S. embassy in Teheran had been sacked had any representative of the Islamic regime been allowed to travel or speak outside the U.N. limits.

There followed a series of letters and phone calls to Madeleine Albright in which I argued that no harm would be done by an NGO's testing the sincerity of Khatami's demarche. Eventually, she agreed that the Ambassador could come on one condition—that Nejad Hosseinian for whose safety the U.S. government would legally be responsible once he left the twenty-five mile limit, could be protected again attacks on his life by Iranians in Orange County who had every reason to feel bitter about his regime.

The FBI's advice to the State Department was, "don't risk it." But Albright over-ruled this. On reflection, her office told me that she accepted my argument that the U.S. should "suck it and see."

To balance Nejad Hosseinian on the World Affairs Council program, I persuaded Bruce Laingen, who as head of the American hostages had spent 444 days in captivity in Teheran, to be the other main speaker at our dinner in the Hilton Hotel in Anaheim. As interest quickened, we turned this into a half-day affair with sessions on Iranian oil and gas, an exposition of the Shiite version of Islam, and presentations on trade and human rights. Two of the best speakers were women, the *New York Times* correspondent Robin Wright and Lady Renwick, the former Homayoun Mazandi who flew in from Britain to join us.

The demand for tickets was overwhelming but as the day of the program drew near unforeseen obstacles arose. Southern California's Iranian language radio stations pumped out daily attacks on the WAC for hosting the representative of a "murderous tyranny." Ali Razi and Bijan Kian, both now trustees of the council were accused of "betraying" freedom in Iran. I personally was described as a "friend of terrorists," and worse, a "secret British agent." The hotel manager then got cold feet. He wanted to cancel the event when two of the public rooms adjoining the ballroom where Nejad Hosseinian was to speak were reserved for a big screen showing of women being half-buried and stoned to death in Iran. I overcame the manager's anxieties on the high ground of our rights to free speech and the low ground of threatening that the council never again would hold meetings at his hotel. The Iranian mission to the U.N. then called with their own demands. The ambassador must not be photographed in the presence of women without veils. No wine or sprits must be served at the dinner. "Preposterous" was my answer. Orange County women don't wear veils, and a meal without wine on offer was unthinkable in California.

I met Nejad Hosseinian at Orange County airport where the police treated the regular Delta flight on which he traveled as if it were carrying a nuclear bomb. The pilot was ordered to taxi to a remote place on the perimeter track where it was surrounded by thirteen police cars. No other passengers were allowed to disembark until the unsmiling ambassador in his mullah's clerical collar was escorted from his economy seat near the rear of the plane and hurried to a black limousine guarded by half a dozen burly Iranians, specially hired by his officials to look after him. Keeping an eye on these Iranians was an even larger squad of heavily armed U.S. security men.

Flashing lights and screaming sirens cleared our ten mile route to the hotel where Nejad Hosseinian was hustled up to his suite and I was left to face a crowd of angry protesters, estimated by the police to number nine hundred. One of them spat in my face. Others waving banners and shouting Persian slogans demanded that the meeting be cancelled and Hosseinian arrested as a terrorist.

It was then that my experience with the British police in facing down very much larger CND demonstrations at U.S. airbases in England stood me in good stead. Offering my hand to the protest leaders, I asked them to sit down with me on a bench and explain their objections. To enable me to hear what they said, the crowd had to quieten down. I also offered to arrange a personal meeting for six of the protesters with Hosseinian if they put aside their banners and agreed to mind their manners. For a while the shouting ceased but none of the demonstrators would meet Hosseinian who instead of joining me on the platform, chose to sit inconspicuously in the front row out of sight of the TV cameras that might send his image back to Teheran, in the presence of women and wine!

The program was a kebab of information and passion. Women speakers described the cruelty and misogyny of the mullahs. A retired Iranian air force general told of the torture and execution of several of his former colleagues. A businessman lamented the loss of Iranian markets for American goods. Bijan Kian told Hosseinian that Iran could not expect a penny of inward investment when foreign executives faced a risk of being dragged before Sharia courts, presided over by a hanging judge, if their companies in Iran ran into labor disputes.

Ambassador Hosseinian's keynote speech was humorless but surprisingly constructive and placatory. He avoided violent attacks on the Shah, sought to explain the origins and objectives of the Revolution and repeated President Khatami's call for a "dialogue of civilizations" and a "nuclear weapons-free Middle East." The sessions that followed were boisterous but never got out of hand. With one exception, there was less violence and fewer interruptions than occur at British election meetings. The exception came at the end as the seven hundred strong audience was listening to Ambassador Laingen's windup. A detective guarding the platform handed me a note saying, "Bomb threat. Do you want to evacuate?"

"What is your advice?" I whispered.

"Your call," he replied.

My mind flashed back to meetings in Northern Ireland at which bomb threats were almost routine. "Keep calm" is the rule of the road.

I tugged gently at Bruce Laingen's jacket. Pointing to my watch, I hissed, "Stop now." And pro that he is, Bruce did in less sixty seconds.

"Show's over." I then announced. "This is the curtain call. There is a problem in the lobby so please help the police by filing out through the kitchen. This will give you a chance to thank the cooks for your meal."

It took less than six minutes to empty the Hilton ballroom. And the only sign of a bomb was a SWAT team of heavily armed cops pinning to the floor of the lobby one of the protest leaders I'd met outside the hotel. Before long he was released. The bomb threat was a hoax. The suspect had nothing to do with it.

Afterwards, I joined Nejad Hosseinian and his staff who were drinking orangeade in his suite. The ambassador placed a call to President Khatami in Teheran. His phone call lasted twenty minutes and when he was done, Hosseinian said that he had reported a "great success," and had been asked by his president to suggest that I visit Iran. Next morning, when he departed, the hotel manager presented me with an extra bill. Nejad Hosseinian's phone call to Teheran had cost $118 and had been billed to me.

There was another and happier outcome. Relieved and, I think, impressed, the State Department agreed that Nejad Hosseinian could speak at other meetings organized by World Affairs councils. Six months later the Iranian foreign minister Kamal Kharazzi, was also permitted to make a non-official visit to Los Angeles where he spoke to an international relations group at UCLA and at an Iranian-

American reception at the Ritz Carlton hotel near my home in Laguna Niguel. At both events, the protesters were out in force. A group of them at UCLA cornered me and Fred Ameri, and threw orange juice on Fred's new suit. But Kharazzi was listened to politely especially when he listed the business opportunities that could open up in Iran if U.S. sanctions were lifted.

Nejad Hosseinian meanwhile addressed thirteen World Affairs Councils in all parts of America. By the time he left the U.N. he had become a different man. The buttoned up Islamic cleric who in Orange County had worried about being seen in the presence of wine and women, doffed his clerical collar and sorrowful mien in favor of a double-breasted suit and the look of a Middle West businessman.

I like to think that the World Affairs Councils played some part in this transformation!

HISTRIONICS AT THE GOLDEN MOSQUE

No one can doubt the reverence, even idolatry that millions
of Iranians still feel towards the revolutionary leader
who dethroned the last of the shahs.
— *Orange County Register*

Following up the suggestion that I should pay another visit to revolutionary Iran, this time wearing my World Affairs Councils hat, I sought advice from U.S. and British officials, think tanks in Washington, London and Paris, and from Iranian exiles who had visited their country since Ayatollah Khatami had won election as president. Opinion as always was mixed. Optimists pointed out that Khatami had curbed the excesses of the regime's religious police and promised action to relieve poverty and unemployment. His approach to the West was said to be "moderate." Pessimists scoffed at this. Khatami in their eyes, was the "smile on the face of the tiger." The regime remained a theocratic tyranny dedicated to the export of Islamic fundamentalism.

Confused by both but convinced by neither of these assessments, I flew to London in May 1998 and caught an Iran Air flight to Teheran on one of the short-bodied 747s the Shah had purchased from Boeing. My fellow passengers included a large number of smartly-dressed Iranian women who before boarding went into the restrooms, removed their lipstick, mascara and jewelry, and reappeared as plain-Janes wearing veils. Iran Air now belonged to the mullahs!

Joining me in Teheran were two other leaders of the World Affairs Councils of America, Dr. Jerry Leach, the national president, a former NSC staff member, and James Nathan, Ph.D., author of a treatise on diplomacy that the State Department recommends as a textbook. At first we did not receive the "warm welcome" Nejad Hosseinian had promised. It took the Iranian Foreign Office thirty-six hours to return my phone calls. To pass the time, we drove around Teheran in a dilapidated taxi, took photographs of the boarded up U.S. embassy and called on an extremely helpful Canadian ambassador.

Stern images of Khomeini and other ayatollahs dominate streets of Teheran and other Iranian cities

Teheran had changed for the worse. Walls and high buildings were plastered with Islamic texts and pictures of grim looking mullahs. Women in public were forced to cover every inch of their bodies. The city had quadrupled in size (to 11 million) generating a haze of smog. Dozens of jerry built skyscrapers, many standing half empty, sprouted in the foothills of the snow-capped peak of Mt. Damavand that dominates the northern skyline. Traffic jams choked the city center (gas was 9 cents a gallon) but Teheran's fashionable boulevards, lined with plane trees and cooled by water running down from the snowfields, still were lined with restaurants and grassy parks filled with young families strolling around the lakes and flowerbeds.

South and west of the capital we saw a shabby hut-filled mass of industry and slums. Close to a million former peasants live there in hovels lacking sanitation, schools and hospitals. Only recently, an outstanding young mayor, Gholam Karbaschi, had made a dent in the squalor by clearing the worst of the slums, opening clinics and extending the Teheran Metro. To finance this, he was said to have levied an extra tax on the *Bazaaris* (merchants) who dominate Teheran business—with the result that the mayor was charged with corruption and jailed by an Islamic court.

Our hosts at the Iranian Foreign Office eventually bestirred themselves. A series of intensive discussions took place at a think tank specializing on Iran–U.S. relations in one of the Shah's former palaces in the hills overlooking the city. We met an under secretary of state carefully chosen to match my former "rank" in the U.K. government and a prominent ayatollah, reputed to be close to President Khatami.

That night, we heard three explosions. Blasts lit the night sky. From our perch in the former Hilton Hotel it looked at first like a fireworks display, then thunder, then mortar rounds. Next morning an excited but anonymous voice informed Jim Nathan by telephone that the explosions had been caused by bombs.

"Whose bombs?" I asked.

The voice had no answer, save only that he had heard this on Radio Israel.

The highlight of our officially arranged program was a visit to the Karaj dam and reservoir which supplies a large share of Teheran's water and power (at whose opening by the Shah I had been present thirty years earlier). This was followed by a drive through the Zagros mountains where winding through ice-bound passes and hairpin bends at 10,000 feet, we saw scores of wrecked vehicles, the fruits of Iranians' penchant for driving around blind curves on the wrong side of the road. Above, on precipitous slopes, goats hopped from crag to crag. Dislodged screed and boulders toppled down onto the highway.

One night, on the shores of the Caspian, we watched fishermen landing their catch, but no longer were there any of the sturgeon I had seen on my previous visit with Janet Milford-Haven. The population of these giant fish has sharply declined in the face of oil slicks from

Azerbaijan's refineries and the contaminants carried down the Volga river from Russia's steel and chemical plants.

We stayed at a French built chateau now serving as a hotel at Rasht and at a modern but far less comfortable U.S.-style motel on the freeway running from Tabriz back to Teheran. The TV programs in these hotels included the BBC and the German West Deutsche Rundfunk, uncensored. Along the way, the provincial cities offered a mishmash of mud walled bazaars and plate glass fronted shops. Their streets teemed with unemployed youths kicking footballs and donkey carts piled high with melons. Everywhere vendors pressed us to buy throw rugs, iced lemonade, glass trinkets, nylon dresses, tin trays, porcelain bangles, Indian teapots, Japanese cameras and Chinese made replica machine guns. Many of the younger women walked freely to work, unveiled. The *komitehs*, religious police, we had encountered in Teheran were nowhere to be seen, but peering down from walls and billboards was the fierce bearded visage of the long deceased Ayatollah Khomeini. Alongside him were life size portraits of "martyrs," Iranian soldiers and Basiji killed in the war with Iraq.

Back in Teheran, we engaged in another round of discussions with Iranian officials and a high ranking mullah with a PhD degree from an American University. Their briefings echoed President Khatami's speech at the U.N. Iran was no threat to the West. Its priorities were reconstruction after the war with Iraq and expansion of its oil and gas exports to help pay for the investment needed to meet the demands of an expanding population for jobs, homes, schools and hospitals. Iran was therefore seeking an end to the hostility between the United States and Iran. "Peace . . . trade" . . . mutual respect" were the words that kept washing over us.

In response I asked why Iran was supporting terrorist organizations like Hezbollah in Lebanon? Why did its Ayatollahs call on all true believers to attack America as the Great Satan? These questions begat counter-questions. Why had America and Britain brought down Iran's first truly elected national leader, Mohammed Mosaddegh? If Americans were still bitter about the fifty-three diplomats held hostage in 1980 in the U.S. embassy, weren't Iranians entitled to feel even more angry about the 296 pilgrims, sixty-six of them children who died when the U.S. cruiser, Vincennes shot down an IranAir 707 en route to Mecca?

This kind of dialogue did not seem to be getting us anywhere so I offered a suggestion arising from my experience as Minister of Sport in Britain. After years of bitter hostility between the West and Communist China, the ice had been broken when a group of young Chinese ping-pong players were given visas to play exhibition matches against table tennis teams in England. Ping-pong diplomacy then crossed the Atlantic paving the way for cultural, then commercial, eventually political exchanges between China and the U.S. as well as Britain. Why not try sports I suggested, as a way of opening the door between America and Iran?

It was an idea the Iranians liked though I cannot claim that it was original. More than likely, the suggestion that the U.S. and Iran should exchange teams of wrestlers was put forward by others with greater influence on Teheran and Washington than I had. But within a year, the American Amateur Wrestling Association sent a team to Iran and scored a huge success. Many thousands of Iranians crowded Teheran's municipal stadium to welcome and cheer the Americans as they took on the Iranian champions at their national sport. Televised to an audience estimated at 30 million, this was not an occasion when American flags were burned. To the contrary, the stadium was filled with a sea of waving Stars and Stripes banners, and chants of "U.S.A." as the Americans won some and lost more of the contests. It was a match that saw the Iranian team come out on top but demonstrated as soccer ever since has done in subsequent rounds of the World Cup, that sport can open doors that politicians close.

The day before we were due to leave Teheran at the end of this 1998 visit, my World Affairs Council group struck lucky. The entire city had been invaded by Shiite pilgrims arriving to commemorate the ninth anniversary of Ayatollah Khomeini's death. From every corner of Iran, these "soldiers of Allah" converged on the enormous Golden mosque and Holy Shrine that contains Khomeini's remains. Next door is the Behesht-e-Zahra, the Middle East's largest cemetery. Joining them were an estimated half-million others from adjoining countries where Shiites comprise majorities, as in Iraq (65 percent), Azerbaijan (75 percent) and Bahrain (76 percent), or significant minorities as in Kuwait (30 percent), Afghanistan (20 percent) and Qatar (16 percent).

It was a once-in-a-lifetime experience to be swept-up by these celebrations. We were the only non Moslems and almost certainly the only Westerners present at this commemoration of the life of a man who Americans regard as an ogre and Iranians honor as a saint. To get to the Golden Mosque we hitched a ride on a bus marked "Foreign VIPs." At the entrance, I got through security by hanging onto the coattails of a turbaned Turkmenistan mullah with steel teeth, no English and a spade beard that between grunts he brushed up and down my red checks. Inside, a crowd estimated at one and a half million displayed all the reverence of a Hajj pilgrimage to Mecca and the same kind of histrionics—and media madness—that marked Princess Diana's funeral in London. Tens of thousands of the faithful wailed and beat their breasts for the departed Ayatollah. Cries of "God be thanked for the Redeemer," were interspersed with shouts of "Down with America." One of the revolutionary guards I at first thought was a boy scout, asked us from whence he came. When Jerry Leach answered, "America," the fellow nodded somberly, smiled, and made room for us to sit on a tennis court-sized carpet stretched across a cobble stoned courtyard near the dais.

As the sun reached its apogee, the temperature soared to 109 degrees. A succession of spellbinders worked the crowd as a tenor and a bass dirge-singer joined Khomeini's handsome grandson on the platform. The main speech was made by Khomeini's successor, the Ayatollah Khameini. He was prayerful and mercifully brief (ten minutes), but his speech roused the giant crowd to a crescendo of lamentation. Sound waves exploded around the mosque gardens, lifting the canvas awnings stretched above us to keep out the sun. My long legs and arthritic knees were about to give out when a young mullah took pity on us foreigners and sprayed rosewater on our heads to keep us cool.

The Ayatollah's memorial service was a revealing as it was disconcerting. In an article I wrote for the *Orange County Register* on our return, I said:

> No one can doubt the reverence, even idolatry that millions of Iranians still feel towards the revolutionary leader who dethroned the last of the shahs. Nor, despite our hopes for better relations between Iran and the U.S. and Britain can there be any doubt that the mullahs, who still control most of the levers of power in Iran, are determined to keep alive the anti-American sentiments that ever since the 1979–80 siege of the U.S. embassy have poisoned relations between two countries that used to be friends.

In a separate note to my government contacts in London and Washington, I reported even more gloomily:

> Over and over again, we were told in Teheran that the U.S. and Britain supported Iraq when Saddam Hussein launched the war that cost Iran more than 300,000 dead. Even the moderate Iranians we met believed that U.S. policy is made in Israel. They told us that America is "seeking

*to destroy the Islamic revolution" by economic sanctions
and CIA support for Iran's enemies at home and abroad.*

Arriving back in London there was an intriguing postscript. Among my fellow passengers were some of the women who had flown with me to Iran. During the return flight from Teheran, they wore long dark gowns and head scarves; some wore chadors that covered their heads completely. On landing at Heathrow these ladies made a beeline for the restrooms from which they emerged, headgear discarded, eyelashes mascaraed, finger nails brightly varnished.

"Does that feel better?" I asked. To which one of the ladies, replied, "We're back in the land of the free."

THE REFORMER WHOSE LIGHT WENT OUT

Liberalism is corrosive in a revolutionary collective. It eats away unity, undermines cohesion and creates dissension.
— Mao Tse Tung

Following our 1998 visit to the Islamic republic, Mohammad Khatami was re-elected to a second term as president of Iran with an even larger majority. Most of his support came from women and young people, and verbally he did not disappoint them. Addressing an audience at Teheran University, the president spoke to ten thousand students. "Freedom of choice and freedom of thought have been frustrated," he said. "Liberty is suffocated in the name of salvation." Speaking of women, Khatami went on, "The traditional outlook based on the erroneous notion of supremacy of men over women does injustice to men, women and humanity as a whole." Younger women were delighted. But that was not what the mullahs were teaching in the mosques. There were mutterings that Khatami was challenging the Holy Writ of the Koran.

President Khatami himself was an ayatollah. But he railed against the mullahs' resistance to change and the excesses of the religious police. "If the clergy distance themselves from the factual realities of present day, they won't be able to fulfill their role," he said in a radio broadcast. This was a courageous stand in a land where one person in twelve serves at one time or another in his life as a member of the clergy or assistant in the mosques. And the Council of Guardians took umbrage. Unlike Khatami, they rejected the notion that church and state can be separate. Iran is theocratic state. The word of God and his priest takes precedence over any elected president.

I kept in touch with events in Iran during Khatami's second term by meeting scores of Iranians who, encouraged by his promise of reform, paid visits to the land of their birth to meet relatives and consider investing. It was the outward and visible evidence that most impressed these visitors. Satellite dishes, theoretically forbidden without an impossibly difficult to obtain license, sprouted over the rooftops of residential Teheran. Shows like *Oracle, Baywatch,* and *L.A. Law* were watched by millions. Tens of millions listened to the now unjammed BBC. American and British publishers attended Teheran's annual book fair offering titles that ten years earlier were banned. Iran got its first woman judge, Shirin Ebadi who eight years later won the Nobel peace prize. Scores more women were elected to parliament, tens of thousands to local councils. Most women still covered their heads, but pushed back diaphanous scarves to reveal the front section of their hair. People in the streets began smiling and greeting one another. Here and there a trace of lipstick and pale pink nail polish appeared.

Among the Western journalists who flocked to Teheran in the late 1990s was Robin Wright who had spoken at my World Affairs Council meeting on Iran. She described "hours spent in government offices listening to Iranian officials haranguing me about the revolution's rejecting the invasion of western values while in the background their TV sets were tuned to CNN."[1] On state run radio and TV stations, the nightly news was followed by Frank Sinatra crooning "Strangers in the Night." Callers put on hold when calling the Ministry of Culture and Islamic guidance, were entertained by recordings of the theme song from *The Sting,* the movie starring Robert Redford and Paul Newman.

Most Iranians seemed to like this. I was impressed by the results of a survey undertaken by an American polling organization which used a battery of computers to comb through the telephone directories of Teheran, Isfahan, Tabriz and Abadan, and randomly selected five thousand Iranians who agreed to answer questions about the regime and its leaders. The responses were compelling:

Q: Do you approve or disapprove of the job Mohammed Khatami is doing as president?

Yes - 63 percent

No - 27 percent

Q: On major issues facing Iran, do you believe that Khatami most frequently sides with the people of Iran or with those in power (i.e., the mullahs)?

With the people - 42 percent

With those in power - 20 percent

Unsure - 26 percent

On November 24, 1998, Iranians celebrated the twentieth anniversary of the seizure of the American embassy. This is now a national holiday, a day of parades and demonstrations against the Great Satan. Against this background I asked my contacts in Teheran how much support there was for Khatami's call for "dialogue" with the United States. A diplomat replied, "It's unanimous—provided the U.S. reciprocates."

But the U.S. did not reciprocate. Khatami's overtures were ignored, his olive branch brushed aside. With nothing to show for his efforts to rescue Iran from U.S. sanctions and isolation abroad, there was a backlash against Khatami at home. He promised reform but could not deliver. Behind his fine words, there was little action. His attempts to legislate changes in economic and social policy were blocked, frustrated, amended to death or dropped. Khatami was also accused of "selling out" the Islamic Revolution. Theologians charged that the Western books and plays that were flooding into Iran were an affront to Shiite values. Persian culture was being devalued by Hollywood movies.

The most powerful resistance to reform in Iran came from its holy warriors, the Revolutionary Guards and the Basiji. Tens of thousands of their comrades had died in the war against Iraq; now, the survivors saw Khatami's calls for an easing of Sharia law as desecrating the memory of their "martyrs" who had sacrificed their lives for God and the Imam. One of the Basiji veterans was a rising political star, named Mahmoud Ahmadi-nejad, a former governor of Arbadil province in north west Iran. The Western media paid no attention to Ahmadi-nejad until years later when he burst into prominence as Mayor of Teheran and in 2005 as the president of Iran who most bellicosely challenged the United States on the subject of Iranian nuclear power.

I was alerted to his potential by Fred Ameri of Orange County, who for several months had Ahmadi-nejad as a student in one of the classes he taught in the engineering department at Teheran University. Ahmadi-nejad was a natural leader. He was in the lead when conservatives in Teheran charged its reformist mayor with corruption and forced him to resign. When a crusading left-wing newspaper that vigorously backed Khatami, published an article proving that Islamic death squads in the 1990s had murdered writers and dissidents opposed to the clerical regime, Ahmadi-nejad sprang to the defense of the regime by demanding the re-imposition of press censorship.

The fundamentalist backlash did not go unchallenged. Tens of thousands of Khatami's supporters surged out into the streets in protest against the press restrictions, and were joined by workers and traders. Violent clashes broke out between the resurgent Islamic tra-ditionalists and Khatami's youthful reformers.

As the demonstrations spread to campuses in all the main towns, the Islamic government's reaction was as harsh as any imposed by the Shah. Troops used tear gas and baton rounds. Armed police invaded the uni-versity dormitories to arrest and beat up students. Helicopters flew overhead and were reported to have fired machine guns into the crowds.

It was the biggest and bloodiest demonstration since the 1979 rev-olution and the Islamic fundamentalists won. Khatami's reformers lost. The counter-attack on liberalization, a phenomenon not unknown in fundamentalist America, destroyed his reform movement. I was reminded of Mao Tse Tung's dread verdict, "liberalism is corrosive in a revolutionary collective. It eats away unity, undermines cohesion and creates dissension."

Why did Khatami fail? I discussed this with Western diplomats who found him courteous, willing to listen, proud of the Islamic revolution, but sincere in his desire to end the hostility between Iran and the United States. Khatami could have played the role of an "Iranian Gorbachov," said one senior envoy. America, he said, missed an opportunity to keep the "moderates" in power in Iran by rebuffing Khatami's offer of dialogue and his pre 9/11 proposals to cooperate in turning down the graph of terrorist violence in the Middle East. Iranians were less forgiving. Some saw Khatami as a lightweight, a front man put up by the mullahs to ease the pressure from the west and gain time for the revolution to recover its strength for further assaults on the Great Satan. "The smile on the face of the tiger," is a fair summation of these views. Other Iranians judged that Khatami's reforms had failed because they offered nothing for the ruling elite. Caught between his promises to change the political scenery and his deference to the principles of the Islamic republic, he didn't know which way to turn. He lacked what the Brits call "stick-to-itiveness." He was more like Bill Clinton than George Bush, facile, persuasive, charming yet lacking the single-minded concentration on a few limited objectives, and to heck with the rest.

Mohammed Khatami by fall 2006, had joined the international lecture circuit that America's ex-presidents and former British prime ministers populate. Looking back on his rise and fall, my sense is that the candle of hope he lit for détente with the west was snuffed out by two forces. One was the Iranian constitution, agreed after years of wrangling only a year before before Khatami took office. This prescribes that the president shall be elected but gives the *faghih*—the unelected Supreme Leader—control of the army, the police, above all the Islamic clergy. These are the levers of power. That is the nature of theocracy. It is the opposite of democracy. The president, Khatami proposed, but the Ayatollah Khameini disposed.

Economics was the other force that precipitated Khatami's downfall. Every productive sector of the Iranian economy ceased to expand as earnings from oil sales fell in the mid 1990s. Output was reduced, exports declined, inward investment dried up. With a million more young people coming onto the labor market each year, unemployment soared and poverty showed up in the streets. Two of my close friends, who paid separate visits to Tabriz and Isfahan, brought back photographs of potholed highways, boarded up shops, and crowds of idle young men standing at the street corners. Police records showed a sharp increase in crime and prostitution. One out of every five Iranians youngsters was reported to be hooked on coke and heroin.

Mohammed Khatami's government tried but failed to tackle these problems. The only way out of the economic mess was to increase oil production but U.S. sanctions prevented this. The irony is that Khatami held out the hand of friendship to America and was rebuffed when oil prices were low. Oil prices are now high, U.S. sanctions are ineffective and an anti-American President, Mahmoud Ahmadi-nejad, has risen to power in his place.

IS MAHMOUD AHMADI-NEJAD
BAD OR MAD?

The mind of a bigot is like the pupil of an eye,
the more light you pour upon it, the more it will contract.
— Oliver Wendell Holmes

Within weeks of his swearing in, Iran's sixth and youngest president, Mahmoud Ahmadi-nejad, made himself a hero among Arabs and a monster in much of America by his crude attacks on Israel. Casting doubts on the holocaust, he claimed that the Germans and Russians had created the Zionist problem "by persecuting the Jews." Europe, not Palestine, should therefore be responsible

for providing a Jewish home, "in Switzerland, or somewhere." Warming to his subject, the Iranian leader said that Israel should be "wiped off the map" of the Middle East, a remark that led the deputy prime minister of Israel to retort that "Iran can be wiped out, too."

Ahmadi-nejad's verbal extravagance quickly made him a bogeyman in the Western media. He was condemned by resolutions in the U.S. Congress and the House of Commons, described by a State Department spokesman as a "threat to world peace;" and by a BBC commentator as a "fruit and nut case."

Mahmoud Ahmadi-nejad

Is he "bad or just mad?" I was asked on a TV program. It was a question that led me to look more carefully into Mahmoud Ahmadi-nejad's background.

He was born in a poverty-stricken village, near Garmsar in north-west Iran, the fourth of seven children of a blacksmith who moved to Teheran in 1957. A bright student, he entered the civil engineering department of the Iran University of Science and Technology (IUST), where he attended classes given by Fred Ameri, my successor as chairman of the Orange County World Affairs Council. He received a PhD in traffic and trans-portation engineering under a program funded by the Islamic Revolution's storm troopers, the Corps of Revolutionary Guards (IRG). Ahmadi-nejad joined the guards in 1986 at the height of the Iran-Iraq war. To judge by the reports of his comrades, there can be no doubt about his physical courage, his fierce Persian patriotism, his intense, even mystical, Shiite religiosity. His fighting record as a special ops trooper inside the Kurdish areas of Iraq won him rapid promotion to be chief engineer of the Guard's sixth army and chief of staff in the western provinces of Iran. After the war, he became a vice-governor (1993–October 1997), then governor of two small frontier provinces and later governor of the newly-created and much larger province of Ardabil.

Ahmadi-nejad was still a comparative unknown in Iranian politics when, reflecting the religious backlash against president Khatami's reforms, he ran for mayor of Teheran as the candidate of a patriotic group dedicated to preserving the Revolution, the Alliance of Builders of Islamic Iran. Campaigning on a platform of "traditional values" and Sharia law, he won easily (on a 12 percent turnout) and once in office, reversed many of the liberalizing measures put into effect by the pro-Khatami moderates. One of his signature moves was to restore the segregation of sexes in Teheran's municipal offices. Elevators were relabeled, Women or Men Only. But the mayor was also a populist. He revoked the Sharia ban on women attending soccer matches, draw-ing protests from his conservative supporters.

Ahmadi-nejad soon clashed at the national level with president Khatami. His tactics reminded me of those of big city mayors in London, Chicago, San Francisco and Tokyo who dump on the national leader to win votes at the local level. His attacks on Khatami led to his being barred from attending meetings of the cabinet, a privilege traditionally extended to the mayor of Teheran. He embarrassed the national government by opening soup kitchens to feed unemployed youths, demanded that the corpses of his revolutionary guard comrades, killed in the war with Iraq, must be dug up and re-reburied in Teheran, and welcomed such figures as Hugo Chavez of Venezuela in whose honor Ahmadi-nejad had a new statue of Simon Bolivar, the liberator of Venezuela, erected in the city's main park.

My Iranian friends said that it was inevitable that Ahmadi-nejad would run for president of Iran when Khatami ended his presidency in 2005. The most obvious successor was Akbar Rafsanjani, the black-spectacled man who I had met when he was speaker of the Majlis. Rafsanjani, a pragmatist, was swamped by a wave of enthusiasm for the fundamentalist mayor's crowd pleasing promises. One of these was a pledge to "safeguard the Revolution." To cheering Basiji veterans, Ahmadi-nejad shouted, "We didn't participate in the revolution for turnabout government." Another applause-line he borrowed from Hugo Chavez—"Put Iran's petroleum income on the people's tables."

Ahmadi-nejad's theme song, then as now, was a "return to traditional values," and the Revolution's duty to carry the Islamic faith to the ends of the earth. "Thanks to the blood of our martyrs," he pledged, "a new Islamic Revolution has risen and will, God-willing, cut off the root of injustice in the world."

Once in office, Ahmadi-nejad's hostility to Israel and opposition to U.S. policies in the Middle East quickly became Iran's official policy. Khatami's proposal for a dialogue of civilizations was shelved:

instead, the new president aligned Iran more closely with Hezbollah in Lebanon, Hamas in Palestine, Chavez in Venezuela, and Castro in Cuba. He also seized on U.S. resistance to Iran's nuclear power program to raise this to the top of the mast in his appeal to Persian

Iranian women demonstrating IN FAVOR of nuclear power

nationalism. The imperialists and the Zionists were "trying to hold Iran down." Building nuclear power stations was a badge of its national honor. Half a million Iranian women were persuaded to join hands and chant for nuclear power along a human chain that snaked four thousand miles along the highways. This was a telling sight. The only crowds of women I previously had seen demonstrating about nuclear issues were the Brits who tried to close down U.S. air bases in England. It was a new and strange experience to see TV pictures of Iranian women in veils demonstrating *in favor* of nuclear power.

On January 2006, Ahmadi-nejad gave notice that Iran would soon be able to make its own fuel for nuclear power stations. In April, he called every foreign correspondent in Teheran to a full court press conference where he announced a "national triumph"—Iranian scientists had successfully enriched uranium to levels sufficient to generate nuclear power. Ahmadi-nejad was careful to deny that his country would reach out for nuclear weapons. Together with supreme leader Ali Khamenei, who issued a fatwa against them, he repeated in speech after speech that Iran will not build and has no need for nuclear weapons. Yet Ahmadi-nejad seems to me to have fused together three strands of Persian endeavor—atomic physics, Iranian chauvinism and evangelical Shiite Islam. All three could be detected in a strange letter that arrived out of the blue at the White House in early May 2006.

Addressed to President Bush, this letter, written by Ahmadi-nejad was the first direct communication between the American and Iranian governments since they broke off relations in 1980. Meandering across six pages, it was an extraordinary document, that at first sight appeared to offer little more than a litany of Iran's traditional charges against America—the CIA "coup" against Mohammed Mosaddegh, support for Saddam Hussein in the Iran-Iraq war, shooting down an Iranian passenger plane, freezing Iran's assets in America and now seeking to kill "the scientific and nuclear program of the Iranian nation—just when all the Iranians are jubilant about its success." The State Department's immediate reaction was to reject this as a ploy. "The United States has nothing to say to Iran until it gives up its reach for nuclear weapons," said John Bolton, U.S. ambassador to the United Nations.

I read Ahmadi-nejad's text three times (see extracts pages 194–6). On first reading, it reminded me of undergraduate debates in college fifty years ago. On second reading, it felt more like an Islamic version of a Sunday night TV evangelist's sermon. On third reading, I pried deeper. Buried in the persiflage, were a number of questions that deserve better than the brush off the Bush administration delivered.

Essentially, Ahmadi-nejad appealed to George Bush to look into his heart and ask if his policies are leading to peace, justice and the relief of world poverty, or to war, destruction, and increased hatred of America. How, he asked, can the U.S. president square his beliefs in God and human rights, with America's actions in invading Afghanistan, occupying Iraq, and supporting Israel's missile attacks on Palestinians?

The author of this book is a conservative who backed President Bush when he put America on the offensive against terrorism, supported him and Tony Blair strongly over Afghanistan, loyally over Iraq, and shares their view that it is iniquitous that the Islamic regime denies freedom of thought and expression to the great and noble people of Iran. But Ahmadi-nejad's charge that two of the administration's central policies—the extension of democracy and open markets—are not working as well as Bush and Blair prophesied, merited a better answer than either the White House or No. 10 Downing Street had offered. All over the world, people are turning back to religion, said the Iranian president. It was a message which in essence, is not very different from that of Billy Graham and the Baptist fundamentalists in the southern States—turn to God and man's earthly problems can be solved.

It is this proposition, as well as the sectarian violence that accompanies and contradicts it, that now lies at the heart of the Islamic challenge to the western world. A Christian president ignores it at America's peril.

EXTRACTS FROM A PERSIAN LETTER

Addressed to President George W. Bush, the Iranian president's letter rambled over six pages. The following extracts capture the main points Ahmadi-nejad sought to convey.

DOUBLE STANDARDS

I am a teacher, my students ask how can you be a follower of Jesus Christ, respecting human rights, making war on terror, opposing WMDS (weapons of mass destruction), yet at the same time, attack and occupy [Iraq] killing 100,000 people, destroying agriculture, pushing the country back fifty years?

WMDs

Saddam was a murderous dictator, but the war was not waged to topple him, the announced goal was to find and destroy WMDS. However, no WMDS existed. This great tragedy that has come to engulf both the people of the occupied and the occupying countries was founded on lies . . .

ISRAEL

Let us assume that six million Jews were murdered in Europe. How does that logically translate into the establishment of the state of Israel in the Middle East and not in Europe?

PALESTINE

The newly-elected Hamas administration recently took office. All independent observers confirm that it represents the electorate, but you have put it under pressure to recognize the Israeli regime. If Hamas had run on that platform, the people would not have voted for it.

SEPTEMBER 11

This was a horrendous incident, deplorable and appalling. [But] could it have been planned and executed without penetration of your security services? Why have some aspects of the attack been kept secret? Why are we not told who botched their responsibilities?

NUCLEAR SCIENCE

Why is it that any technological and scientific achievement reached in the Middle East region is portrayed as a threat to the Zionist regime? All scientific research can be applied for military purposes; is that reason to oppose all scientific disciplines, including physics, mathematics, medicine, engineering, etc.?

JUDGMENT DAY

The day will come when all humans congregate before the court of the almighty so that their deeds are examined. I trust both of us believe in such a day when we must be answerable to our nations and all others whose lives have been affected by our actions.

(continued on next page)

Do you not think that if all of us come to believe and abide by the principles of one God, justice and respect for human dignity, we can overcome the present problems of the world and improve our performance? Will you not accept this invitation for a genuine return to the teachings of the prophet's belief and preservation of human dignity and obedience to almighty God?

GOVERNMENTS AND RELIGION

The people of the world are not happy with the status quo and pay little heed to the promises of world leaders. [They] oppose the spreading of insecurity and war . . . the increasing gap of haves and have nots . . . increasing corruption . . . attacks on other people's cultural foundations . . . disintegration of families. Yet your solutions, liberalism and western style democracy have failed. Those with insight can already hear the sounds of the shattering and fall of the ideology of liberal-democratic systems.

Instead, the people of the world are flocking towards one main focal point—Almighty God. My question to you is do you want to join them?

[Signed]

— Mahmoud Ahmadi-nejad, President of the Islamic Republic of Iran

PART TWO

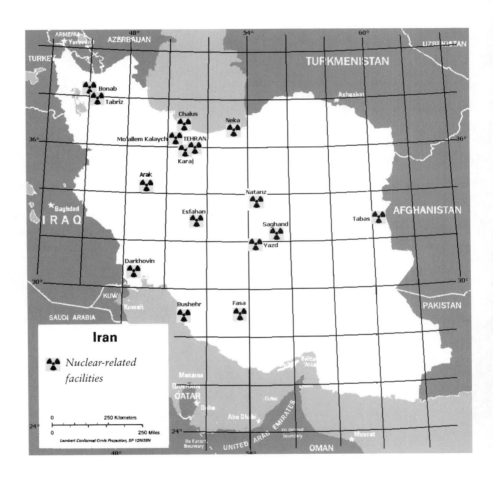

IRANIAN NUCLEAR TURBULENCE

The great ocean of truth lay all undiscovered before me.
— Sir Isaac Newton, 1642–1727

On the last day of July 2006, the United Nation Security Council took time out from its consideration of the collision between Israel and Hezbollah in south Lebanon to address an even greater potential threat to the balance of power in the Middle East—Iran's reported reach for nuclear weapons.

The United States accused the Islamic regime of secretly building atomic bombs. The Iranians denied this, but indignantly asserted their right as a sovereign nation to build nuclear power stations and their ability and intention to do this in accordance with the Non Proliferation Treaty to which Iran and the U.S. have been parties since 1968.

The treaty operates through its inspection arm, the International Atomic Energy Agency (IAEA). This is charged with offering help for its member countries' civil nuclear programs and checking their compliance with its ban on the construction or acquisition of nuclear weapons.

The nuclear weapons powers at the time of the treaty signing, the U.S., Britain, Russia, France and China were—and are—exempted from the NPT's ban on atomic weapons. Israel subsequently built up a sizeable—but still unrevealed—arsenal of nuclear warheads with surreptitious help from the United States and France. India and Pakistan which did not sign the NPT have since acquired nuclear weapons, but are not subject to IAEA inspection. North Korea signed but withdrew and is now building its own atom bombs *(See pages 220–222 for further details of the NPT).*

In the run up to the August vote, the Security Council was persuaded that the dangers of an Iranian nuclear weapon was so great that action must be taken to "strangle it in the cradle," as an American official put it. By fourteen votes to one, with support from the first time from Russia and China, the Council passed a binding resolution drafted by two of its permanent members, Britain and France, plus their E.U. partner, Germany with support from the United States. This ordered Iran to cease its enrichment activities or face U.N.-mandated sanctions.

Iran immediately declared the resolution to be "destructive and unwarranted." The British foreign secretary urged the Iranians to think again. The American ambassador declared that the Iranians for many years have "consistently defied the international community." Iran must come into line with the Security Council's instructions before August 31 or else.

China backed the resolution as part of a broader strategy to offer Iran a choice between cooperation or isolation. Its envoy agreed with the Russian delegate who said that any future measures designed to enforce compliance must "rule out in advance the use of force."

Such then were the outward signs of the latest storm over Iran's nuclear program. Behind the scenes, the Bush administration accused Iran of cheating. By concealing facilities in which covert work on nuclear warheads may be going on, Iran, it says, forfeited the right to IAEA help with its civil nuclear program. The issue turned on a technical question: are the Iranians enriching uranium to the relatively low levels (3.5 percent) that are needed for nuclear power or to the much higher levels (90 percent) that would enable them to make atomic weapons?

To tackle this question, I sought help from many sources, starting in the United States where intelligence on the ground about Iran is patchy. Satellite observation is limited to surface inspection and many of the Iranian nuclear installations are located underground for safety reasons. A good deal of the U.S. evidence is derived from Iranian defectors and Mossad, the Israeli intelligence agency. Some of it, put out by congressional committees, is regarded by the IAEA as "biased" and "inaccurate." More objective sources of information are the IAEA's own experts who by mid-2006 had paid twenty-six visits to Iran's nuclear facilities, and the French, German and British diplomats and technical advisers who for more than a year negotiated—but failed to find a compromise that would allow the Iranians to generate nuclear electricity while ensuring that nuclear weapons would not be built.

To access these and other sources, I sought the advice of a nuclear engineer and safety expert with thirty-seven years experience, Vojin Joksimovich who worked in Britain's Atomic Power construction company while completing his PhD in nuclear engineering at Imperial College of Science and Technology in London. Emigrating to America, Joksimovich has been a nuclear engineer at NUS/Halliburton, General Atomic and Westinghouse Corporations, director of nuclear safety projects for the U.S. Nuclear Regulatory Commission (NRC) and Department of Energy (DOE); and has worked for Japanese and Korean nuclear utilities and nuclear safety research institutes. Using probabilistic risk assessment (PRA) techniques, he directed studies of nuclear proliferation scenarios for the U.S. Arms and Disarmament Agency.

The following survey reflects Joksimovich's research and that of former Iranian finance minister, Jahangir Amuzegar.[1] Essentially, it reveals that the U.S. and its allies helped the Iranians design and build nuclear power plants while the Shah was on the throne but cut off their sources of fuel when the Islamic regime seized power.

HOW IT STARTED

Iran has been in the nuclear power business for fifty years. It all began when President Eisenhower in 1950 made his Atoms for Peace proposals at the United Nations. Countries with the bomb should begin to disarm, he proposed. Nuclear material from their stockpiles would be contributed to a "bank" controlled by an international atomic energy agency. From this, other countries would draw nuclear fuel and know-how enabling them to build atomic-powered electricity plants, thereby reaping the benefits of the peaceful atom.

The International Atomic Energy Agency (IAEA) was set up in 1957, Iran was one of the first countries to sign up and ask for American help in building its own civil nuclear power program. The U.S. agreed to help Iran build nuclear power plants. In 1959 the Teheran Nuclear Research Centre (TNRC) was established to be run by the Atomic Energy Organization of Iran (AEOI). The TNRC was equipped with a U.S.-supplied 5MW nuclear research reactor, which was fuelled with highly enriched uranium (HEU) and became operational in 1967. The following year, the Shah asked President Lyndon Johnson for help in moving from research to nuclear power generation, and LBJ agreed. He told Abbas Hoveyda, then the Iranian prime minister that the U.S. would cooperate with Iran in building nuclear power stations. Iran then signed the Non Proliferation agreement in London and ratified it in 1970.

On April 13, 1974, the U.S. ambassador to Iran handed the Minister of Court, Asadollah Alam, a U.S. government memorandum proposing "to deepen and broaden the already strong ties" (between the two countries) by cooperation . . . in the development of Iran's potential for nuclear energy.[2] In August 1974 the Shah declared, "Petroleum is a noble material, much too valuable to burn . . . We envision producing, as soon as possible, 23,000 megawatts of electricity using nuclear plants."

That went far beyond Iran's own resources but later that year an American firm, Stanford Research Institute was hired by the Iranian government to help design and advise on construction of nuclear plants. U.S. Secretary of State, Henry Kissinger, issued National Security Decision 292, titled "U.S.-Iran Nuclear Cooperation." This set out details of the sale of American nuclear equipment to Iran, which was projected to bring Westinghouse, General Electric and other U.S. corporations more than $6 billion in revenue.

In 1976 President Ford signed a directive offering Teheran the chance to buy and operate a U.S.-built reprocessing plant for extraction of

President Ford (right) meets Iranian Ambassador Ardeshir Zahedi. The U.S. saw no problem in giving Iran control of enriched uranium

uranium and plutonium from the spent fuel. The deal was to deliver a "complete fuel cycle" to Iran. The nuclear fuel cycle consists of mining and milling of natural uranium to produce uranium oxide concentrate; a plant to covert this into uranium hexafluoride gas; uranium enrichment equipment to produce low enriched uranium (LEU); fuel fabrication facilities; a nuclear power plant; safe storage of spent fuel; reprocessing of the spent fuel to separate wastes from reusable uranium and plutonium; and final disposal of nuclear waste. The U.S. would provide the nuclear fuel and was paid in advance to do this.

Because Iran had signed the NPT the White House saw no problem in giving Iran control of large quantities of plutonium and enriched uranium, two avenues to a nuclear weapon. "I do not think the issue of proliferation came up," said Dr. Kissinger.

ENTER THE FRENCH AND GERMANS

The first Iranian nuclear power plant was to be constructed at Bushehr (see page 50). As the first installment of a 20mw power grid, a light water reactor was commissioned at Bushehr in the early 1970s. In 1974, a contract worth $4–6 billion was placed with Germany's Kraftwerk Union (KWU) to build two 1196 mw pressurized water reactor. Coincidentally I flew over this site during the early stages of its construction. The plant was supposed to come on line in 1981. The Germans were paid in advance.

The Shah had also signed a contract with the French company Framatome for two 950mw PWRs to be built on the Karun river in southwest Iran. Site preparations began but construction was cancelled by the Islamic regime which in its early days was opposed to nuclear power.

To secure its supplies of nuclear fuel for the Bushehr plant, the Shah had made an investment in Eurodif, a joint company formed in 1973 by France, Belgium, Spain and Sweden. In 1975 the Swedes sold their 10 percent share to Iran as a result of a deal the Shah made with the president of France. Iran lent $1 billion and another $180 million in 1977, for the construction of Eurodif's uranium enrichment plant in return for the right to buy 10 percent of its production.

Uranium ore for this program was purchased by Iran from France and its former colonies. Reporting on his April 8, 1976 meeting with the ambassador of Gabon, Minister Alam recorded in his diary:

> *I told the Shah that the ambassador expects us to give his country full financial support.*
>
> *"Why on earth should we," the Shah replied. "They promised to sell us uranium but now it appears the French control their entire supply."*
>
> *According to the poor old ambassador, they've already arranged to supply 120 tons of unrefined uranium below the marked price . . .*[3]

By 1977, three nuclear power plants were under construction in Iran. According to the head of its Atomic Energy Organization, Dr. Akbar Etemad, two were on course to achieve 80 percent of their 4000 KW capacity. Etemad was exaggerating. None of Iran's nuclear reactors achieved anything like that level of output while the Shah was on the throne, nor have they under the mullahs.

Dr. Etemad also wrote in his memoirs that neither he nor the Prime Minister Hoveyda "inquired too deeply into the question of whether the fuel would be enriched to make plutonium for nuclear weapons. But early on we easily understood what [the Shah] had in mind. I pretended not to know, but I could see the pieces of a large mosaic were coming together."[4]

Alam was more specific. Describing the Shah's "great vision for the future of Iran," he said, "This, though he denies it, probably includes our manufacturing a nuclear deterrent."

NO REVOLUTIONARY REACTORS

The Islamic Revolution changed everything. The United States at first continued to cooperate with Iran but broke off relations and terminated all support for Iranian nuclear activities when the U.S. embassy was seized in 1980.

Ayatollah Khomeini had no knowledge of, nor interest in, nuclear power. He denounced nuclear weapons as "immoral." The Islamic regime abandoned Iran's nuclear power program as "costly and wasteful" and made no provision for nuclear research or to complete the Bushehr power plant. The number of Iranian scientists and technologists employed in its nuclear industry fell from 4,500 to barely 800.

Only after Saddam Hussein launched his attack on Iran did the Islamic regime authorize a "fresh start" to be made on nuclear development. Iran, in 1982, informed the IAEA that it planned to restart a nuclear program, using indigenously made nuclear fuel. In 1983 the IAEA agreed to help in producing LEU under The Technical Assistance Program. the IAEA was forced to terminate this under pressure from the U.S. and its allies.

The U.S. neither delivered the fuel nor returned the billions of dollars payment it had received from the Shah. Eurodif also refused to provide enriched uranium to Iran, and France held onto the down payments. During the squabble that followed, the French accused Iran's intelligence agents of putting pressure on Eurodif in Lebanon where Hezbollah took several French hostages. In 1986, a Eurodif manager was assassinated.

In 1991 France refunded $1.6 billion and Iran remained a shareholder of Eurodif. Its representatives abstained from Eurodif discussions of enriched uranium.

KWU of Germany stopped work at Bushehr in January, 1979 with Unit One 85 percent finished and Unit Two 50 percent complete. The Germans withdrew completely from Iran in July that year having received $2.5 billion of the total contracts payments.

In 1984 KWU did a preliminary evaluation of the work that would be needed to complete the project but declined to proceed because Iran was at war with Iraq. The Bushehr plant was damaged by six Iraqi air strikes between March 24, 1984 and November 1987. France which had helped design and build it now supplied the air re-fuelling equipment required by the Iraqi bombers that attacked it.

These operations destroyed the entire core area of both Bushehr reactors. The Germans estimated that it would cost an estimated $2.9-4.6 billion to repair the damage, but refused to supply the components or nuclear fuel required to bring it on line. The Islamic republic filed a $5.4 billion lawsuit against KWU in 1996. This has got nowhere.

OVER TO RUSSIA AND CHINA

After the war with Iraq ended, Iran invited several western nuclear suppliers to help in refurbishing Bushehr. A consortium of German, Spanish and Argentine companies put in a bid to complete Unit One in the late 1980s, but diplomatic pressure by the U.S. put an end to this deal.

Teheran then attempted to procure components from Italian, Czech, Polish and Ukranian companies. All four refused, citing American objections.

Unable to find a Western supplier, Iran turned to the Soviet Union and China for nuclear technology. In 1990, the Soviet Union agreed to complete the Bushehr plant with two new 440 mw plants at a cost of $800 million. When the Soviet Union collapsed, work on this project stopped. The contract remains unfulfilled.

In 1993 Iran signed an agreement with China for construction of two 300 MW PWRs at Darkhovin in western Iran. China conducted seismic surveys at the site and received initial payments. Subsequently, the U.S. convinced the Chinese to cancel the contract. In 1996, the U.S. also tried, without success, to block China from selling to Iran a uranium conversion plant together with the uranium hexafluoride gas necessary for enrichment. The same year China and Iran informed the IAEA about their plans to build a uranium enrichment facility in Iran. Later, China withdrew in response to a request from President Reagan reportedly transmitted by his then Vice President George H. Bush, who previously had served as U.S. ambassador to China. Iran advised the IAEA that it planned to pursue construction anyway.

Iran meanwhile was scouring the world for suppliers of uranium. In 1984 a state radio station announced that negotiations with the African republic of Niger for the purchase of natural uranium were nearing completion. Geologists identified a number of uranium-bearing formations at several sites in Iran itself. In 1985 another Iranian radio program referred to the discovery of uranium deposits at Saghand in eastern Iran. IAEA inspectors visited and reported on all of Iran's known uranium sites in 1992.

PAKISTAN'S INVOLVEMENT

In February 1986, Dr. Abdel Qader Khan, the father of Pakistan's Islamic bomb visited Teheran. Khan who later confessed to running the world's first international black market network for nuclear components, signed a nuclear consulting agreement with Iran. This was not reported to the IAEA nor discovered by western intelligence services until 2003.

Full details of the Kahn network's support for the Iranian Atomic Energy Authority still have not been disclosed. Khan is now in prison but Pakistan refuses to make him available to U.S. experts for questioning.

What is known is that Khan's network of scientists, engineers, businessmen and government officials procured huge quantities of highly sophisticated equipment to make centrifuges. These could enrich uranium 235 isotopes not only to the 5 percent levels required to fuel power stations but also, if his clients were willing to pay, to the levels needed to make nuclear bombs. The technology involved in enrichment is complex. Gordon Corera in his masterly survey of Khan's activities, explains it as follows:

> *A rotor within each centrifuge cylinder spins uranium gas at incredibly high speeds, separating out the lighter U235 isotope so it can be gradually siphoned off. Each machine only enriches the gas a tiny amount so the slightly more concentrated output of one machine is fed into the next centrifuge in a connected-machine series called a cascade. Each consists of a hundred parts and many of these have to be engineered to within a thousandth of a millimeter and be able to withstand incredibly high speeds. One tiny mistake and the centrifuge will spin out of control, often crashing into the other machines and destroying the entire cascade.[5]*

A.Q. Khan stole the blueprints and technical drawings required to build and connect centrifuges from URENCO, an international consortium set up in the 1960s by Britain, Germany and the Netherlands to produce fuel for their nuclear reactors. From private companies in America, Europe and Asia, he then procured tens of thousands of the components required to build cascades of centrifuges, using dummy corporations and false addresses to evade international controls set up to prevent proliferation. His reward for this illicit trafficking which led George Tenet, director of the CIA to describe Kahn as "more dangerous than Osama bin Laden," was the highest honors that the Republic of Pakistan can bestow and a vast fortune tucked away in international banks.

Khan justifies his activities by recalling the humiliation his country suffered in 1971 when the vastly superior Indian army forced Pakistan to surrender, allowing its eastern wing, now Bangladesh, to secede. Only by building an A bomb, said Khan, could

A.Q. Khan, father of Pakistan's nuclear bomb, was regarded by the CIA as "more dangerous than Osama bin Laden."

Pakistan avoid any further defeats. Nuclear weapons, he argues, "level the playing field," for developing countries, enabling them to resist, "bullying by big powers like America." Poor nations with atomic bombs can "stand tall again."

Such thinking led Khan to offer his services to a number of third world countries. One was Libya to which he conveyed all the know-how and most of the equipment needed to build nuclear bombs. Only when U.S. and British intelligence tracked down the BBC *China*, a German freighter operating out of Antigua with a cargo of centrifuge enrichment equipment heading from Dubai to Tripoli was Khan's network unmasked. This was a major factor in Mommar Gadaffi's decision to abandon his nuclear arms program.

Shortly before then I visited Libya and interviewed Gadaffi. When later he handed over all the equipment and documents the Libyans had acquired from Khan, four trucks were needed to carry them.

There is no firm evidence that Khan provided the same data to Iran. If he did, one may surmise that it may have received a turn-key gas centrifuge facility, requiring 10,000 centrifuges, piping to connect them together, detailed project designs for the centrifuge plant, electrical and electronic equipment, uranium feed and withdrawal equipment.

Suppose Gadaffi had continued with his program and the Khan network had not been exposed? Libya might have succeeded in four or five years in assembling the centrifuge plant and producing significant amounts of HEU. Iran, by comparison, announced on April 11, 2006 that it had connected 164 centrifuges and produced a small quantity of low-grade enriched uranium (LEU). To move from 164 to the 10,000 centrifuges available to the Libyans requires a vast amount of technological expertise and industrial engineering experience. It was doubtful in mid-2006 if Iran possessed such capability. Even if its atomic energy agency were to launch an all-out crash program, the best advice I can obtain is that the Iranians are almost certainly five years away from being able to make an atomic bomb on the basis of Khan's facilities.

"SECRET SITES"

Could Iran be operating a second "secret" network of military nuclear sites, unknown to IAEA? On August 14, 2002, a prominent Iranian dissident, Alireza Jafarzadeh, reported the existence of two such installations in Iran, a uranium enrichment plant at Natanz (part of which is underground) and a heavy water plant in Arak *(see map)*. Anti-regime groups inside Iran were the main sources of Jafarzadeh's revelations. This information was provided to the United States by the National Council of Resistance, officially a front for an outlawed Iranian opposition group, Mojahedeen Khalq.

Israel and the U.S. accused Iran of using these concealed facilities to make nuclear weapons. Photos of the Natanz site taken in September 2002 and another taken in February 2003 were published in the Los Angeles Times and British newspapers. The chairman of Iran's Expediency Council, former president Akbar Hashemi Rafsanjani, sought to make light of this by saying, "if we wanted to conceal anything there were other places to do this than a construction site where 250 loaded trucks arrive daily."

To assuage suspicion, the Islamic regime invited IAEA inspectors in February 2003 to examine all its nuclear facilities for an extended period. No evidence of nuclear arms activities was found. In December 2003, Iran signed the Additional Protocol to the NPT, allowing unannounced and more intrusive inspections by IAEA agents; but this did nothing to resolve U.S. and Israeli suspicions. Nor did it staunch the flow of "inside information" proffered by Mojahadeen sources.

In June, 2004, a mysterious laptop, allegedly procured from a senior Iranian nuclear engineer, reportedly showed a test shaft and drawings of missile modifications that might be related to a nuclear weapon program. Separately, U.S. sources drew attention to nine sites where activities related to nuclear power production are underway in Iran *(see map page 198)*. One is the uranium mine at Saghand in the eastern province of Yazd, two are "yellow cake" production plants, one at Ardakan in central Iran and the other near Bandar Abbas on the Persian Gulf. Atomic research centers at Bona and Moallem Kaleyeh in northern Iran are suspected by the U.S. of housing gas centrifuges that could be used to enrich uranium. Neka on the Caspian coast is thought to have two ageing Russian or Chinese 400 Kw reactors stored there since 1995. Fasa near Shiraz is said to be the location of the uranium hexafluoride plant supplied by China in 1996, and there are James Bond-like "rumors" that other sinister facilities supplied by China and Russia may be hidden at Darkhovin near the Shatt al Arab border with Iraq, and at Tabas near the Afghan frontier. North Korea is said to have assisted in the development of other nuclear facilities at Katateh between the cities of Damghan and Shamrun.

All these sites have been visited by IAEA inspectors. After 2,600 man-hours of inspections, the agency's chairman Mohamed El

Baradei, said that his technical advisers found no evidence that Iran is attempting to build a nuclear weapon but that "Iran failed to report certain nuclear materials and activities." IAEA requested "more cooperative action" from Iran.

Mohammed El Baradei, chairman of the IAEA. His agency could find no proof that Iran is building nuclear weapons, but needed more information.

E-3 ENGAGEMENT

By fall, 2004, there was an impasse. The U.S. continued to assert that Iran might be concealing a secret push to build an atomic device. Iran vehemently denied this. The European powers, Britain, France and Germany (E-3) decided to engage Iran in "intensive negotiations" on the basis that the E.U. would provide civilian nuclear technology in exchange for the Iranians "terminating uranium enrichment, permanently." Hawks in Washington called this "appeasement" but the Administration eventually said that it supported this initiative, though refusing to take part in the E-3 negotiations.

Iran agreed in November 2004 to suspend its enrichment activities for the duration of the E-3 talks. The IAEA placed seals on the centrifuge plant at Natanz. Ayatollah Ali Khameini issued a fatwa forbidding the production, stockpiling and used of nuclear weapons. The full text of this was released in Vienna as an official statement.

While the E.U. talks were proceeding, El Baradei on June 14, 2004, accused Iran of "less than satisfactory" cooperation during his Agency's latest investigation. The first round of E.U.-Iran talks broke down. On June 27, Iran removed the seals the IAEA had placed on the Natanz facility and resumed construction of centrifuges.

On August 1, 2005, Britain, Germany and France offered Iran a compromise package. A second set of negotiations offered E-3 security assurances, further economic cooperation, and a guaranteed supply of fuel for civil power reactors. In exchange, Iran must permanently forgo production of fissile material used in nuclear weapons. The Teheran government rejected the Europeans' "implementation document." This was described as vague and offering only "minor incentives" in exchange for Iran's permanent abandonment of an "inalienable right" and no commitment by the United States to give up plans to attack Iran.

Shortly afterward, Iran announced the resumption at Isfahan of uranium conversion, ie. turning yellow cake into a gas that could be further purified and used as a fuel in nuclear reactors.

ENTER PRESIDENT AHMADI-NEJAD

The election in 2005 of Mahmoud Ahmadi-nejad raised the profile of the Iranian nuclear power program. Internally, the new president presented this as a patriotic drive for energy independence and pride in Iranian technology; internationally he engaged in belligerent rhetoric, threatening Israel and denouncing America. On September 15, 2005, he addressed the U.N. General Assembly reiterating his attacks on the U.S. and Israel and repeating that Iran had an "inalienable" right to develop a civil nuclear program. Ahmadi-nejad used more moderate language when he suggested that foreign companies would be permitted to invest and participate in this. The State Department dismissed his offer, one official calling it "moonshine."

Iran then gave the E-3 a six-point proposal, which included an offer to again suspend uranium enrichment for two years pending the outcome of further negotiations.

Ahmadi-nejad presented nuclear power as Iran's "patriotic duty" while threatening to extinguish Israel

Russia, in the meantime, had offered to supply uranium for Iran's reactors and remove it when spent for reprocessing in Russia. Iran did not accept this. Teheran complained that it had not received from Russia the fuel it had been promised to bring the power reactors at Bushehr on stream. Dismayed by Ahmadi-nejad's truculence, the E-3 concluded that Iran was stalling. The E-3 reported to the IAEA that their negotiations had failed.

THE PROBLEM GOES PUBLIC

In the context of this breakdown of two rounds of European talks, international concern about the pace of development of the Iranian program intensified in spring 2006. An IAEA report issued at the end of January 2006 said it had found evidence suggesting a link between Iran's officially peaceful nuclear research program and its military work on high explosives and missiles under a so-called Green Salt Project. According to Dr. Amuzegar, this was the first such declaration by the agency, which previously had refused to back Washington's claim that at least some of Iran's nuclear activities had links to a military project.

A heavy water production plant was also reported to be nearing completion at Arak where a further 40 MW (th) heavy water moderated research reactor, identified at IR-40, is scheduled to be built. It is technically possible for this reactor to produce weapons-grade plutonium if Iran could link it to a plant to reprocess spent nuclear fuel. As of June 2006, the IAEA had no information to confirm that Iran has such a reprocessing plant.

Leaks and background briefings by Pentagon, CIA and NSC officials heightened tensions in the run-up to the IAEA's February 2006 meeting in Vienna. Espousing Israeli-originated claims that Iran could "surprise the world" (as Pakistan had already done) by testing a nuclear warhead "in a matter of months, not years," various U.S. Congressmen and their aides began calling for military action, "before it is too late." TV programs recalled Israel's June 7, 1981 pre-emptive air attack that destroyed Iraq's nuclear power plant at Ozirak. Retired U.S. generals appeared on Fox television to draw lines across maps showing how and where the U.S. air force could strike at Iran's facilities.

It was in the context of this American and Israeli "war-talk" and the ever-increasing bellicosity of Iran's retorts that an emergency meeting of the IAEA board took place in Vienna on February 4, 2006. This charged Iran with sixteen documented violations of the NPT, most of them refusals to comply with requests for information about its enrichment activities. A European-drafted resolution reporting this to the U.N. Security Council was passed by a vote of twenty-seven to three with five abstentions. Only Cuba, Syria and Venezuela voted against it.

At the U.N. there followed a flurry of backstage negotiations among the five veto-wielding permanent members. This produced a draft resolution directing Iran to (1) resume its suspension of all enrichment and reprocessing activities (i.e., shut down its centrifuge facility at Natanz); and (2) give IAEA inspectors free rein for spot inspections including access to documents, workshop visits and interviews with Iran's atomic scientists. In addition, the Islamic Republic was asked to "reconsider" its plans to build a heavy water reactor at Arak.

The U.S. described this as a victory and insisted that world opinion was "virtually unanimous" in condemning Iran. That was wishful thinking. The resolution in fact delayed for another month any action by the Security Council until receipt of a new progress report by the IAEA's director general. Russia excluded from the text the word "non-compliance," a phrase that under the IAEA's statute would trigger enforcement action. Washington also had to back down and accept a clause referring to the goal of a nuclear-free zone in the Middle East (implicitly questioning Israel's nuclear weapons status).

A month later, in March 2006, El Bareidi reported to the Security Council that his agency "has not seen any diversion of nuclear material to nuclear weapons or other nuclear explosive devices," but added that it was "not in a position to conclude that there are no undeclared nuclear materials or activities in Iran." His report confirmed a number of specific violations of the NPT by Iran, chiefly arising from suspected links between its nuclear research program and the Green Salt projects on explosives and missiles.[6]

This report alarmed the E.U. Its politicians joined in the chorus of American denunciations. Collecting the voices, Dr. Amuzegar wrote in March 2004:

> The French foreign minister, Philippe Doutse-Blazy, representing a country with long-standing and sizeable commerce with Iran, expressed his concerns in the bluntest terms: "It's very simple: No civilian nuclear plan can explain Iran's nuclear program. Therefore, it's a clandestine military program." Echoing his exasperation, Germany's chancellor, Angela Merkel, said, "We must prevent Iran from developing its nuclear activities." Moscow and Beijing also talked on various occasions about the world's "lack of confidence" in the Iranian nuclear activities. President Putin emphasized that Russia has "a very close position with England and the United States" in objecting to an Iranian nuclear bomb. After years of silence, some Persian Gulf states also expressed worries about a nuclear Iran and called for tougher actions. Saudi, Jordanian and Kuwaiti officials similarly expressed worries about threats of environmental disaster in the region.[7]

Washington and London by now were concerned that Iran might be "duping" the IAEA while clandestinely completing its Isfahan and Natanz facilities for enriching nuclear fuel to weapons-grade levels. Reflecting these anxieties, all fifteen members of the U.N. Security

Council on March 29, 2006, unanimously adopted a non-binding statement calling on Iran to suspend its nuclear-enrichment program within thirty days and return to negotiations with the IAEA.

The Bush administration once again hailed this as a breakthrough, but it still did not commit the United Nations to any action against Teheran. In fact, the U.N. statement masked a persistent disagreement among the Council's five major powers. Russia and China wanted the issue to be handled exclusively by the IAEA. The U.S., Britain and France sought Security Council enforcement action. There was no U.N. agreement on what kind of measures the U.N. should take. Two weeks later, Teheran openly defied the Council by announcing that it would not be "pressured or intimidated" and that its decision to go on enriching uranium was "irreversible."

THE U.S. TURNS FROM ATTACK TO DIPLOMACY

Exasperation in Washington led to a renewal of media speculation on the possibilities of a U.S. air strike. The White House made known the public version of its latest National Security Strategy which included a statement that Iran had forfeited its right under the NPT to enrich uranium because of its "clandestine" nuclear activities. President Bush reiterated his administration's determination that "The Iranians should not have a nuclear weapon, the capacity to make a nuclear weapon, or the knowledge as to how to make a nuclear weapon." Vice President Richard Cheney, addressing the American Israel Public Affairs Committee (AIPAC) on March 7, 2003, spoke of "meaningful consequences" if the regime continued on its present course.

Then came the sea-change in Washington. In May and June 2006, talk of armed action to "take-out" Iran's nuclear facilities died down in the corridors of the White House and the Pentagon. President Bush changed course. The State Department was authorized to join in E.U. and Russian efforts to find a diplomatic solution to Iran's nuclear challenge.

Exactly why and to what extent the administration had modified its approach to Iran was something of a mystery as this book went to press. In the uncertain aftermath of yet another Middle East crisis in south Lebanon, there were conflicting assessments and fierce disagreements in the White House and the Pentagon. Hawks blamed Iran for Hezbollah's attacks on Israel. Most of the missiles fired into northern Israel were built or assembled in Iran. Arab sympathizers retorted that virtually all the warplanes, helicopters, howitzers, tanks and missiles used by the Israelis were manufactured (and paid for) by America. Some U.S. diplomats with a lifetime of Middle East experience expressed the view that the Islamists in Iran were using Hamas in Palestine and Hezbollah in Lebanon as "forward shock groups" in the jihad to wipe out Israel that Mahmoud Ahmadi-nejad had proclaimed. Others with no less experience pointed out that both these groups provide schools and social services that their governments are unable to offer and that Hezbollah was first in the field in offering relief for the villages destroyed by Israel in south Lebanon. Hamas and Hezbollah have also won places in the parliaments of Palestine and Lebanon in free elections of the kind the U.S. had urged them to hold in pursuance of George Bush's call for democracy for the Middle East.

Facts on the ground meanwhile were changing fast. Politics in America and Britain, diplomacy at the U.N., above all events in the

Middle East were in a state of flux. With sectarian violence rampant in Baghdad and Basra, the American public's support for Bush's strategy in the Middle East was evaporating. Blair was on his way out. Opposition to the war in Iraq had brought the popularity rating of both men to its lowest ebb since they first were elected. Afghanistan, too, was looking less like a "victory" against Al Queda than a resurgent civil war as Taliban attacks on U.S. and British-led NATO forces revived. Neither country in autumn 2006 could hope to start bringing their troops home from Iraq if the United States simultaneously was girding up for a third Middle East conflict with Iran.

And then there was North Korea. Whether Pyongyang's missile firings over the Sea of Japan would increase or decrease George Bush's determination to "go after" Iran was a matter for speculation in Teheran as well as in Washington and London, but two things seemed clear as the Bush administration strove to define a "new direction" for U.S. policies in the Middle East following its repudiation by the American electorate in the November 2006 elections that gave control of Congress to the Democrats. First, North Korea presented a clearer and more pressing nuclear danger than Iran. Second, Iran—unlike Korea—is unlikely to be able to produce a usable atomic warhead even if its leaders are determined to do this, for at least four and more likely five or six years.

In brief, there was no need—and no support from the electorate of the U.S. or U.K.—for any extension of the war in Iraq to Iran. Force cannot be ruled out but in its efforts to head off an Iranian A-bomb, America's policy of choice has now swung back to "jaw-jaw" not "war-war." A fresh approach has been mandated. The last part of this book is devoted to a number of radical suggestions designed to help achieve this.

NUCLEAR NON- PROLIFERATION TREATY

The atomic bombs dropped by the United States on Japan in 1945 ended World War II, but the nuclear genie could not be kept in the bottle. The Soviet Union detonated its first atomic bomb on August 29, 1949. The U.S. launched a crash program to develop hydrogen bombs with its first successful test at Eniwetok-Atoll in 1951. Within nine months, the Soviet Union exploded its own first H-bomb. Britain followed in 1952.

Seeing no advantage—and huge danger—in an escalating nuclear arms race, President Eisenhower delivered his historic "Atoms for Peace" speech at the U.N. in December, 1953. This led to the establishment of the International Atomic Energy Agency (IAEA) with headquarters in Vienna to promote the peaceful uses of nuclear energy and to inhibit its use for military purposes. Rapid progress was made in the use of nuclear power to generate electricity but the IAEA was unable to halt efforts to use nuclear science for military purposes. France exploded its first A-bomb in 1960. China began work on its nuclear weapons. These and the introduction of intercontinental ballistic missiles with nuclear warheads, led the U.S., Britain and Soviet Union to sign the Nuclear Test Ban Treaty and to negotiate the Nuclear Non- Proliferation Treaty (NPT).

RENOUNCING NUCLEAR WEAPONS

The NPT has three pillars: disarmament, non-proliferation and the right to use nuclear technology for peaceful purposes.

As Nuclear Weapons States (NWS), the U.S, Britain, Russia, France, and China committed themselves to reducing their nuclear arsenals and not to transfer nuclear weapons technology to Non-Nuclear Weapons States (Non-NWS).

Nuclear disarmament has stalled since the collapse of the Soviet Union, Russia has substantially reduced its armory of nuclear weapons. Britain and France have done so too. China has added to the number, range and throw-weight of its nuclear missiles. The United States, though destroying most of its older ISBMs has added new ones e.g., bunker-busters and future A-bombs in space.

NON-PROLIFERATION

All non-NWS that signed the treaty must open their nuclear facilities to inspection by the IAEA and guarantee that nuclear materials are not diverted to military uses. The IAEA investigates suspected violations under the mandate of the U.N.

One hundred and eighty-eight nations have signed the NPT. A dozen have given up nuclear weapons, e.g. South Africa and the former Soviet republics, Ukraine, Belarus, and Kazakhstan which destroyed or transferred the nuclear weapons to Russia. Libya renounced a nuclear weapons program in 2003.

Three countries declined to sign the treaty, India, Pakistan, and Israel. The IAEA has no authority to inspect their nuclear facilities. The Israeli stockpile of fissile material is estimated to be sufficient for up to 200 nuclear warheads, India's for 100 to 150 warheads, Pakistan's for sixty to 100.

(continued on next page)

PEACEFUL USES

The treaty gives every state an "inalienable right" to use nuclear energy for peaceful purposes. Most nuclear power plants, being based on Light Water Reactors (LWR) which run on Low Enriched Uranium (LEU) fuel, it follows that states are allowed to enrich uranium or purchase nuclear fuel on the international market. Natural uranium ore, most of it mined in Africa, contains less than 1 percent (0.71 percent) of fissionable material (U-235). In an enrichment plant, natural uranium is converted into LEU (with between 3 and 5 percent fissionable material). For nuclear weapons purposes, the U-235 content must be enriched to 90 percent (HEU). This is extremely difficult, requiring "cascades" of gas spinning devices. Only a few NWS have mastered this technology. It can be argued that enriching uranium to the lower levels required for atomic power is only a step away from enriching it to weapons grade: but no country subject to NPT inspection, as yet has successfully developed a nuclear weapon.

North Korea ratified the NPT but withdrew in January 2003, following U.S. accusations that it had started an HEU enrichment program. On February 10, 2005, these charges were confirmed when North Korea declared that it now possesses nuclear weapons. In six-party talks hosted by China, North Korea said it would abandon its nuclear weapons, rejoin the NPT and readmit IAEA inspectors—but only in return for the supply of two LWR plants that the U.S., South Korea, and Japan had agreed in the 1994 Framework Treaties.

The experience gained in negotiations with North Korea more than likely will guide the U.S. and E.U. approach to Iran.

PART THREE

TIME TO TALK

Of this I am quite sure, if we continue our quarrels between the past and the present, we shall find that we have lost the future.
— Winston S. Churchill

O n December 26, 2003 an earthquake struck the ancient city of Bam in southern Iran killing not less than 30,000 people. That's ten times as many as died in the 9/11 terrorist attack on the World Trade Center in New York. As the world's disaster relief agencies rushed to Bam to help dig out the victims, the number of dead and injured kept rising until the true awfulness of this tragedy became known. More than 41,000 Iranians had died, many of them choking to death as the roofs of their clay homes collapsed, engulfing them in centuries old dust. Tens of thousands more had been injured, and at least 100,000 homeless were huddling together for warmth in make shift shelters and tents on the arid windswept plateau surrounding Bam, where night time temperatures in mid winter seldom rise above freezing.

The Bam earthquake moved me deeply. Its magnitude and drama triggered memories of two other disasters that had punctuated my lifelong association with

Ancient Bam and an aerial photo of Bam after the devastating earthquake of 2003

Iran. One which devastated Tabas in the northeast province of Khorasan, killing more than 25,000, occurred in the final violent days of the Shah's long reign. A second, some of whose after effects I saw in the Azerbaijan province of Iran killed another 21,000 people in 1990.

Virtually no help had been provided by western governments to the victims of these disasters. In Bam I was determined to do better.

A small group of us in California, where earthquakes are no less frequent (though less devastating) than in Iran, launched a project to help Bam to recover. This was an uphill task in the face of the U.S. government's ban on trade, or visits to Iran. As always, we had to consider whether help intended for Bam would end up in the pockets of henchmen of the Islamic regime. Most members of Orange County's World Affairs Council had applauded President Bush when he condemned the theocrats in Teheran as partners in a global Axis of Evil but they were moved, as I was by the suffering of the people of Bam and wanted to help them recover.

I wrote an open letter to the people of Bam which was signed by several hundred members of the Council and copied to President Bush and President Khatami. This proposed that a team of California seismic engineers should share their expertise in reconstructing earthquake-damaged buildings with their Iranian opposite numbers engaged in rebuilding Bam.

This offer of technical help by members of American Society of Civil Engineers (ASCE) was accepted by the Iranians. Three Californian engineers traveled to Bam and carried out a survey of the damage.

Their report revealed that many of the victims died when the roofs of recently built multi-story structures, including hospitals, police and fire stations, collapsed as a result of shoddy workmanship and inadequate steel beam supports. Hundreds of adobe dwellings, many of them rebuilt after previous earthquakes had also crumbled as the earth moved. The engineers' recommendations were simple. Iran needs building codes of the kind that require California's high-rise buildings to be fortified with enough supports to make them resistant or immune to earth tremors. Bam's adobe dwellings need also to be reinforced by steel and nylon ropes that fasten around the mud walls like the belt on a pair of trousers.

The Iranian local authorities adopted these suggestions. As Bam gradually recovered, steel "belts and braces" were strapped around the newly built adobe homes into which its people returned. To help pay for this an auction of Bam style adobe bricks at $100 a piece was organized at Orange County's best known Iranian American restaurant "The Caspian." This raised a large sum of money to help the orphaned children. Many other Americans contributed to a Bam relief fund headed by the Iranian poet, Shirin Ebadi, who won the 2003 Nobel Prize for literature.

I recount this tale of disaster and one small effort to help mitigate its human consequences to underline two points. First, politics apart, people-to-people relations can help bridge the gap between nations whose leaders are at daggers drawn. Americans and Iranians, despite decades of government-to-government hostility, do not hate one another. My experience is that they get on well together. Second Iranians because of their greater exposure to earthquakes are more aware—and more afraid—than contemporary Americans of the consequences of nuclear weapons. Children in Iranian schools are taught to compare the number of casualties caused by earthquakes with the even greater numbers killed in Hiroshima and Nagasaki. Public attitudes in Iran are therefore not unlike those of Americans in the late 1950s when millions built atomic bomb shelters. Many Iranians with whom I have discussed nuclear weapons, are as opposed as the Japanese are, to their country having anything to do with them.

Given the complex history—and potentially dangerous consequences—of Iran's nuclear program, American policymakers in fall 2006 nevertheless were rightly worried. They also gave the impression of being divided, confused and frustrated. The United States agreed to join the Europeans in negotiations with Iran but imposed conditions and deadlines that the Iranians proceeded to ignore. This brought the worst of both worlds, accusations by the hawks in Washington that the U.S. was "going soft on Iran" and charges by the Europeans that America's preconditions were unrealistic.

The administration took comfort from the U.N. Security Council's near-unanimous call for Iran to cease its enrichment activities. But with Russia and China dissenting from enforcement measures, there was no U.N. agreement on how to overcome Iran's refusal to obey.

Nuclear technology meanwhile had become a source of national pride in Iran. Far from cowing the regime, U.S. threats had assisted Mahmoud Ahmadi-nejad in using it to boost his populist appeal. Former Iranian finance minister Jahangir Amuzegar, a bitter opponent of the ayatollahs put this well when noting Khameini's statement that "using nuclear technology is a national obligation . . . indispensable to Iran's honour and glory," he wrote.

> *"American neo-cons" open advocacy of regime change, Secretary of State Rice's assertion that Iran is a 'menace beyond the nuclear issue,' her $75 million budget request to 'promote democracy' in Iran, leaked reports about the Pentagon's war preparations and U.S. special forces operations inside Iran's ethnic minorities, and the passage of a stiff sanctions bill by the U.S. House of Representatives all played into the mullahs' hands. The price of oil skyrocketed. Sympathy for Iran's case increased.*

The United States case against Iran has evolved over the years. Washington at one point maintained that Iran does not need nuclear electricity because of its abundant oil and natural gas reserves. This is a weak argument. Iran is a net importer of petroleum because its refineries cannot meet domestic demand for gasoline. Many other big oil producers, outside the five NWS (nuclear weapons states), also have nuclear power programs. Brazil for instance produces large quantities of oil and gas but in defiance of previous U.S. efforts to prevent this, has also built two large nuclear power plants and has a third one under construction. Most of the fuel for these Brazilian reactors is enriched at its own Resende plant.

The U.S. later argued that Iran forfeited its right as a sovereign nation to develop nuclear power stations by undertaking the "clandestine" nuclear projects that the defector Alireza Jafarzadeh claimed to have revealed in 2002. This is still the subject of debate in the intelligence communities of the United States and Britain as well as at IAEA; but the Iranians retort that three of their near neighbors who refused to sign the NPT, have developed nuclear weapons in "clandestine" programs that the United States encouraged or took no action to prevent—Israel, India and Pakistan. Iran, by contrast, says it operates (as of this writing), within the NPT!

Is Iran in violation of the NPT? The answer is, probably not. The text of the treaty says that "nothing in the NPT shall be interpreted as affecting the inalienable right of the Parties to the Treaty to develop research, production and use of nuclear energy for peaceful purposes without discrimination." There is no sterner critic of the Islamic regime than Ardeshir Zahedi, who signed Iran into the NPT during the Pahlavi dynasty, but even Zahedi agrees that Iran's civil nuclear program is its "inalienable" right.

The crucial issue is nuclear weapons. Many Americans believe that the religious extremists who control Iran not only are determined to get their hands on nuclear weapons but would make use of them to overawe their neighbors, to threaten and possibly "wipe out" Israel, and eventually to achieve the Islamic Revolution's declared intention of overcoming "the Great Satan." Ilan Berman, vice president for policy at the Washington-based American Foreign Policy Council, interprets this as a virtual declaration of religious war on the United States. Berman wrote in spring 2006:

> *Iran's ayatollahs have unleashed a new wave of global instability . . . Iran is now in control of terrorism in Israel . . . Iran has a strategy for uprooting the Americans and English, and in the words of one of its mullahs, plans to strike at these [global infidels] by means of suicide operations and missiles.*[1]

Such language sounded like war-talk. Convinced that it reflected the views of hawks in the Pentagon and NSC, Iranian propagandists translated it into Arabic and publicized it widely in the Moslem world. Berman's tirade alarmed America's friends and helped its enemies to paint the United States as a warmonger. Yet the neo-cons' anxieties about an Iranian bomb are premature. As of September 2006, the best estimate IAEA's observers can make of Iran's potential ability to produce an atomic weapon, assuming its rulers, despite their denials, have launched a crash program to do this, is a minimum of four years and probably much longer. It follows that there is time to let diplomacy work.

QUESTIONS

To that end, the U.S. and Britain need answers to some basic questions that in recent years have gotten lost in the hubbub of charge and counter-charge between Washington and Teheran.

First, why should Iran *want* a nuclear bomb? The short answer is that nearly all Iranians—except those living abroad—have a strong sense of vulnerability. Few countries have been invaded so often, classically by Greeks and Romans, later by Mongols and Tartars, Seljuk and Ottoman Turks, more recently by Russians and Brits. Iran's neighbors, Afghanistan and Iraq have also been attacked in the 1980s by U.S.-led invaders, leading a Teheran official to ask, "which country, other than Canada, has Americans on every border?" Iran, too, is surrounded by nuclear weapon states—Russia, China, India, Pakistan and Israel. U.S. forces in Iraq and the Persian Gulf could also call up nuclear weapons, for instance to respond to attacks on Saudi Arabia and the U.A.E.

In these circumstances, if I were an Iranian, I too would ask, what is the surest way of discouraging any further invasions? The answer, I suspect, is the same one as led Britain, France, China, India, Pakistan and Israel to build their nuclear arsenals—to deter an enemy attack.

A second question is, would the Iranians, in the event they were to build a nuclear weapon, ipso facto, be likely to use or threaten to use it?

There can be no certain answers. But the last time Iran started a war was in 1850 in an attempt to win back territory it had lost to the Afghans. Its last invasion of another country was in 1738.[2] The Iranians may be unpredictable but for all their president's wild talk and mullahs' aim to spread militant Shiite Islam to the unconverted world, I find it hard to believe that Iran intrinsically is more aggressive or more unstable than any of the other nuclear weapons wielders with which the United States is currently engaged. For instance, North Korea. Is Iran more likely to attack its neighbors than North Korea? The odds are the other way round. North Korea attacked South Korea. Iran was attacked by Iraq.

Question three is whether Iran might seek to advance its aggressive Islamic ambitions by transferring nuclear materials to terrorist organizations, enabling them to make "suitcase" A-bombs? This is a terrifying possibility. Few things are more likely to bring it about than an American attack on Iran. Meanwhile, the most pressing danger of terrorists getting their hands on such devices arises from nations that already possess atomic weapons. Pakistan is the main culprit. It was from Pakistan's nuclear weapons laboratories that A.Q. Khan and others exported bomb-making materials to Libya, possibly Iran and probably North Korea.

Last but not least, there is the question posed mainly by Iranian refugees living in the U.S. and Europe. What about human rights? Iran is a brutal theocracy. Its elections are flawed, its press and television subject to government interference, its religious courts can still impose grotesque punishments on women and dissenters. But Iran is no more of a tyranny than its central Asia neighbors, such as Uzbekistan or Azerbaijan, or most of the African and central American states with which the U.S. does business. China, too, though it sits on the Security Council as one of the judges of Iran's behavior, is scarcely a paragon of freedom and justice. If Iran is ruled by Islamic mullahs, China is ruled by Marxist Leninists. Iran's mullahs have executed thousands. China's Communists murdered millions . . .

OPTIONS ON THE TABLE

So what is to be done? Some, a few Americans and rather more Israelis, still recommend military action to eliminate Iran's nuclear facilities. Plans to do this exist. Suggestions still appear in the U.S. press, based on leaks from the Pentagon that Iran could be "de-nuked" by "a swift, massive, devastating force that decapitates the regime" and that this could be done "in a single night."[3] I do not think this is feasible. Iran is a far more formidable adversary than Iraq whose nuclear research plants the Israelis bombed at Osirak. Iran's 125 or more identified nuclear research and development facilities are widely dispersed and many are in the vicinity of large centers of population, making the civilian cost of bombing them unacceptably high. The United States would also be on its own if it were to launch a pre-emptive strike. The British Foreign Secretary said in November 2005, "I don't foresee any circumstances in which military action would be justified against Iran, full stop."

The same goes for the rest of the E.U. and Turkey. Russia and China would object. So would Japan. India, Brazil, South Africa and

Egypt would condemn America, not Iran. Only Israel would support pre-emptive U.S. attacks and the result would be an Arab and Islamic Asian backlash against American and Jewish interests of the kind that led to the U.S. to bar Israeli participation in both the 1991 Gulf War and the war with Iraq.

Threatening to attack Iran is also counter-productive. It did the United States no good when President Bush had to disown as "wild speculation" a leak from the Pentagon about a USAF contingency plan to use atomic bunker bombs to destroy Iran's underground nuclear facilities.[4]

Such threats not only alienate America's E.U. allies, including the British; they stir up resentment, anger and hatred throughout the Muslim world and reinforce the perception that America is engaged in an anti-Islamic conspiracy.[5] Worse, they strengthen the hands of the "peacocks" in Iran who recommend a crash program to acquire an Iranian nuclear deterrent. The net effect is to push the Iranian people back into the camp of the regime that many of them want to replace.

Can sanctions be more effective? The United States has been applying unilateral sanctions against Iran for thirty years, nearly as long as against Cuba. America has also pressured its allies and international organizations to deny or limit financial transactions with Iran. These measures may have helped to bring down Mohammed Khatami, the only Iranian leader since the Islamic revolution to hold out an olive branch to America; but they have been no more effective in bringing about regime change in Teheran than they have been in Havana.

U.N.-mandated multilateral sanctions might be more effective. A blockade on Iran's oil and gas exports would deal a severe blow to its economy. Four-fifths of Iran's international earnings and half its Government's revenues, arise from sales of energy. Choking off oil supplies at a time when world demand for energy is surging in response to the rise of China and India would nevertheless be a classic case of cutting off one's nose to spite one's face. U.S. and E.U.

consumers would be the first to feel the impact in terms of higher gasoline prices. The global economy would face a sharp upward push in inflation. Nor would Russia or China be likely to bar Iran's energy exports by way of their pipelines to Europe and Asia. Russia is a major arms vendor to Iran's defense establishment and is still the sole contractor to build Iran's atomic reactor in Bushehr. China receives 12 percent of its oil imports from Iran; Chinese firms are active in many Iranian development projects including the Teheran metro; Behjing recently signed a $100 billion energy agreement with Teheran.[6]

Targeting Iran's individual leaders by preventing them from travelling or investing abroad potentially is a better bet. The U.S. Treasury and the Bank of England are on the trail of large sums of cash that some of the Iranian mullahs, like the Shah's courtiers thirty years ago, have stashed in dummy accounts in tax havens. There is much to be said for seizing and freezing this, but it is not easy to see how a travel ban would greatly inconvenience the ayatollahs who rule the roost in Teheran. Few members of their decision-making Expediency Council venture far outside their monasteries, let alone travel abroad.

CHANGE FROM WITHIN

President Bush proposed in spring 2006, to step up America's psychological warfare against the Iranian leadership. Congress added $50 million to U.S. spending on programs beamed into Iran by the Voice of America and Radio Farda, a U.S.-funded Farsi language broadcaster aimed at Iran's young people. The U.S. also increased its support for opposition parties in Iran and promotes limited (covert) action against the Islamic regime. Supporting this, the State Department recalls that one reason why the Iron Curtain collapsed in Europe at the end of the Cold War is that East Germans and Poles saw and heard on Western TV programs how far their countries under Communism had fallen behind the free world. Many members of the Iranian diaspora, including the

Shah's son, Reza Pahlavi, believe the same thing could happen in Iran. They point to widespread disenchantment and growing resistance "back home" to the regime's Islamic intolerance; to the rising levels of unemployment and stagnant living standards; to the possibility of strikes and civil disobedience.

Sooner or later, the Iranian people can be relied on to change their form of government. Like the Chinese they may already be doing this from within. Whether U.S.-driven outside efforts to destabilize and unseat the Islamic regime in Teheran will do more good than harm to the cause of reducing the nuclear threat, remains to be seen. As in the case of Cuba they may do more to impress the hardliners in Congress and appease the Iranian diaspora than to separate the Iranian people from their rulers.

Does this mean that nothing can be done? Not at all. As Bruce Laingen suggests in his foreword to this book, statecraft of the highest order is needed to prevent a further spread of nuclear weapons into the volatile security situation of the Persian Gulf region. The challenge is to combine U.S. and E.U. efforts to contain and reverse Iran's reach for nuclear weapons with fresh proposals for a Persian Gulf non-aggression pact and beyond that, a broader regional settlement, based on a nuclear weapons-free Middle East.

ENGAGING WITH IRAN

The United States does not have the luxury of engaging only
pleasant, democratic and tolerant governments.
The great challenge of effective diplomacy is to deal with,
and get results from, regimes that most Americans would
prefer did not exist.
           — Ted Galen Carpenter
           CATO Institute

Following the Bush administration's U-turn, it took the E-3 and the U.S. most of the spring and summer of 2006 to devise a new strategy towards Iran's nuclear activities. The European Union's foreign policy chief, Xavier Solana, former Secretary General of NATO and himself a nuclear physicist flew to Teheran with an "incentives and penalties" package designed to coax and pressure the Iranians into a fresh round of negotiations in which the Americans could be expected to take part.

On his arrival, Solana told the Iranian foreign minister that he hoped this would open the door to "a new era of collaboration" between Iran and the rest of the world. This must be based on "trust and mutual respect." The Iranians received Solana courteously. President Ahmadi-nejad described the still closely-guarded package as "helpful," promised to study it carefully, and said that Iran would reply with "some ideas of our own."

Seasoned diplomat as he is, Xavier Solana emphasized to the Iranians the advantages of a "deal" with their critics. Among the "incentives" he had to offer in return for their ending enrichment of uranium were:

- Affirmation of Iran's legal right to nuclear energy for peaceful purposes in line with Article IV of the Nuclear Non-proliferation Treaty
- Effective aid in building new light-water reactors in Iran through joint ventures
- Participation as a partner in an international fuel-cycle center in Russia
- Establishment of an inter-governmental regional forum aimed at guaranteeing each member state's political sovereignty and territorial integrity
- Support for Iran's membership in the World Trade Organization
- A strategic energy partnership with Europe
- Increased foreign investment

And the "penalties?" Solana was careful to avoid the threatening language that emanated from the White House and Pentagon. He still made it clear that a failure to cooperate would lead to a ratcheting up of E.U. and U.S. sanctions. Penalties on the nuclear front would include an international embargo on the sale to Iran of all types of equipment and know how relating to atomic research and development; a ban on contact with Iranian scientists and technicians; and prohibition on their travel outside Iran. Further escalating "disincentives" Iran would face if there is no agreement, include E.U. and U.S. action to halt all trade in arms and dual-use high-tech equipment; barring loans from private banks or international agencies to Iran; freezing Iran's assets in foreign institutions; banning foreign investment in or transfer of

Xavier Solana, European Union's foreign policy chief

technology to Iran. The most severe economic action would be to forbid all sales of foreign products to Iran including critically needed gasoline; an embargo on all oil and non-oil exports by Iran; and, finally, expelling the Islamic Republic from all international organizations.

Iran's response to these "carrot and stick" overtures was reported by Solana to E.U. and American leaders at their July G8 summit in Moscow and considered again by the U.N. Security Council. The outcome was the Security Council's demand that Iran must terminate its enrichment activities by August 30. The deadline passed by without progress, Iran refused to budge. The council's permanent members were preoccupied with Lebanon. The prospect was for a long hot period of behind-the-scenes diplomacy, interrupted by events on the ground in Iraq, Afghanistan and Palestine, and threats and counter-threats by politicians who lost and won in America's November 2006 Congressional elections.

Yet one clear message rang out from the noisy exchanges between the West and Iran. The United States had re-engaged. For the first time in twenty-seven years, America had broken the "angry silence" that five successive U.S. presidents had maintained vis-à-vis Iran.

Sooner or later this was bound to happen. There is a perverse progression in these matters. Unlike most countries which recognize and deal with governments that de facto, control their territory, the United States, since Woodrow Wilson, has sought to isolate and dislodge regimes it does not like, (e.g. Communist China, Vietnam and Libya), only to end up years later recognizing and talking to them because America's interests require this. Thus, the U.S. for half a century refused to sit at the same table as the aggressive and unpredictable North Koreans—yet today, American diplomats meet unobtrusively with Pyongyang's representatives for behind the scenes exchanges aimed at negotiating an agreement on a non-aggression pact and a nuclear-free Korean peninsula.

President Bush should now apply a similar approach to Iran. U.S.

envoys now engaged with the E.U. and Russia in talks with Iran on its nuclear program should be authorized to extend this re-engagement to other issues that divide the two countries. Already, American representatives unofficially are talking to Teheran about Iran's role in facilitating—or impeding—a draw-down of U.S. and British troops from Iraq. The U.S. and NATO are also in contact with the Iranian military in regard to the resurgence of Taliban activities in Afghanistan and through France on Iran's support for Hezbollah in Lebanon. But a U.S.-Iran dialogue cannot be confined to military and nuclear weapons issues. The net should be cast wider. Both sides need to attend to a raft of other sores that have poisoned their relationship ever since the seizure of the U.S. embassy in 1980.

Thus, the United States accuses Iran of complicity in the 1980s bombing of the American embassy in Lebanon and blowing up the U.S. marines' base in Beirut, killing more than 200 Americans; of arming and financing terrorists throughout the Middle East; and since 9/11 of lending support to Al Queda, though no evidence of this has been found. Iran supplies weapons and funds to Shiite warlords whose forces attack Americans and British troops in Iraq. A ship carrying Iranian weapons for Hezbollah was intercepted by a Spanish frigate en route to Lebanon. The State Department lists the Islamic regime at the "No 1 State sponsor of terrorism."

The Iranians, who have longer memories, level even more charges against America, starting with the 1953 removal of Mohammed Mosaddegh. They accuse the U.S. of prompting the Shah to waste Iran's oil revenues on weapons it did not need; of "stealing" the Iranian assets deposited in American banks by the Shah but ever since frozen by the U.S.; of siding with Saddam Hussein in the Iran-Iraq war; shooting down an Iranian air liner with 290 pilgrims to Mecca and scores of children aboard; and ever since of "systematically punishing" the Iranian people by sanctions. The president of Iran calls America "the Great Arrogant." Its spiritual leader, Seyed Ali

Khameini, charged President Bush with leading a "crusade" to destroy the Islamic revolution.

THE IRAQ DIMENSION

The nuclear standoff has exacerbated this cold war between Iran and America. Both sides intensified their actions against the other. The Iranians originally played a constructive role in Iraq, welcoming the overthrow of Saddam Hussein, helping to rebuild the Iraqis' water, energy and electricity infrastructure, signing a billion dollar aid and trade deal with the first post-occupation Iraqi government. Iran now exerts a powerful anti-American influence among the Shia majority in Baghdad and southern Iraq. Its leverages arises from a shadowy network of intelligence operatives, armed gangs and religious militias who look to Iranian sources for funds and inspiration. Increasingly, public figures in Iraq proclaim their ties to Iran. Senior party spokesmen such as former prime minister Jaafari and the current prime minister, Nouri-al-Maliki, spent years of exile in Iran and remain close to its Islamic leaders. Iran has also developed ties with Muqtada al-Sadr, who once inflamed passions with his virulent anti-Iranian rhetoric. According to Vali Nasr, arguably the most authoritative commentator on Iran-Iraq relations who currently teaches course on Political Islam at the U.S. Naval Postgraduate School, Iran's Revolutionary Guards supported Sadr's Mahdi Army in its confrontation with U.S. troops in Najaf in 2004. Since then Iran has trained Sadrist military cadres, bankrolled Shiite parties in Iraq during two elections, used its popular satellite television network al Aalam to whip up support for them, and helped broker deals with the Kurds. Iraqi Shiite parties he says, attract voters by relying on political and social service networks across southern Iraq that, in many cases, were created with Iranian funding and assistance.[1]

The coalition authorities in Baghdad were caught off guard by this revival of Iranian influence in Iran. Washington in response complains that Iran supports insurgents and criminal gangs; accuses Teheran of poisoning Iraqi public opinion with anti-Americanism; of arming insurgents—and now of reaching out for nuclear weapons.

It is in this context that the Bush administration expanded U.S. efforts to isolate Iran. Under its Proliferation Security Initiative (PSI), Washington forced international banks to stop offering credits to Iranian companies. In 2005, the U.S. defense department organized air and naval exercises in the Persian Gulf, the east Mediterranean and, surprisingly, the landlocked Caspian Sea to increase military pressure on the Islamic regime. With Poland and the Czech Republic, the Pentagon proposes to locate anti-missile batteries capable of shooting down Iranian long-range missiles in the event that Iran at some future date was to deploy them. Special offices in the State Department and Pentagon have been set up to assist opposition forces in Iran to bring down the Iranian government.

Until the administration changed course in June 2006, these actions and counter-actions pointed in the direction of armed conflict. Israeli claims, endorsed by the U.S. that Iran was the armourer and "long-distance commander-in-chief" of Hezbollah's offensive against northern Israel revived calls in Washington for U.S. air attacks. The change of control in the U.S. Congress, coming on top of and in protest against the deteriorating situation in Iraq has quieted down such talk.

The diplomatic and political challenge is now to reverse the slide towards a war that the U.S. still describes as one of its options, that the Iranians say they "will not shrink from" but that cooler heads on both sides are now determined to avoid.

The new mantra in the White House is "give diplomacy its best chance."

PROPOSALS FOR PEACE

It is always easier to convince a people to follow a proposal which seems bold and certain, even if danger lurks behind it, than to follow one which appears cowardly and uncertain, even if it contains security.

— Machiavelli, *The Discourses: Book I, Chapter 53*

The first task for American diplomats engaging with Iran is to break down the plethora of disagreements between the two countries into bite sized portions and tackle them, one by one, at separate tables. For instance:

A—IRAQ

Venue	Baghdad/Basra
Attendees	U.S., British, Iraqi and Iranian commanders
Agenda	Ending or reducing the infiltration of Iranian "volunteers" who smuggle arms and cash to insurgent Shiite militias; liaison between Coalition and Iranian military as Americans and Brits hand over to Iraqis; future border security between Iran and Iraq; policing of Shatt al Arab waterway.

B—AFGHANISTAN

Venue	Kabul

| Attendees | Afghan and Iranian ministers, U.S., British and NATO representatives |
| Agenda | Defeating the resurgent Taliban (which Iran regards as menace); pacifying its western provinces; stabilizing the border with Iran; returning 280,000 Afghans who fled to Iran for refuge; cracking down on narco-trafficking, a key Iranian priority. |

C—COMPENSATION

Venue	United Nations
Attendees	U.S. and Iranians only
Agenda	U.S. claims for 1980's damage to its embassy in Teheran, restitution of property and assets of U.S. firms and citizens seized by Islamic regime; Iranian claims for increased compensation for shooting down of Iranian airliner. Unfreezing of Iranian assets held by Washington.

SOLVING THE NUCLEAR CONUNDRUM

Issues of this kind can be handled at first instance at the official level. The nuclear impasse requires political input. The problem is to find a compromise between the West's demands that Iran shall not build nuclear weapons and Iran's insistence on enriching its own nuclear fuel. This is a conflict of right with right. The Non Proliferation Treaty and its Safeguards Protocols cover both (see box on pages 220–2). The challenge is to enforce them, lacking the two essential ingredients—credible inspection and trust.

The key to a nuclear detente turns on unlocking a technical conundrum: how to supply Iran with nuclear fuel for legitimate energy production while at the same time satisfying U.S. and E.U. concerns that Iran might secretly use this to develop nuclear bombs.

One approach to resolving this reaches back to the World Bank's proposals made as long ago as 1953 to defuse the crisis over Mohammed Mosaddegh's seizure of the Anglo-Iranian oil company's assets. An updated version of this would create a multi-national consortium under the aegis of the World Bank to invest and participate in Iran's civil nuclear power program. The governors of the World Bank in which the U.S. is the most prominent participant would exercise on oversight role. An international advisory board would supervise its enrichment activities.

Another possibility is to apply to Iran's enrichment facilities the "dual key" arrangements that apply to American nuclear weapons deployed at U.S. air force bases in my former constituency in Britain. At all times these remain in the possession of the United States and under the control of the president. U.S. law requires this. But these weapons cannot be deployed, much less used for any military purpose, without the consent of the British prime minister. Could the principles of this "dual key" approach be applied to atomic fuel intended for Iran's civil nuclear power stations? The Iranians would own and control it but its use would be subject to IAEA inspectors' consent.

The most hopeful approach, as of this writing, could be the one devised by a group of experts chaired by Bruno Pellaud, IAEA's deputy director general for safeguards. A Swiss nuclear safety engineer, Pellaud was asked to recommend measures to bridge the gap between Iran's "inalienable right" to generate its own nuclear power, and international fears that it might secretly use the fuel to develop nuclear weapons. His expert group proposed a "voluntary conversion" of Iranian nuclear facilities into "multi-national nuclear assets" (MNAs). Scientists and technicians from other countries would work alongside the Iranians. For Iran this would ensure a supply of nuclear fuel and international investment in its nuclear energy program while at the same time providing the U.S. and E.U. with assurances that its enrichment activities are kept under the microscope of what Pellaud describes as "scrutiny from international peers and partners." Non-proliferation and security guarantees would be strengthened. "It is difficult to play games if you have multi-nationals at a site," says Bruno Pellaud.

NON AGGRESSION PACT

Any resolution of the standoff over the technical issue of enrichment needs to be placed in a wider context. Today's diminished U.S. and British priority is to leave behind in Iraq a government that is sufficiently broad-based to avoid civil war and externally is secure against outside interference, eg from Iran. Only the Iraqis themselves can ensure their country's unity and stability and neither is assured as Sunnis war with Shi'as and Iraqi Kurds increase their pressure for autonomy and control of the northern oilfields. Securing Iraq's borders is another matter. Outside help to do this will be required for many years to come. The challenge is to protect Iraq against interference from its neighbors, notably Iran, while at the same time assuaging Iran's fears of being invaded and the Gulf State's fears of being over-awed or attacked by Iran.

The best way to do this is to construct a non-aggression pact along similar lines to the one now being contemplated in Korea. Following the first successful Gulf War, then U.S. Secretary of State James Baker called for such a security arrangement among the Gulf States that would include Iran. "Fifteen years later" says Bruce Laingen, who spent 444 days as a hostage in the U.S. embassy in Teheran, "it

President Bush appointed James Baker to advise on a fresh approach to Iraq

is time, indeed high time, for a further U.S. policy initiative along the lines of the Baker proposal."[1] Appointed by President Bush to advise on a fresh approach to Iraq, Jim Baker's instinct remains—a regional approach is required. Over time says Laingen, a Persian Gulf security pact "could build on the existing Gulf Cooperation Council (GCC), and a continuing U.S. naval presence. It would also recognize that Iran's size, population and location dictate the reality of Iran's being the principal residual power in the Persian Gulf."

There is a precedent for such a pact—the "five powers" Central Treaty Organization (CENTO) set up with U.S. help between Turkey, Iraq, Pakistan and Britain as custodian for the Gulf States, as long ago as the 1960s, CENTO, whose headquarters were in Baghdad, was designed to defend its members and the Middle East generally against aggressive Soviet moves to push south to the oil of the Persian Gulf and the blue waters of the Indian Ocean. Today's nightmare among the Sunni Arabs of the Persian Gulf, no longer is Russia, it is Iran. From Kuwait and Iraq to Saudi Arabia and Oman the Arab states bordering the Persian Gulf have a combined population smaller than Iran's. I believe they would gladly embrace an updated version of CENTO, underwritten by the U.S. and NATO, with the object of safeguarding themselves from attack by Iran while at the same time assuaging Iran's fears of invasion.

President Bush or his successor would therefore serve Arab as well as American and European interests by exploring the possibilities for a regional non-aggression pact in which the Iranians and their neighbors (and past invaders) enjoy mutually assured security.

All members of such a pact including Iraq and Iran would bind themselves never to initiate or to support attacks against one another. By so doing they could pave the way for an end to the confrontation between the U.S. and Iran. The context would be a step-by-step approach to a nuclear weapons-free Persian Gulf, a neat fit with the proposals put forward by Iranian president Khatami in his 2000 "dialogue of civilizations" address to the U.N. Security Council.

NUCLEAR TRADE OFF

To move towards this, the president should let it be known that he would not be averse to meeting the Iranian president and Ali Khamenei, at next year's U.N. General Assembly or in some neutral country, e.g. Singapore.

This would be a breathtaking move. Iran haters would cry appeasement. The diaspora would feel betrayed. Instant opposition could be expected not only from neo-cons but from many of those in Congress as well as in Israel who see the Iranian version of Shiism as implacable and Iran's chauvinistic ambitions as an incorrigible menace to the future of the Middle East, if not to the entire world.

But there is a time for boldness in politics and courage in world affairs. Richard Nixon changed the world when he went to China to meet the murderous boss of a Communist regime that Americans had been brought up to believe was the Red Menace. Ronald Reagan met the leaders of the Soviet Union whose nuclear missiles were targeted on American cities, in search of a strategic arms limitations agreement. Successive British prime ministers have also taken risks in their largely successful attempts to transform mortal enemies into friends. Welcoming the leaders of more than forty heads of government at a commonwealth summit, Prince Philip commented that Tony Blair and the Canadian, Australian and New Zealand prime ministers were the only heads of government who previously had not served time in British jails as terrorists!

There is no greater prize on the diplomatic horizon than a stable and sustainable settlement in the Middle East. Nine successive American presidents and nineteen U.S. secretaries of state have striven mightily—and unsuccessfully—to achieve this. Iran, Iraq and Afghanistan are now part of the problem and critical to a solution that henceforth must include a grand bargain over nuclear weapons.

That indeed is the message from Lebanon, Palestine, Israel and Iran. It is time for the United States to try, try, try again.

STEP ONE

Step One should be a trade off similar to the one now being contemplated in Korea. In return for Iran's abandonment of its reach for atomic bombs nuclear weapons, the U.S. Navy would remove its nuclear weapons from the Persian Gulf and the British island of Diego Garcia.

STEP TWO

Step Two would be more ambitious—nuclear detente between Iran and Israel. Both countries would need to work towards a nuclear weapons free zone reaching from the Mediterranean to Afghanistan.

Impossible? I don't think so. Israel started making nuclear weapons in the 1980s with help from the U.S. and France. It is now believed to possess as many as two hundred free-fall atomic bombs and warheads for its short- and medium-range missiles. Secretly maintaining and updating this nuclear arsenal is expensive and increasingly difficult. Some of Israel's nuclear bomb making facilities at Dimona are getting old and before long will need to be updated if their weapons are not to become unusable. Only the United States can provide the technology and the funds from private sources with which to do this; but will it? What happens to U.S. claims to be opposed to any further proliferation if it equips the Israelis with a new generation of nuclear weapons?

Some of Israel's hardest headed strategists have recently begun to question whether this is the wisest use of the Jewish state's resources. Nuclear weapons do nothing to deter the attacks by terrorists and suicide bombers or Hezbollah rockets that are the most menacing threats to Israeli security.

NATO GUARANTEE

It is still hard to visualize any Israeli government reducing, let alone giving up the nuclear arsenal the U.S. surreptitiously helped to create unless Israel's national ability to deter or destroy its enemies is replaced by no less reliable international guarantees of its security. One of these must be a verifiable and enforceable ban on Iranian nuclear weapons, the other a NATO-style guarantee by the U.S. and E.U. to go to the aid of a nuclear-renouncing Israel in the event that it were to be attacked.

Pipedreams? Again, I do not think so—if only the *sine qua non*, a mutual security pact can be achieved.

Alistair Horne, one of the shrewdest Middle East observers, author of seven books translated into Hebrew by the Israeli Defense forces, says Israel as well as the Arab states would be "safer in a nuclear-free Middle East." As the Lebanon crisis wound down, Horne wrote:

> For Israel the danger is that in a few years time, Hezbollah's rockets might carry Iran-made nuclear-tips, fired not from neighboring Lebanon, but from the unreachable remoteness of Iran. Thus more urgently than ever before, there is a need for a new strategy to break the logjam. Most important—and most radical—would be for an internationally-backed, total clampdown on Iranian nuclear development and at the same time, Israel's relinquishment—or at least mothballing—of its nuclear capability.

The United States as well as Israel has much to gain from a nuclear-free Middle East. Henry Kissinger recalls that Israel's possession of its doomsday weapons meant that every Middle East crisis he confronted carried with it "a threat of the Israeli tail wagging the American dog," because it enabled Israel's leaders to argue that they would have no alternative but to use or threaten to use their nuclear weapons if America failed to provide them with the air-supremacy weapons they needed for survival. Alistair Horne's conclusion is that "de-nuclearising Israel would be the surest way to get support from the moderate Sunni Arab states to apply pressure on Iran." Trading Israeli nuclear weapons to get rid of the

Iranian nuclear menace "would be worth almost any price to (ensure) the security of Israel."

The author's conclusion is similar. Long term, it is inconceivable that four million Israelis can retain a monopoly of nuclear weapons in a turbulent Middle East. Within ten years the populations and economic power of Iran and the Arab states are likely to be twenty times greater than Israel's. And the time to grasp this is now while most Iranians want their country to use non-polluting nuclear power to generate a growing share of their future energy needs, but have no wish to see it armed with nuclear weapons unless they face invasion or attack.

Sooner rather than later, NATO-style guarantees of the security of Israel and a trade of its nuclear weapons for a secure peace in the Middle East needs to be part of any resolution of the dangerous, if as yet unrealized possibility of a nuclear-armed Iran. Hence this book's concluding question to George W. Bush in the concluding years of his presidency. It is derived from one that the Iranian poet Hafez used to describe an eagle:

He is a bird of many storms. Will he shrink from this one?

END NOTES

BRITS AND PERSIANS
1. For a revealing narrative of these early Brits in Iran, see Denis Wright (British Ambassador to Iran 1963–1971), *The English Among the Persians* (William Heinemann Ltd., London, 1977)

MOSADDEGH LIFTS HIS NIGHTGOWN
1. For a detailed description of this visit see Rudy Abramson, *Spanning the Century: The Life of W. Averell Harriman, 1891–1986* (William Morrow & Co, 1992)
2. Stephen Kinzer, *All the Shah's Men: An American Coup and the Roots of Middle East Terror*, (John Wiley & Son, 2003)
3. Kinzer, *All the Shah's Men*

THE AMERICANS MOVE INTO IRAN
1. Kinzer, *All the Shah's Men*
2. Kinzer, *All the Shah's Men*
3. Farah Pahlavi, *An Enduring Love: My Life with the Shah* (Hyperian. New York, 2004)
4. Ardeshir Zahedi in personal letter to the author.

THE SHAH'S DREAMS AND ILLUSIONS
1. William Shawcross (son of Hartley, later Lord Shawcross, Attorney General), *The Shah's Last Ride: The Story of the Exile, Misadventures and Death of the Emperor,* (Chatto & Windus Ltd, London, 1989)
2. Akbar Etemad, *Iran's Atomic Energy Program*, edited by Reza Agkhami (Bethesda Press, 1997)
3. Asadollah Alam and Alinaghi Alikhani, *The Shah and I: The Confidential Diary of Iran's Royal Court, 1969-1977* (St Martins Press, New York, 1993)

AMBASSADOR EXTRAORDINAIRE
1. Revolutionary Iran has renamed this Enghelab Avenue.

PARTY AT PERSEPOLIS
1. Houchang Nahavandi, *The Last Shah of Iran: Fatal Countdown of A Great Patriot Betrayed by the Free World, A Great Country Whose Fault was Success,* (Aquilon Ltd., 2005)

AMERICA'S IRANIAN U-TURNS
1. Peter Lord Carrington, *Reflecting on Things Past: The Memoirs of Peter Lord Carrington,* (Harpercollins, 1988)
2. Houchang Nahavandi, *The Last Shah of Iran,* 70

AN AMBASSADOR POISONED, A PRIME MINISTER SACRIFICED
1. See Abbas Milani, *The Persian Sphinx: Amir Abbas Hoveyda and the Riddle of the Iranian Revolution* (MAGE Publishers, Washington DC, 2001) for a revealing account of Hoyveda's personal relationships as well as political achievements

BLACK FRIDAY
1. Houchang Nahavandi, *The Last Shah of Iran*
2. Houchang Nahavandi, *The Last Shah of Iran*
3. Houchang Nahavandi, *The Last Shah of Iran*

REAPING THE WHIRLWIND
1. David Rockefeller, *Memoirs* (Random House, 2002), 359
2. Houchang Nahavandi, *The Last Shah of Iran,* 101
3. For a fascinating description of the trial see Abbas Milani, *The Persian Sphinx*
4. Peter Lord Carrington, *Reflecting on Things Past,* 214
5. John Keay, *Sowing the Wind: The Seeds of Conflict in the Middle East* (W. W. Norton & Company, 2003), 364

THE FLYING DUTCHMAN
1. Farah Pahlavi, *An Enduring Love*
2. William Shawcross, *The Shah's Last Ride*
3. William Shawcross, *The Shah's Last Ride*
4. For a play by play account of the Shah's experiences in Nassau see William Shawcross, *The Shah's Last Ride*
5. William Shawcross, *The Shah's Last Ride*

ESCAPE FROM PANAMA
1. Hamilton Jordan, *Crisis: The Last Year of the Carter Presidency,* (Putnam Pub. Group, 1982)
2. Hamilton Jordan, *Crisis*
3. William Shawcross, *The Shah's Last Ride*
4. William Shawcross, *The Shah's Last Ride*
5. Hamilton Jordan, *Crisis*
6. Hamilton Jordan, *Crisis*
7. Jehan Sadat, *A Woman of Egypt,* (Simon and Schuster, Inc., New York, 1987)

OLLIE NORTH'S IRANIAN FOLLIES

1. See article on Terrorism Part 1. *Security Gazette*. Pub. London Dec. 1984.)
2. For a detailed account of Reverend Terry Waite's involvement in Colonel North's attempts to barter U.S. weapons for prisoners held by Iranian-backed terrorists, see Terry Waite, *Taken on Trust: An Autobiography*, (Quill, 1995). This also gives a vivid but low-key account of Waite's four and one-half year imprisonment.
3. Harold Evans, *The American Century*, (Alfred A. Knopf, 1988)
4. Terry Waite, *Taken on Trust*, 343
5. Terry Waite, *Taken on Trust*

ORANGE COUNTY OPENS A DIALOGUE

1. Robin Wright, *The Last Great Revolution: Turmoil and Transformation in Iran*, (Vintage, 2001)
2. Robin Wright, *The Last Great Revolution*, 64
3. For her interview with Khatami and later reporting on the war with Iraq, Amanpour was awarded the World Affairs Council's 2003 Journalist of the Year Award.

THE REFORMER WHOSE LIGHT WENT OUT

1. Robin Wright, *The Last Great Revolution*

IRANIAN NUCLEAR TURBULENCE

1. See *Nuclear Iran*, article in Middle East Policy, Vol XIII, Summer 2006
2. Asadollah Alam, *The Shah & I*
3. Asadollah Alam, *The Shah & I*
4. Akbar Etemad, *Iran's Atomic Energy Program*
5. Gordon Corera, *Shopping for Bombs: Nuclear Proliferation, Global Insecurity, and the Rise and Fall of the A.Q. Khan Network*, (Oxford University Press, 2006)
6. "Atomic Agency Sees Possible Link of Military to Iran Nuclear Work," *New York Times*, February 1, 2006
7. Jahangir Amuzegar, report, *Middle East Policy*, Volume X133, Summer 2006

TIME TO TALK

1. Ilan Berman, *Tehran Rising: Iran's Challenge to the United States*, (Rowman & Littlefield Publishers, Inc., 2005)
2. Sir Percy Sykes, *History of Persia Vol II*, (RoutledgeCurzon; Third Edition, 2003), 258–60
3. See Facing Down Iran, *City Journal*, Spring 2006, Pre-empting Iran's Ambitions, *Washington Times*, March 3, 2006.
4. Seymour Hersch, article "Iran Plans," *New Yorker*, April 17, 2006

5. Anwar Husain, article "Dear Neo-Cons," *Baltimore Chronicle*, February 7, 2006

6. Jahangir Amuzegar, "Nuclear Iran: perils and prospects," *Middle East Policy*, June 22, 2006, 87

ENGAGING IRAN
1. Vali Nasr, *The Shia Revival: How Conflicts within Islam Will Shape the Future*, (W. W. Norton, 2006)

PROPOSALS FOR PEACE
1. See his foreword to this book, pages vii–ix.